The Art of
TAPESTRY
WEAVING

The Art of
Tapestry
Weaving

A COMPLETE GUIDE
to Mastering the Techniques for
Making Images with Yarn

REBECCA MEZOFF
FOREWORD BY SARAH C. SWETT

Storey Publishing

The mission of Storey Publishing is to serve our customers by publishing practical information that encourages personal independence in harmony with the environment.

EDITED BY Michal Lumsden and Gwen Steege
ART DIRECTION AND BOOK DESIGN BY Michaela Jebb
TEXT PRODUCTION BY Liseann Karandisecky
INDEXED BY Nancy D. Wood

COVER AND INTERIOR PHOTOGRAPHY BY Mars Vilaubi, © Storey Publishing

ADDITIONAL PHOTOGRAPHY BY Courtesy of Andrew Neuhart, 211, 223; © Carolyn Wright, 11 b.; © Cecilia Blomberg, 12; © Cecil Hayes, 225; © Charles L. Harris, 6, 181 r., 252 t.; © claudio.arnese/iStock.com, 87 r.; © Cornelia Theimer Gardella, 138; © Craig Kolb, 181 l.; © Danita Delimont Creative/Alamy Stock Photo, 9 r.; © Donald Sandoval, 189 l.; © 2013 Elizabeth J. Buckley, 175 l.; © Gary Mirando Photography, 163 b.; Courtesy of Glimåkra, 29; Courtesy of Gregory Case Photography, 96, 169, 182, 191 b.; Hervé Cohonner, 231; 'Homage to Carl Emmanuel Bach', 2003, Jørn Utzon, woven at the Australian Tapestry Workshop by Cheryl Thornton, Pamela Joyce, Milena Paplinska, Chris Cochius, wool, cotton, 2.67 x 14.02m. Collection: Sydney Opera House. Photograph: John Gollings AM, 22 b.; image this photographics inc., 203; James Hart, 94, 183; Courtesy of Jim Marshall, 11 t.; © Jim Smith, 22 t.; © johncameron.ca, 8; kajsfoto.dk, 175 r.; © Lialia Kuchma, 91; © Marcia Hanson Ellis, 222; © Margo Macdonald, 221; © Mark LaMoreaux, 101; © Michael D. Walsh, 95; Courtesy of Michael F. Rohde, 33 b.; Michael Gauvin, 59 ex. b.l.; Michael Lichter, 25 t.l. & r.; © Molly Manzanares, 28; © Pat Williams, designer/weaver, 89 b.; © Photo Josse/Leemage/ Getty Images, 174; Courtesy of Rebecca Mezoff, 25 b.r., 121 t., 220, 226, 269 b.; Courtesy of Robbie LaFleur, 189 r.; © Ruth Manning, 216; © Sam Elkind, 227; © Sarah C. Swett, 33 t.; © Simon Nadin, 88 b.; Courtesy of Susan Maffei, 100, 163 t.; © Taylor Dabney, 147; © Tim Barnwell, 252 b., 274 b.; Courtesy of Tommye McClure Scanlin, 233; © Ulrika Leander, 27; In the permanent collection of Whitman College, Princeton University, Princeton, NJ, © Bhakti Ziek, 9 l.

ILLUSTRATIONS BY Missy Shepler, except 279, 282 & 283 by Ilona Sherratt, © Storey Publishing

CHAPTER OPENER TYPE DESIGN BY Sébastien Hayez + contributions by Jérémy Landes

Text © 2020 by Rebecca Mezoff

Storey Publishing
210 MASS MoCA Way
North Adams, MA 01247
storey.com

Printed in China through World Print
10 9 8 7 6 5 4 3 2

Library of Congress Cataloging-in-Publication Data

Names: Mezoff, Rebecca, author.
Title: The art of tapestry weaving : a complete guide to mastering the techniques for making images with yarn / Rebecca Mezoff ; foreword by Sarah C. Swett.
Description: North Adams, MA : Storey Publishing, [2020] | Includes index. | Summary: "Rebecca Mezoff shares her techniques in this in-depth guide to every aspect of the process, from developing a color palette to selecting yarn, warping the loom, and weaving the image"— Provided by publisher.
Identifiers: LCCN 2020024105 (print) | LCCN 2020024106 (ebook) | ISBN 9781635861358 (hardcover) | ISBN 9781635861365 (ebook)
Subjects: LCSH: Tapestry. | Hand weaving.
Classification: LCC TT849 .M49 2020 (print) | LCC TT849 (ebook) | DDC 746.7/2—dc23
LC record available at https://lccn.loc.gov/2020024105
LC ebook record available at https://lccn.loc.gov/2020024106

DEDICATION

*For my students, who have taught me so much more than
I've taught them and who asked for this book.*

*And for my wife, Emily, without whom I would never have
had the courage to do the thing I love the most.*

CONTENTS

Foreword Sarah C. Swett ix

FOREWORD

The loom is the length of my forearm, the warp between its bars no wider than my palm. Two tapestry bobbins (one wound with indigo-dyed wool, the other with hand-spun flax), are tucked behind an ear, yarn tails brushing my cheek. I'm ready to dive back into this book.

I have to prepare, you see, for even as the ideas hold me spellbound, my fingers clamor to weave. "Let us at it," they cry, twitching the pages. Best to begin with a loom at my elbow. With yarn in hand, I can linger over meticulous instructions (today a technique for outlining a shallow curve with split weft), hone my skills in real time, and relax into a new tapestry adventure guided by my friend Rebecca Mezoff.

For Rebecca has the ability to illuminate the path from selvage to selvage even if you've never walked it before. And if you have, she makes the path fresh. Her words are precise, engaging, trustworthy, and challenging. "Notice this," she says. "It'll show up later in another guise." And sure enough, I notice, weave on, then when my hands and brain are ready for the next step, it is there.

This is no mean feat. Handwoven tapestry is a demanding medium by any measure, and to make it approachable at the beginning and compelling after a lifetime is Rebecca's particular skill — and a gift to us all. For this medium is both timeless and utterly of our time, one of the few means of expression that cannot be replicated by machine.

Our world needs more tapestries.

It needs your tapestries.

Just remember, this book is best commenced with a warped loom by your side, and if you don't yet have one, instructions await in chapter 4.

SARAH C. SWETT
Moscow, Idaho
December 2019

PART 1
LEARNING

Why Tapestry?

I've always been fascinated by the creation of cloth. As a little girl, I remember standing next to the Macomber floor loom of my grandfather, who was an engineer. I would watch him throw the shuttle to make vast swaths of cream-colored cloth for curtains in his two-story greenhouse. Click, swish, click. Click, swish, click. The rhythm of the shuttle, the dance his feet made on the treadles, and the cloth inching forward on the loom until he stopped and wound it onto the cloth beam enthralled me. He had taken this weaving machine, added some thread, and made huge pieces of useful fabric from them.

Twenty-five years later I found myself standing next to the Macomber loom of James Koehler, master tapestry artist, in a workshop at North Carolina's Penland School of Craft. There was no shuttle this time. Just the clank of the harnesses shifting and the mesmerizing sight of James's fingers dancing over the warp, creating even lines of weft bubbles before — thud — he beat them in with the beater on the loom, opened the other shed, and began again. I watched, mesmerized, as a blue-violet-hued tapestry grew, the subtle shifts in color and the gentle curves of the design creating optical illusions in the fabric. And then I sat at my own loom and tried to make the magic happen for myself. I had found my path.

My journey as a weaver started with that little girl watching her grandfather weave curtains and, as an adult, led me to become a tapestry artist apprentice in Koehler's studio, and finally, to run my own tapestry school and studio. This tapestry life has been full of experimentation and the joy of exploring my own creative impulses while learning through making with my hands. For me, making tapestry is more a process than a wish to reach a particular goal. The deep satisfaction of being immersed in a tactile and richly colored way of expressing ideas keeps me going back to the loom day after day.

Why Weave Tapestry?

Cloth-making metaphors are deeply embedded in our language. We "weave through traffic" to get somewhere quickly or "spin a yarn" to tell a good story. The word *tapestry* is used frequently in common language to indicate a mixing of various parts into one narrative: "a tapestry of cultures" or "nature's rich tapestry." This use of weaving terms in common language to refer to concepts that are not about the act of weaving cloth is an indication of how deeply the process of making fabric is part of the human experience.

The process of weaving a tapestry connects with something primal in our experience as dexterous creatures. There is something sensuous and attractive about tapestry weaving. Its slow rhythm has a very peaceful, repetitive quality to it. And the step-by-step problem-solving nature of the process brings a sense of accomplishment and allows a gentle reconnection with self. The depth of color in a simple piece of yarn, the endless variations of expression when colors are woven next to each other, and the accomplishment of a finished expression that represents something important to you — these are the reasons many of us engage with this historied art form.

Tapestry allows for a variety of expressions. Your work could be monumentally large or remarkably tiny or any size in between. It could be bright and loudly colored or soft and subtle. It could be full of bumpy texture or present a perfectly flat surface. You'll find your way among all these choices as you work through the techniques in this book. My hope is that you come out on the other side with the confidence to take these foundational skills and create your own tapestries. The journey of making art in any medium never ends. And for that, I am grateful.

How to Be a Beginning Tapestry Weaver

Most of us live in success-focused cultures. Even as children we are taught to produce particular outcomes. There are expectations placed upon us, and we quickly learn to place expectations on ourselves. This can lead to the belief that anything we try has to result in perfection or it isn't worth doing.

If you allow it to do so, tapestry weaving can provide a challenge to that perfectionism. Those of us drawn to weaving often love structure in our lives, and many of us are a bit particular about the outcome of our projects. I am most certainly one of these people. But tapestry is a medium that resists perfectly square corners and gorgeously rounded curves because our images are woven on a gridded structure. The joy comes when you learn to accept the medium as it is and use the natural structure of tapestry techniques to inform your own woven forms.

As with any new skill, there are many components to tapestry weaving that you'll need to learn before you can produce the tapestry you imagine in your mind. There is an intellectual component (understanding how it works) and there is a motor-skills component (teaching your body to manage tools and materials effectively). Add to those the challenge of artistic design and you'll realize you are learning a fiber art form that requires some practice to master. It is not possible for you to produce a "perfect" tapestry on your first try. Realizing that will free you up to have some fun.

Because of its long history and the reverential way we tend to treat old tapestries today, tapestry weaving as an art form is often understood as something belonging to the experienced or highly trained practitioner. Even today, tapestry workshop apprenticeships at places like France's Manufacture Nationale des Gobelins can be two to five years long. Once we know a little about tapestry weaving, it feels unreachable from our living rooms and home studios. I'd like to challenge that notion. Start at the beginning, allow yourself to play with simple design, and embrace sampling. Step by step, you can definitely do this.

I often hear my students express anxiety about their weaving. They are afraid of doing it wrong, of not following the rules. In this book, I'll teach you a lot of those rules, but right from the beginning I encourage you to question them. Yes, you need to learn the techniques to create a firm foundation for your work. But experimentation is the bedrock of any artistic process. As you practice the techniques throughout this book, consider what you want to express. If your method deviates from mine, ask yourself if your method is structurally sound. Will your piece fall apart when you take it off the loom or hang it on the wall? If not, continue your experiment and look

◄ *This is my very first tapestry. The selvages are wildly uneven, and it is full of technical problems. I keep it under my loom bench as a reminder of where I began. Start where you are and dare to follow the journey of weaving wherever it leads you.*

at it with a critical eye when it is done. Find ways to express your idea and use these techniques as your starting point. There aren't any fiber art police. Remember that this is your own journey. Experiment. Be curious. Make stuff. Because making is a powerful way to experience the world.

How to Use This Book

This book presents the foundational techniques of tapestry weaving in the order I feel is easiest to experience them. I've developed this sequence of topics over a decade of teaching thousands of students, both in person and online. You don't have to follow my lead, but I do suggest that you work through the chapters in order at least through chapter 7. This basic information is critical for you to understand before tackling the techniques presented in the rest of the book. There are parts that won't pertain to you, depending on what kind of loom you are using, but that is made clear by section headings.

Starting in part 2, I guide you through how to weave each of the techniques I introduce. I encourage you to follow these step-by-step instructions in a sampler. Making samplers may not sound very fun, but it is a great way to experiment with these new skills without feeling like you have to produce something exceptional at the end. It takes a lot of practice to learn the skills of tapestry weaving, so warp your loom and weave along with me.

The images of tapestries throughout the book are intended both to illustrate the point I'm making but also to give you some inspiration for your own work. Most of the artwork is from tapestry artists who are still producing, so look them up online and see what they've finished lately. The community of tapestry weavers is worth dipping into not only for inspiration but also for support. There are many online groups and forums, as well as local guilds and study groups all over the world. Finding other people who enjoy working in tapestry can be a wonderful way to enrich your life and your tapestry practice.

One of the first things to master when learning a new skill is the terminology. Weavers have their own set of jargon, and tapestry weavers have an even more specific set of terms. Because weaving has been done all over the world in every culture for millennia, the terms used today are varied and can be confusing. I have defined the terms you'll find in this book starting on page 13.

Tapestry is an art form and a practice that can become a fun lens through which to experience the world. Anyone can learn to weave tapestry, and that definitely includes you. It is time to dive in.

◄ *Detail from* Feathered Relief *by Silvia Heyden. Full tapestry on page 181.*

1 This Is Tapestry

At its simplest, weaving involves two sets of threads: weft threads and warp threads. The warp threads are held tightly by a device called a loom. The process of weaving involves passing a weft thread over and under successive warp threads. This is the basic procedure to weave most kinds of cloth.

In tapestry weaving, the warps are spaced widely enough that the weft slides down over them and completely hides the warp. Because the warp is hidden and the image we see is created by the weft alone, the weaving is called *weft-faced*.

Unlike the weft in most functional textiles, the weft in tapestry weaving is usually discontinuous. In most cases the weft does not travel from one side of the textile to the other. Weft yarns of different colors are wound in small bundles known as butterflies or on tapestry bobbins and are introduced in sections across each row. These color changes are what create the patterns or images.

Tapestries are very often two-dimensional pieces of art produced to hang on the wall as artistic decoration. The definition at the bottom of this page does leave room for other uses for a piece of tapestry cloth, and many artists take tapestry off the wall and create a three-dimensional statement with it as Jane Kidd's piece shows on the next page. Tapestry can also be used for smaller decorations on clothing or for functional items.

When you're a beginner, tapestry weaving can seem a little complicated. There are many combinations of tools and materials you can use to create a tapestry, and those options can seem overwhelming. Simplifying those choices so that you can get started is one goal of this book.

Tapestry *is a discontinuous weft-faced woven structure that creates an image.*

Stacked like Bricks

I find one of the most magical things about tapestry is that the structure of the fabric and the image are created at the same time. This is unlike a medium such as painting, where the image is created by applying paint or pigment to another surface and color can be added to any part of that surface at any time.

Tapestry is woven from bottom to top much like a brick wall is formed: each brick supports the ones above it. If we don't weave from bottom to top, open warps will be trapped beneath woven sections. It is very difficult to "fill in" areas of open warp, because the weaving above restricts your shed (the space you create between two sets of warps and into which you insert the weft to make cloth) in such a way that you are unable to open it. Attempting to do things such as weaving a shape in the middle of the warp and then filling in the space around it not only creates the most challenging weaving environment, but it also makes it much more difficult to create a stable textile and consistent-looking fabric.

This bottom-to-top weaving approach means you need to plan before you start weaving, as the shape at the bottom has to be woven before the shapes farther up the warp. This fact leads most tapestry weavers to use a cartoon (or full-scale mock-up of the design) to guide their work.

Jane Kidd, *Curiouser and Curiouser #2*, 2015.
Wool, cotton, rayon, and linen, mounted on a wooden shelf, 18" × 71".
▲ *This tapestry is part of Jane Kidd's* Wonderland *series, which is about seeds and genetic manipulation. It is displayed on a shelf with one end rolled to suggest an unknown conclusion to this human story.*

What Tapestry Is *Not*

There are many ways to interlace fiber to create a textile that contains an image. Tapestry is just one of these, but often other techniques are confused with tapestry. True tapestry can only be woven by hand. Complicated looms can approximate the effect of tapestry, but the structure of the cloth is very different from handwoven tapestry.

In Europe, the stitched practice of embroidery is also often referred to in its finished form as "tapestry." Be careful about European yarns labeled "tapestry wool," as they are often intended for embroidery and may not be appropriate for tapestry weaving.

To add to the confusion about what a tapestry is, tapestry techniques can be used to create textiles that are not hung on the wall and are sometimes made into functional garments or accessories instead. For example, tapestry techniques are used in the construction of many kinds of rugs. Is a rug a tapestry?

It could be. Diné (Navajo) textiles are often called rugs even when they are thin and hang on the wall. Traditional Diné textiles are woven using tapestry techniques and can all be called tapestry even if they are used on the floor or worn as a *manta*. But other types of rugs from other traditions are often knotted, and those are not tapestry. Many woven rugs with patterns are made with tapestry techniques and could be called tapestries, even though they are used to cover the floor.

Bhakti Ziek, *Stardust* (detail), 2014.
Silk, tencel, and metallic yarns handwoven weft-backed jacquard, 16' × 28" (each panel).

▲ *Frequently called "tapestry," jacquard weaving is created by a sophisticated loom. Originally the patterning was controlled by strings of cards with holes punched in them, but today's jacquard looms are computer operated. Each warp thread can be raised independently of all the others, which allows for vast possibilities in design. Both embroidery and jacquard can produce art pieces that are cloth, but they are not tapestry. Stardust is a permanent installation at Whitman College, Princeton University, Princeton, New Jersey. The weaving consists of six large panels that cover one wall of the Community Hall.*

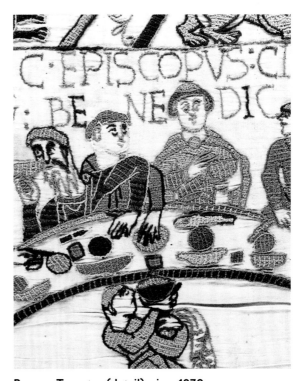

Bayeux Tapestry (detail), circa 1070.
Wool and linen, 20" × 224'.

▲ *This famous "tapestry" is actually a huge embroidery from the eleventh century. The images are stitched — not woven — onto a ground cloth. The Bayeux Tapestry depicts the events leading to the Norman Conquest of England. It has resided in France for more than 900 years, being hung in the Bayeux Cathedral for centuries. It is currently housed in the Musée de la Tapisserie de Bayeux.*

Tapestry's Storied History

Humans in all corners of the earth have been weaving for tens of thousands of years to decorate themselves and their environments. Cultures separated geographically have individually developed their own ways of weaving. This has led to a rich variety of expression in all forms of weaving and in tapestry designs, tools, and materials.

At its most basic, tapestry is a decorative piece of cloth that may or may not have other functions. In the archaeological record, images depicting tapestry weaving have been found on ceramics and carved in stone that date back as far as 2500 BCE. Homer mentions tapestry weaving in approximately 700 BCE, and the Old Testament also refers to this form of creative expression. Ovid describes tapestry in his *Metamorphoses* of approximately 8 CE, and the creation story of the Diné people of the American Southwest describes Spider Woman weaving the universe and passing on her weaving knowledge.

Tapestry weaving is solidly rooted in the past. The art form of woven tapestry brings to mind faded, monumentally sized fabric hangings depicting battles, unicorns, bloodied martyrs, and the courts of kings. Royalty and rich patrons commissioned these large tapestries, which were an opulent way to communicate status, but also a way to communicate with a largely illiterate populace. Tapestries in the Middle Ages were rather like today's social media. They could be carried in the streets to line parade routes or fill the large entertaining halls of the wealthy, and their images told all sorts of stories. Many subjects were biblical, including the Apocalypse Tapestry, whose approximately 1,000 square yards of weaving illustrates the Book of Revelation. Other tapestry series, such as the unicorn tapestries of the fourteenth and fifteenth centuries, told stories of wars or took on more secular subjects. Elites paid for the tapestries and used them for decoration and communication, and to exhibit their considerable wealth.

Most of these medieval tapestries now spend their time meticulously rolled in museum collections, and an unknown number of long-forgotten tapestries from centuries gone have disintegrated into dust in attics. Some of the surviving tapestries from the Middle Ages, such as the massive Apocalypse Tapestry (woven in the fourteenth century and now on display in the Château d'Angers), make us realize how big an industry tapestry production was in medieval times and continuing right through the nineteenth century.

These monumental reproductive tapestries were first designed by an artist who generally painted a full-scale cartoon and then woven by skilled artisans who copied the painting. Multiple workshops, each employing many weavers and almost always supported by patrons, might work for a decade to produce one set of tapestries. A few weaving workshops that operate in this manner still exist in the world, notably the Australian Tapestry Workshop in Melbourne, the Manufacture Nationale des Gobelins in Paris, and Dovecot Studios in Edinburgh, Scotland. But for most tapestry practitioners the world over, creation in this medium has gone the way of the artist-weaver, and the person who creates the design is also weaving the final textile.

As such, tapestry remains a living art form. Throughout time, cultures that came in contact with each other influenced each other's artistic practices. This continues today, and in our global society that sharing of information occurs much more quickly. For example, in the United States, tapestry weaving is practiced in New Mexican Hispano, Diné, Mexican, South American, Asian, Scandinavian, and an array of other European-influenced styles. Sometimes those traditions remain distinct, and sometimes practitioners mix styles. The images on the next two pages start to give us some idea of the range of styles used just in the United States.

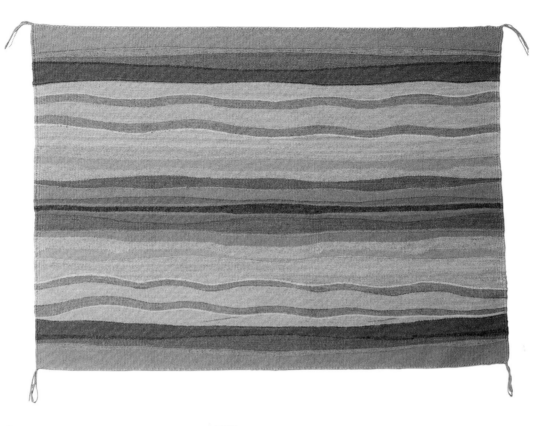

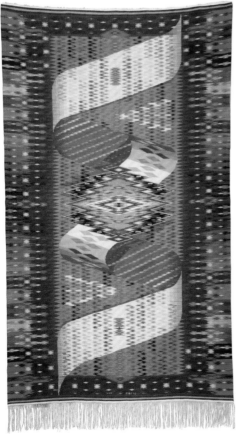

D. Y. Begay, *Pollen Path*, 2007.
Wool, dyed with goldenrod, madder roots, purple onion skins, *Coreopsis tinctoria*, *Hydnellum peckii*, *Phaeolus schweinitzii*, and aniline, 25" × 36".
▲ *A Navajo weaver trained in the traditional Diné approach, D. Y. Begay has created her own contemporary tapestry style that reflects her roots.*

Irvin Trujillo, *Saltillo Shroud*, 2014.
50/50 merino wool/silk blend, 88" × 50".
◄ *Traditional Hispano Rio Grande weaving has its own distinctive style, as seen in this tapestry by Irvin Trujillo of Chimayo, New Mexico.*

Cecilia Blomberg, *Point Defiance Steps*, 2015.
Wool, linen, and cotton, 36" × 50".
▲ *Cecilia Blomberg's work is woven in the European-based tapestry style I teach in this book. This way of weaving tapestry spread from Europe in the Middle Ages to places around the world, eventually reaching the United States and Australia, where weavers still use these ancient methods to create modern images.*

Most modern-day tapestry weavers have the challenge of being both designers and technicians. In the United States, there were a few workshops weaving from artists' cartoons in the late twentieth century, but since their closures, U.S. weavers have designed their own tapestries for the most part. The American Tapestry Alliance, founded in 1982 by Jim Brown and Hal Painter, has worked hard to support independent artist-weavers in this new world of individual work. Artist-weavers in the United States usually work alone in private studios and tend to create works of a smaller size — most often a few inches to a few feet square — than the monumental tapestries of Europe. This smaller expression has a different feeling from the large tapestries of medieval Europe but is manageable for both the equipment typically found in home studios and time constraints of modern life.

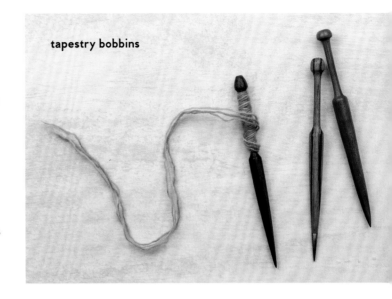

tapestry bobbins

Terms to Know

In the fiber world, many terms are used similarly, no matter what fiber activity they refer to. Many of these are probably very familiar to those of you who have done other kinds of weaving or other fiber crafts. But there are some terms that are used in special ways in tapestry weaving, and this section will help you understand them better.

Aubusson bone. A form of bobbin often called a flute, which has two rounded ends and carries the weft yarn while weaving on low-warp looms.

Batten. A long, thin stick inserted in the warp and turned on its side to hold open the warp. The term *batten* is typically used to refer to something larger than a shed stick, which serves the same purpose but is finer and used on smaller work.

Bobbin. A device to hold yarn. Tapestry bobbins have a point on one end and a ball on the other end; they are used both to hold the weft yarn and to beat (or push) it into place.

Butterfly. A way of organizing the weft yarn to make it more manageable for weaving without using another tool to wrap it around. Also called a finger skein.

Cartoon. An actual-size drawing of the major forms and color areas in a tapestry that is used as a reference guide while weaving.

Castle. The part of many beamed looms that holds the shafts.

Chromatic neutral. A less saturated version of a hue made by adding some of that hue's complementary color.

Color harmony. Relationships between colors on the color wheel that can help guide color choices in design. See chapter 5.

Cutback. A way of breaking up a large area of a single color by weaving it in sections bordered by angles. Traditional Diné weavers often use cutbacks in their weaving. Cutbacks have often been referred to as lazy lines, a term considered offensive to many Diné weavers.

Dent. The space in a reed or warping coil. Specific dent spacing helps keep the warps at a certain number per inch.

Eccentric weaving. When the weft travels in a way that is not perpendicular to the warp.

Fell line. The top line of weaving at any point during the tapestry creation. If you're weaving line by line, the fell line will be straight across the weaving.

Float. A weft thread that goes over two or more warps instead of going over and under successive warps. Floats can be intentional in a particular technique or the result of a weaving error.

Grattoir. A type of tapestry fork used by low-warp weavers, primarily in Europe.

Harness. *See* shaft.

Hatching. A common tapestry technique in which two adjacent colors are woven over each other in alternating sequences to create an area where the two colors are blended.

Heddle. A wire or cord with an eye in the center through which a warp is passed. In tapestry, two sets of heddles, one on each shaft, open one of two sheds.

High-warp loom. A tapestry loom that has the warp perpendicular to the floor. Also called haute-lisse.

Hue. The name of a color; e.g., red or yellow-green.

Ikat. A dyeing technique that uses resist dyeing to change colors along a length of yarn. Resist dyeing is a method of tightly wrapping parts of the yarn with another material so that portions of the fiber remain undyed.

Immersion dyed. The result of yarn or other fiber material submerged in a vat of dye. Generally immersion-dyed material is uniform in color.

Jacquard. A computer-controlled weave structure used to make cloth with images.

Locking treadles. A way of mechanically holding down a lever on a beamed floor loom for long periods so the weaver doesn't have to maintain pressure on it with their foot.

Loom. A device for holding a set of warp threads under tension so weft can be woven into it, creating cloth.

Low-warp loom. A loom for tapestry in which the warp is parallel to the floor, also called basse-lisse.

Meet and separate. A method of weaving in which adjacent wefts move in opposition to each other.

Micron count. A laboratory test that measures the diameter of a fiber. The larger the number, the coarser the fiber.

Optical mixing. The tendency for the human eye and brain to mix colors, resulting in an experience of a color that doesn't actually exist in the physical object.

Ordering cord. A strong thread that travels across the warp three or four times at the base of the weaving. It provides a firm foundation for the weaving and helps to evenly space the warp before putting in the waste yarn.

Pass. The there-and-back movement of a weft thread across a portion or the whole width of the warp; a sequence of two picks.

Pick. A single length of weft across a portion of or the whole width of the warp; also called a half-pass or demi-duite.

Pick and pick. A technique that creates narrow vertical stripes parallel to the warp.

Ply. Each individual strand making up a piece of yarn. Many tapestry yarns are 2-ply, meaning there are two strands of yarn twisted together.

Put up. The way a length of yarn is packaged for sale. Yarn for weaving often comes wound on cones or tubes, but you will also find it in skeins, hanks, and balls.

Raddle. A comblike device that helps organize the warping of large beamed looms.

Reed. A metal comblike object, attached to some beamed looms, through which the warp passes. It assists with spacing the warp and beating in the weft.

Relay. The point where the weft turns around a warp and returns in the opposite direction in the other shed.

Saturation. The purity of a color. A fully saturated color does not have any black, white, or other hue added to it.

Selvage. The outside edge of a woven fabric.

Sequence. Two picks, or rows, of weaving that together create a solid line in tapestry; also called a pass or duite.

Sett. The number indicating how many warp ends occur in a unit of measurement. In the United States, sett usually is designated as warp ends per inch (epi).

Shade. The result of adding black to a pure hue.

Shaft. On a beamed loom, the shaft is the part of the frame that holds the heddles, which helps organize the warp threads and open different sheds. Also called a harness.

Shed. The opening in the warp that allows the weft to pass through. In tapestry there are generally only two sheds.

Swift. A device for holding a yarn skein open and under tension so it can be wound into a ball. A popular version is called an umbrella swift, which collapses for storage.

Tapestry. A discontinuous weft-faced woven structure that creates an image.

Tapestry beater. Also called a tapestry fork, this is a tool for beating, or pushing, the weft into place.

Temperature. In color theory, the warmth or coolness of a color.

Tint. The result of adding white to a pure hue.

Tone. The result of adding gray to a pure hue.

Value. The relative darkness or lightness of a hue when compared to the range of grays from black to white. Tints, shades, and tones all change the value of a hue.

Warp. The set of threads held tightly by a loom so that weft can be woven across them to create cloth.

Waste yarn. The weft yarn you weave before and after your headers to establish spacing and hold the piece together when it comes off the loom. Use your regular weft yarn as your waste yarn.

Weft. The yarns that weave across the warp to create images or patterns in tapestry weaving.

Weft tension. The amount of weft that goes into any one portion of a tapestry.

Woolen preparation. A fiber preparation method used by handspinners in which the fibers are carded and spun in a more disorganized fashion than in worsted preparation. Spinning "woolen" creates a loftier, more air-filled yarn than spinning worsted does. Because woolen-spun yarns squish and stretch significantly, they are not as desirable for most tapestry weaving.

Worsted preparation. A fiber preparation method used by handspinners in which the fleece locks are lined up with cut ends and tip ends matching, the fibers are combed, and they are spun with a short forward draw. This is different from a worsted weight yarn, which designates the yarn thickness primarily of knitting yarns.

2 Looms Large (and Small)

There are many tools we can use to weave tapestry. Some are very simple, some are more complicated. Each weaver will prefer a unique combination of equipment. As you begin your tapestry journey, understanding the characteristics you should consider when choosing tools and materials will help you decide what might work best for you.

Characteristics of a Good Tapestry Loom

Virtually any piece of equipment that can hold a set of warp threads in order with some tension will work as a loom. However, there are certain loom characteristics that will make your tapestry weaving more successful. An inadequate loom can not only be frustrating to weave on, but it can produce visible irregularities in your tapestry.

There are five important qualities to consider when choosing your loom:

1. The ability to achieve and adjust tension
2. The presence of a shedding device
3. A way to space the warp
4. A sturdy construction
5. Ergonomic comfort

Each weaver will develop their own preferences around these loom characteristics, and your preferences may well differ from mine. If you haven't yet settled on a loom to start with, read through this chapter before deciding which options feel right for your needs.

TENSION. The best looms for tapestry weaving have adjustable tension. Tapestry is easier to weave when the warp is fairly tight. Tension can change as you weave for a variety of reasons, and it is helpful to be able to adjust for these changes by re-tensioning the loom. Warps naturally get tighter as you weave the weft threads over and under them. This can be particularly problematic on very small looms without tensioning devices, as the warp can feel too loose to start and too tight after you've been weaving for a while. Using a warp thread with some stretch, such as cotton seine twine (see page 46), for small untensioned looms helps keep the tapestry easy to weave on.

A warp can also get looser depending on what it is made of, how much humidity is in the air, and how long it has been under tension. Being able to increase the tension on the loom means you can return to easy weaving quickly and you won't see the effects of changing warp tension in your tapestry. Some looms are not capable of holding a high tension due to their construction, and these looms are not recommended for tapestry weaving.

SHEDDING. A shedding mechanism is a way of opening each layer of warp for ease and quickness of weaving; however, a loom does not need to have a shedding mechanism at all. I have spent many happy hours on simple looms using a shed stick or needle to pick up every other warp thread to pass the weft through. However, this method of weaving is somewhat slower. We'll talk about sheds later in this chapter, but for now realize that having such a mechanism on a loom will make weaving faster and manipulating close-together warp threads much easier.

WARP SPACING. Some looms have mechanisms that evenly space your warps. Examples include looms with pegs, slots, or a coil that allows the weaver to warp the loom with a certain number of warp threads in each inch (called the sett). Floor looms often have reeds, or combs, that are made of steel and have slots in them through which each warp thread passes.

Some of these spacing mechanisms can be altered so that you can change the number of warp threads in an inch. On looms with warp-spacing coils, for example, you can use various coils that have different spacing between slots. Floor loom

Over/Under Weaving Pattern

Tapestry is a form of plain weave, meaning that the weft travels over and under successive warps in the first pick, then over and under alternate warps in the second pick. All of the techniques in this book follow this simple pattern. In tapestry weaving, we make sure the weft completely covers the warp and we change the colors of yarn we are using to create images. But the basic structure is just over, under, over, under.

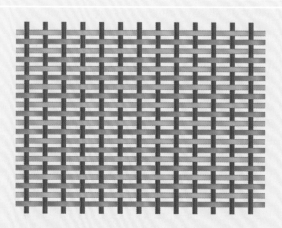

reeds come with different spacings, and you can use a different reed for each sett. Most slot or peg frame looms, on the other hand, do not have a built-in spacing mechanism, so you must use other methods to change the number of warps per inch.

Some looms do not have a mechanism that spaces the warp for you. In these instances, you'll rely on counting inch marks on the loom to get the sett you want. These looms have the advantage of being able to warp with any number of warps per inch without changing the equipment.

STURDY CONSTRUCTION. Tapestry weaving creates a lot of force on the loom. The equipment has to be able to withstand this force without bending, breaking, or twisting. It should maintain a square relationship between the warp threads and the top and bottom beams. The beams or the rods you tie the warp to should not bend significantly when tension is applied.

ERGONOMIC. Tapestry weaving takes a lot of time, and you'll be spending many fun-filled hours with your loom. Using a loom that fits your body is important for your long-term health. People come in all different sizes, but each kind of loom is generally offered in only one size. If you are a small person, weaving at a very large floor loom may be uncomfortable. People with large hands may struggle to manipulate warps on looms without shedding devices. Some people love to weave with the warp oriented horizontally; other people prefer to weave on a loom where the warp is vertical. Both are possible in tapestry, but it might take a little experimentation for you to figure out what works best for you.

▶ *Treadles on a countermarche beamed loom. The weaver steps on the treadles to change the shed.*

Anatomy of a Tapestry Loom

Looms are used for many different types of weaving, so it is important to use one that will work for tapestry. While tapestry looms come in many forms, they all accomplish the basic function of holding a set of ordered warp threads under tension. Some looms have devices built into them that help open the sheds and space the warp threads evenly.

WING NUT AND THREADED ROD. Many tapestry looms use threaded rods and nuts to increase the tension on the loom after it is warped. The loom can be made taller by turning the wing nut, which puts pressure against the warp and makes it tighter.

WARPING BAR. As the warp is wound on the loom, it turns around this bar. The warping bar provides a way to rotate the tapestry around the loom so you can weave longer tapestries.

WARP SPACING COIL. Many tapestry looms have mechanisms for spacing the warp. The Mirrix loom shown on the opposite page has a metal coil at the top. You can use different-size coils depending on the number of warps you want per inch. Other looms have pegs, slots, or a steel bar with slats (called a reed) to maintain the warp spacing. Some looms don't have any mechanism to space the warp; the weaver manages this when setting up the loom by counting warp ends carefully.

SHEDDING BAR AND HANDLE. A bar with heddles attached that rotates when the weaver turns the handle and allows each of the sheds to be easily opened.

OPEN SHED ROD. On a loom without any shedding device, like the one pictured on page 112, you can place a thin rod in one shed at the top of the loom and leave it there while you weave. This thin rod makes it much faster to find one of the sheds with a shed stick.

▲ *Heddles on a Mirrix loom*

HEDDLES. On the loom above, the heddles are short pieces of thread looped around every other warp. One set goes on a thin bar on each side of the bigger shedding bar. Heddles on other looms may be metal or take the form of leashes, which are long loops of thread tied to a bar at the front of the loom. See more information about leashes on page 284.

SHED STICK. A thin pointed batten that can be inserted in the warp and turned on its side to hold the sheds open. It is removed after each piece of weft is inserted. When weaving in the shed that the shed rod is holding open, a shed stick is slid into the gap and turned sideways to widen the opening. For the second shed, the shed stick or your fingers must "pick" every other warp to bring it forward.

warp spacing coil

ANATOMY OF A LOOM

shedding bar
and handle

heddles

warp

wing nut and
threaded rod

weft

tapestry

warping bar

Mirrix tapestry loom

Small-Format Tapestry

Traditional tapestry of the past was monumental in size. One panel of a multipanel piece might be many square yards. Today, tapestries this large are mostly woven only in workshops such as Scotland's Dovecot Studios and the Australian Tapestry Workshop, by teams of weavers working from a design made by a non-weaver. In the United States, artist-weavers are the current trend, meaning the designer also weaves the piece. Smaller size tapestries, mostly less than a square yard, are the most common. Many juried shows define small-format tapestries as about 1 square foot. These sizes make the medium accessible to people who have smaller equipment and less time to weave.

Helen Smith, *Dancing for Joy*, 2017.
Wool, silk, and cotton, 16" × 12" (including fringe);
12¼" × 12" (excluding fringe).
▶ *Smith's small-format tapestries are a riot of color and movement.*

Jørn Utzon, *Homage to Carl Emmanuel Bach*, 2003.
Wool and cotton, 105" × 46'. Woven at the Australian Tapestry Workshop by Cheryl Thornton, Pamela Joyce, Milena Paplinska, and Chris Cochius.
▲ *Tapestries can be many yards square, as the works woven at the Australian Tapestry Workshop often are.*

Types of Looms

Tapestry can be woven in a few different ways, and some types of looms are better suited to a particular weaving approach than others. If you're not sure what you want to weave yet, don't worry! You can start with a simple loom, and if you find you want to weave larger pieces or want more features on your loom, you can upgrade your equipment later. Remember that tapestry can be woven on the very simplest of equipment. Everything else is just for convenience, speed, ease of use, and comfort.

You can divide tapestry looms into three categories: untensioned frame looms; tensioned frame looms; and looms with rollers (or beams). Both frame-type looms are similar in form and function. Looms with rollers that hold the warp tightly are more complicated. The beams provide tension and serve as a place to store the unwoven warp and the tapestry as it is produced.

Frame Looms

The majority of tapestry weavers today, especially those who are weaving small-format pieces, use some kind of frame loom. These looms are usually rectangular, and they can be as small as a few inches square or large enough to create a tapestry 8 feet wide or more. These looms may or may not have tensioning ability.

UNTENSIONED FRAME LOOMS are the simplest kinds of looms. They come in one piece and don't have any moving parts. They often have slots or pegs at the top and bottom of the loom to wrap the warp around. They usually don't have shedding mechanisms, and the warp spacing is limited by how many slots or pegs are in each inch. They are most often rectangular or I-shaped.

When warping these types of looms, it is helpful to use a slightly stretchy warp, such as cotton seine twine, to make up for the inability to adjust the tension. If the warp becomes loose while weaving,

▲ *The Lost Pond loom and Schacht Easel Weaver are both examples of simple, untensioned frame looms with evenly spaced pegs.*

you can weave some thin sticks into the warp to make it tighter, but you can't make a tight warp looser on an untensioned loom. These looms are generally small in size, not larger than 18 inches in either direction. When the loom is larger than that, it is difficult to keep a firm tension on your warp without a tensioning device.

Because these looms don't generally have shedding mechanisms, you can use the open shed rod and shed stick method, outlined on page 20 and explored further in chapter 6, to speed up the weaving a little bit.

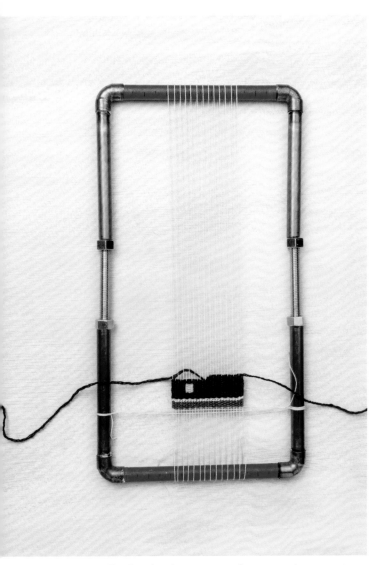

▲ *This handmade copper pipe loom provides tensioning with threaded rod and nuts. You can make your own tensioned frame loom fairly easily with a few simple tools. Copper pipe, galvanized threaded pipe, black threaded pipe, or PVC are all materials I've seen used successfully for looms. You can even make a very large loom out of scaffolding pieces. See pages 289–293 for instructions to make two types of these looms.*

TENSIONED FRAME LOOMS include a way to increase the tension on the warp. They may or may not have shedding mechanisms and ways to help you space the warp evenly.

Many tensioned frame looms are made of some kind of metal. They adjust tension through a mechanism that lets the loom get longer after it is warped so that more or less force is applied to the warp threads. For example, a copper pipe loom is just a rectangle of pipe with pieces of threaded rod and four nuts inserted into the sides of the loom. After the loom is warped, the nuts can be turned in the direction that lengthens the loom and thus increases the tension on the warp.

Some tensioned frame looms do have shedding mechanisms. A Mirrix loom, for example, has a rotating shedding device to which heddles are attached and a handle is rotated up or down to open each shed (see page 21). Other handmade pipe looms have a leash bar on the front. Tensioned looms that don't have any shedding mechanisms can use the open shed rod and shed stick methods shown on page 112.

Some of these looms have devices to help you space the warp evenly. Mirrix looms have a metal coil that is attached to the top of the loom. The coil stretches out to give you a space between each wire where a warp thread can be inserted. Different-length coils allow different numbers of warps per inch.

There are some tensioned frame looms that are made of wood. These tend to have either plastic pegs or metal combs attached to space the warp with a particular number of warps per inch. Popular examples of these looms are the Glimåkra Freja and the C. Cactus Flower Navajo-style loom. The Schacht Arras loom is an example of a wooden loom with tensioning that, similar to the Mirrix, has coils to space the warp.

▲ *The Schacht Arras loom has a rotating shedding mechanism along with plastic coils to help you space the warp*

On handmade pipe looms, there is not usually a warp-spacing mechanism. Instead, you typically mark the bottom and top of the loom at even intervals, which allows you to space the warp threads manually. In the United States we generally use inches for measurement, and I like to mark these looms at ¼-inch intervals.

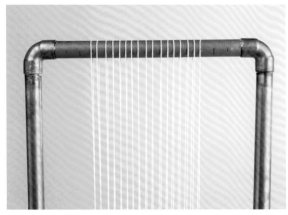

▲ *Inches are marked on tape at the bottom and top of this copper pipe loom.*

High-Warp, Low-Warp

Tapestry weavers often refer to their looms as either high-warp or low-warp looms. (Sometimes books use the French terms *haute-lisse* for high-warp and *basse-lisse* for low-warp.) These terms refer to the orientation of the warp and the way that you weave on the loom. A high-warp loom is one that holds the warp threads in a vertical orientation, while a low-warp loom orients the warps horizontally. (See page 27 for an example of a high-warp loom.) It is impossible to tell whether a tapestry was woven on a high- or low-warp loom once it is finished. The difference is how weaving on the loom feels to the weaver: some people prefer to weave on a warp that is upright, and other people's bodies work better weaving a horizontal warp.

▲ *The Cranbrook loom, made by Schacht Spindle Company, is a low-warp countermarche loom.*

Christine Pradel-Lien, *Herbes Folles*, 2019.
Wool, cotton, linen, and Lurex.
▲ *This work in progress is being woven on an Aubusson low-warp loom, a traditional French loom with treadles underneath that pull the two sheds downward.*

Looms with Beams

The final category of looms uses rolling beams to hold both the warp and the finished tapestry. As a result, looms with beams are capable of creating very long lengths of tapestry, something frame looms cannot do. Looms with beams come in many sizes. Some, including rigid-heddle and table looms, sit on a table, while floor looms of all sizes sit right on the floor. These looms can have the warp oriented horizontally, as in low-warp looms, or vertically, as in high-warp looms. The two-beam structure remains the same; only the orientation changes.

As with frame looms, the job of beamed looms is to hold the warp tight so the weft can be woven through it. Beamed looms have more complicated mechanisms than frame looms for controlling which warp threads are raised or lowered to create a shed. When the beams and corresponding hardware are very small, the loom is unable to provide a high tension. As a result, smaller beamed looms such as table or rigid-heddle looms tend to be poor choices for tapestry weaving, though there are exceptions to this.

Fortunately for us, we only need two sheds in tapestry weaving, so we don't have to worry about using multiple harnesses and complicated threading patterns, as weavers of patterned fabric do. These looms with beams work in the following ways.

- The unwoven warp is rolled on a beam called the warp beam, and the finished tapestry is rolled on a beam called the cloth beam. The warp is stretched between these two beams, and you turn the beams to apply tension. Brakes keep the beams from rolling on their own.

- As the warp passes through the center of a low-warp loom, it goes through the castle, the part of the loom where the patterns are created. The castle is the structure that supports a series of rectangular frames called shafts.

- Each shaft holds multiple heddles, which on a beamed loom are often made of metal but could also be made of string or Texsolv (a polyester material with very little elasticity). Every warp thread goes through a heddle on one of the shafts. The shafts are connected to treadles on the floor that your feet control.

- When you push a treadle, it moves a shaft, causing all the warp threads going through the heddles on that shaft to rise. This creates a shed. The way the shafts are raised or lowered, along with the configuration of the structural part of the loom, determines whether it is a good choice for tapestry or not.

- Between the castle and the front beam, a beater holds a steel comb called a reed. The reed contains evenly spaced slots, and on most beam looms, the reed spaces the warp. Reeds with different numbers of slots (also called dents) per inch are available, and you must purchase a reed for each sett you want to use.

HIGH-WARP TAPESTRY LOOM

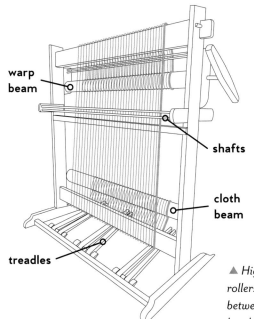

warp
beam

shafts

cloth
beam

treadles

LOW-WARP TAPESTRY LOOM

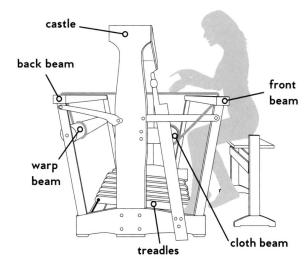

castle

back beam

front
beam

warp
beam

cloth beam

treadles

▲ *High- and low-warp tapestry looms work in similar ways. Both have two large rollers that hold the warp and the finished cloth, with the weaving happening between them. On high-warp looms, the warp is held on a beam above the weaver's head; on low-warp looms, the warp is on a beam at the back of the loom.*

High-Warp Looms with Beams

A high-warp loom with beams is the quintessential tapestry loom. The big tapestry workshops like the Australian Tapestry Workshop and Dovecot Studios in Scotland use huge versions of these looms, but they also come in smaller widths for home use. These looms may or may not have shafts to change the shed, but all of them are designed for tapestry weaving: the warp travels directly between the two beams and is held tight by hefty hardware. Though high-warp looms with beams are no longer being manufactured for commercial sale for the most part, you can frequently find used ones on the Internet.

These tapestry looms may or may not have a beater and a reed. If they do, the reed will help space the warp evenly. If they don't, you may put the warp on with the help of a similar comblike tool called a raddle, which will be removed once the warp is on the top beam. The tapestry weaving itself will maintain the warp spacing as you weave the weft.

Ulrika Leander, *Unfinished Sky* (working title), 2020. Wool and cotton, 80" × 67".
▲ *This work in progress is being woven on a 96" high-warp beamed loom designed by the artist and custom built.*

There are three types of low-warp beamed looms you should know about if you're considering a large loom for tapestry.

COUNTERBALANCE LOOMS have balanced shafts, meaning they generally have either two or four shafts that are attached to rollers at the top of the loom. When one or two shafts go up, the paired shafts on the other side of the rollers go down. Because tapestry only requires two sheds, and thus two shafts, and the tension on these looms is excellent, counterbalance looms are good choices for tapestry weaving. (See page 29.)

COUNTERMARCHE LOOMS have a much more complicated shedding mechanism. The shafts are connected to upper and lower lamms, or bars, which raise and lower each shaft. The lamms are paired so that when one combination of shafts is raised, all the other ones are lowered. This means that the tension on the warp as a whole is always even. When half the warp goes up, the other half goes down. These looms provide excellent tension and are great choices for rug weaving and tapestry. (See the Cranbrook loom on page 25.)

JACK LOOMS are the most common type of floor loom and are often used for weaving functional fabrics. These looms have shafts that are pushed up when you step on a treadle. Often the warp does not run straight from the front to the back beam, and as tension on the warp is increased, the jacks start to float upward, making it difficult or impossible to create a shed. In my experience, many jack looms, especially the ones that are made to fold up in an X-shaped pattern, won't hold a high tension at all. Jack looms made by Macomber are the exceptions: Macomber looms that are at least 40 inches wide have very heavy hardware and will provide excellent tension for tapestry weaving.

The Walking Loom

Rio Grande weavers in the American Southwest use a particularly excellent form of counterbalance loom called a walking loom. These looms have a counterbalance mechanism and are traditionally used by New Mexican Hispano weavers to make tapestries and rugs. The weaver stands while weaving, and their body weight shifts the shed on the loom as they "walk" from one treadle to the other. My very first tapestry loom was a walking loom that I built in a college course in New Mexico.

◂ *Lara Manzanares of Tierra Wools in Chama, New Mexico, weaves on a walking loom in the company's weaving and teaching studio.*

Choosing a Tapestry Loom

The loom you choose may not be quite as permanent a decision as you'd like to think. First of all, used looms are fairly easy to buy and sell in today's Internet age, so if you purchase something that you don't like, you can probably find someone else who will. Secondly, you don't know how your practice of tapestry will evolve. Maybe one day you'll want to weave very large pieces and need a very large loom. Or perhaps you'll become a maker of miniatures that you produce on pipe looms you make yourself. Don't let the process of choosing a loom trip you up.

Most people new to weaving who want to try tapestry will start with a frame loom. These looms are portable, less expensive, and provide an easy entry into tapestry weaving. If you don't already own a loom that works for tapestry, I recommend you start with a tensioned frame loom.

If you do want a larger loom, consider one of the beamed floor looms. High-warp looms require less space than low-warp looms with shafts, which are large pieces of furniture and might well replace your dining room table. On a high-warp loom, you can also see more of the work in progress and view it in much the way it will be seen on the wall. On a low-warp loom where the fell line must be kept close to the weaver's body for ergonomic reasons, you're able to see less of the work in progress before rolling it around the front beam.

The two kinds of looms also require different body positions. High-warp looms demand more upright arm and shoulder motion than low-warp looms. Some people find that working at a low-warp loom is more comfortable, since you can sit with the work right next to your torso and directly under your shoulders.

The chart on the next page can help you in choosing a loom.

▲ *Glimåkra counterbalance loom*

TYPE OF LOOM		PRICE	STORAGE FOOTPRINT	SIZE OF TAPESTRY WOVEN	PORTABILITY	
Untensioned frame looms	Slot or peg loom	$	Tiny to small; some fit in your shoulder bag	2" to 8" square	Very portable	
	Copper pipe loom	$	Small	Tiny to about 20"	Very portable	
Tensioned frame looms	Galvanized or black pipe loom	$$	Small to medium	Tiny to very large	Small looms somewhat portable, large not	
	Mirrix	$$	Small to medium, folds flat	Tiny to 36" wide, variable lengths	Looms under 22" very portable	
Looms with beams: high- and low-warp examples	Countermarche/ counterbalance	$$$$$	Large	Up to weaving width of loom; as long as needed	None	
	Jack: Macomber 40" and larger	$$$$	Medium	Up to weaving width of loom; as long as needed	None	
	Large high-warp tapestry loom	$$$$	Medium, but smaller than Macomber	Up to weaving width of loom; as long as needed	None	

Weaving Both Tapestry and Functional Fabrics

Many people who start weaving tapestry already weave functional textiles. Since most of us don't have a lot of space for multiple large looms, being able to do both things on one loom might be a good compromise for you. If you like the smaller footprint that a jack loom provides, you'll want a 40-inch Macomber. If you have a little more room, a counterbalance or countermarche floor loom is an excellent choice.

My favorite loom for tapestry is the Harrisville Designs rug loom. Like all countermarche looms, it is more complicated to tie up, but the tension is outstanding. It has both a warp extender, which keeps the warp at the same tension at all times, and a worm gear, which allows incremental tensioning of the warp. The Schacht Spindle

Company and Glimåkra also make excellent countermarche looms, and Leclerc and Glimåkra make nice counterbalance looms.

Approaches to Weaving

Over thousands of years, many different approaches to tapestry weaving have developed around the world. This means that today we have a wide variety of choices for equipment and weaving style. I describe two of those choices here.

Weaving from the Front or from the Back

Whether you weave with the back or the front side of the tapestry facing you is a matter of preference. Both methods have been used throughout the long history of tapestry. The most

TENSIONING	WAYS TO SPACE THE WARP	BEATER PART OF LOOM	TYPE OF SHEDDING DEVICE
Fair to poor; no tensioning device	Depends on width of slots or pegs	No	None
Excellent; threaded rod and nuts	Any sett; weaver adjusts	No	Most often, none
Excellent; threaded rod and nuts	Any sett; weaver adjusts	No	Often, leashes
Excellent; threaded rod and wing nuts	Change coil; 6, 8, 10, 12, 14, 18, 20, 22 epi; can be warped without the coil	No	Rotating shedding device; can be attached to a foot-operated treadle
Excellent	Change reed	Yes	Shafts
Excellent	Change reed	Yes	Shafts
Excellent	Any sett or change reed	Maybe	Shafts or leashes

famous tapestry workshops in the world today, France's Manufacture Nationale des Gobelins and Manufacture de Beauvais (both of which have been in existence for hundreds of years), weave everything from the back on both high- and low-warp looms.

Every tapestry weaver has an opinion about whether weaving from the back or the front is best, or at least reasons why they weave the way they do. Archie Brennan, perhaps the most influential tapestry weaver in modern times, started weaving from the back as a 16-year-old apprentice at the Dovecot workshop in Scotland in the 1940s. Eventually he switched to weaving from the front, which he did for the rest of his career. Brennan said that weaving from the back is technique based and weaving from the front is image based. There is some truth to this distinction, and here's why.

When you weave tapestry from the front, you can see exactly what you're weaving without becoming a contortionist, using a mirror, or just plain guessing. If what you want to weave is largely pictorial instead of abstract, you may choose to weave from the front. It is more difficult to flip a design over in your head when you are creating a picture. Making decisions about color and form based on what you see right in front of you is easier from the front, and your view of the weaving will not be obscured by tails as it would be when weaving from the back.

One drawback to weaving from the front is that your hands are in direct contact with the front of the tapestry and, as a result, it may get somewhat dirty or worn. There are also some techniques, such as double weft interlock (see page 210), and some hatching forms (see page 167) that are very difficult to accomplish from the front. And there is a harder-to-describe quality of mind when weaving from the front: because it is easier to become focused on the image, I find it is also easier to lose sight of the feeling of the overall work.

My work is more abstract than pictorial, and several of the techniques I use work better from the back. I could absolutely weave almost everything in my tapestries from the front if I wanted to, but I was taught to weave from the back, and my brain likes the added challenge of flipping the image. When some of the image is obscured, I am less constrained by making the picture "look right" and more invested in the overall feeling of the work. Even if you weave complicated realistic pictures, you definitely could weave them from the back — European weavers have done it for hundreds of years.

A technical benefit of weaving from the back is that the yarn tails are facing you, so their bulk is not in the way of the cartoon fastened on the far side of the weaving. I also do a lot of splicing and sewing slits, and sometimes I stitch in yarn tails as I go, which is more easily accomplished when the back side of the work is facing me.

The ways of warping various looms also affect the side from which you may find it easier to weave. When using a tensioned loom with a continuous warp, such as a Mirrix loom, there is a second layer of warp on the back of the loom. If you are weaving from the back, this layer obscures the front of the tapestry. If you use a Mirrix or a pipe loom with a continuous warp and you hate the fact that you won't be able to see the front of the tapestry at all, you'll be happier weaving from the front. If you are using a tensioned loom warped in the figure-8 manner (see page 79) or a high-warp beamed tapestry loom, you can turn the loom over or walk around to the back to see the other side and even weave from either side if a technique requires it. Now that is the best of both worlds!

NOTE: Being able to weave from either the front or the back depending on what the equipment and design demand is a good skill to have. You'll develop the ability to do this with experience. Most techniques shown in this book can be done from either the front or the back. But because over the last 50 years most tapestry weavers in the United States have moved to weaving from the front, the material in this book is presented that way.

Weaving across in a Line versus Building Up Shapes

How you approach weaving your weft also has implications for the type of loom you use. You can weave one line at a time, covering all the warps across your piece with as many different-colored wefts as you need to make your image. You can also weave one shape at a time, building it upward until you complete it. Some weavers use both techniques in the same piece. Which way you weave a tapestry or even a section of a tapestry will depend on the equipment you are weaving on and the techniques you're using to create the image.

Historically tapestry has been an art form that created very large or even mural-size images. Often multiple weavers sat side by side and wove on the same piece. To accomplish this, they had to weave the area right in front of them, so they wove a shape at a time. Weavers in workshops and ateliers all over the world still work collaboratively this way, building up shapes on both high- and low-warp looms.

For some weavers, ergonomics play a part in which weaving approach they use. With a large woven area, weaving all the way across in a line requires that the weaver move their body constantly to access that line of weaving. Weaving this way can be harder on the weaver's body than sitting in one place. Many all-in-a-line weavers solve this by standing to weave, while others use sliding benches.

In the United States, many tapestry weavers use countermarche or counterbalance floor looms. These looms have a beater with a reed, and weavers commonly weave all the way across the warp in a line so that they can use the beater to pack in the weft. Use of the reed has a distinct advantage for weft tension control and makes weaving line by line a fantastic way to get perfectly straight selvages. I'll talk more about this very important concept in chapter 7.

Which technique you use may also be related to the image you're creating. If your image has a lot of horizontal elements or hatching (see page 161), your forms may be interlocked side to side, which may require you to work across the whole warp to create them. Weavings that contain lots of shading made with hatching will have larger areas where the weaving progresses a line at a time. In contrast, if the work is more graphic with distinct shapes, it can be woven one shape at a time. There are also techniques like eccentric outlining (see page 253) that can only be accomplished by weaving up in shapes.

If you're a beginner, you don't have to figure out right now which way you prefer to weave. Dive in with whatever loom you have, and as you learn you may decide you prefer other equipment and one particular method of weaving. It should be noted that it is possible to build shapes using a tapestry fork instead of the loom beater on a low-warp loom and to weave all in a line on a high-warp loom.

In this book we'll start out by weaving one line at a time. This makes it easier to understand the structure of the weaving and helps you grasp important concepts such as meet and separate (see page 132). However, I do want you to understand that individual shapes can also be woven, and we will practice this in chapters 12, 13, and 14.

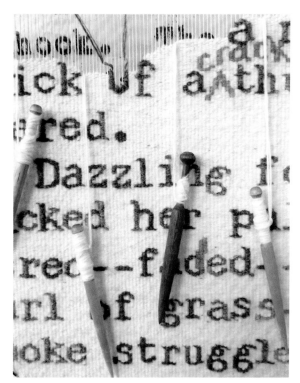

Sarah C. Swett, *Dinner Dazzle* (detail), 2015.
Wool, 15" × 9".
▲ *Weaving up in shapes on a high-warp loom.*

Michael Rohde, *Florid* (working title), 2020 (in progress).
Wool, approximately 80" × 49".
▲ *This work in progress shows Michael Rohde's line-by-line weaving on a low-warp loom.*

Additional Tools

Besides a loom, you'll need a few other tools before you can start weaving. You need something such as a bobbin or a butterfly to hold the weft yarn. If your loom doesn't open the shed mechanically, you also need a way to pick up the shed; battens or shed sticks serve this purpose. Finally, you need a way to beat the weft into place. Weavers use a tapestry fork, the reed on a loom, or the point of a tapestry bobbin to accomplish this. Depending on how the yarn you buy is packaged (for example, on cones or in skeins), you may need a few tools to wind it into other forms. And of course, you'll need some incidental tools and supplies along the way.

For Managing Yarn

The type of loom you're using will influence the other tools you need, especially how you manage your weft yarn and beat it into place.

Weavers who use low-warp looms (where the warp is horizontal) often use Aubusson bones to organize their weft bundles. This tool, sometimes called a flute, is generally made of wood and holds a length of weft wrapped around it. It lacks the point of a tapestry bobbin.

Weavers using high-warp tapestry looms (where the warp is vertical) most often use tapestry bobbins to hold the weft. The bobbins hang down on the surface of the weaving or are stuck in the

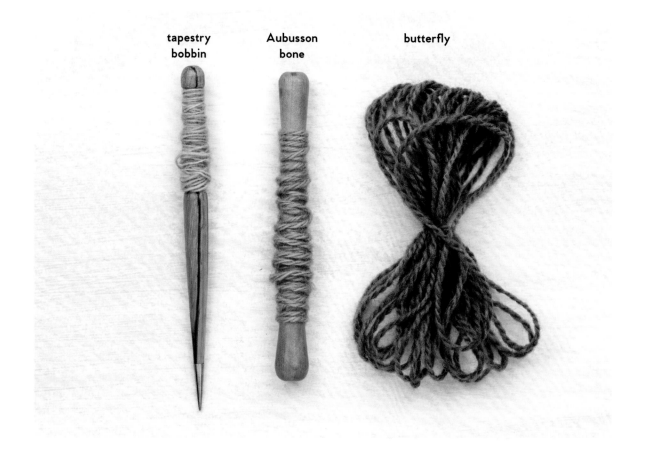

tapestry bobbin   Aubusson bone   butterfly

warp when not in use, then picked up again when needed. A tapestry bobbin is perhaps the most iconic symbol of this medium. The shaft of the bobbin holds a length of weft yarn, and the point is used for tapping it into place.

Bobbins are often made of wood, though there are less expensive plastic versions available. Wooden bobbins can either be entirely wood or have metal tips. The metal tips last longer, but they aren't necessarily more functional. Wooden-pointed bobbins do wear down with use, but you can sharpen them again or use them for areas where you don't need the point to beat in the weft.

Tapestry bobbins come in many sizes and even different shapes. Matching the bobbin to the loom you're using is important. A very long metal-tipped bobbin that hangs down over the edge of a table or gets wedged against part of your loom could easily injure you. If you're making smaller tapestries, smaller bobbins are appropriate since you don't need as much yarn length. A set of 5-inch bobbins will work well regardless of the kind of loom you're using. If you have a high-warp tapestry loom and are weaving very large pieces at wider setts, you will need more weft yarn in your bundle and should use larger and longer bobbins to accommodate that.

You don't, however, have to use a physical device to hold your yarn at all. For the most part, I use butterflies to manage my weft yarn. Also called finger skeins, butterflies are small bundles of yarn that can be passed through the shed. Butterflies work on all kinds of looms, but if the shed is too small, they tend to unravel.

Butterflies or Bobbins?
How to Choose

Bobbins are most often used on large high-warp tapestry looms. They keep the weft organized and wrapped around the shaft. The point of the bobbin is used to beat in the weft. When weaving on high-warp looms, tapestry weavers often manipulate the weft with one hand and, with the point of the bobbin in the other hand, tap the weft into place after it is inserted. Having one tool that both holds the yarn and packs it in is efficient, and when the weaver no longer needs that color, the bobbin can hang down the front of the weaving until it is needed again.

Bobbins don't work well on low-warp looms because, due to the horizontal surface of the weaving, they can't hang vertically when not in use. Low-warp weavers who want to use bobbins usually choose Aubusson bones, which lie nicely on the surface of the weaving and aren't likely to stab the weaver. On small frame looms, bobbins help keep fragile yarns from being abraded.

Because they are handmade, butterflies are free, meaning you don't need to buy a tool at all. But if you're using a lot of weft bundling (see page 49) with multiple strands of yarn, the yarns can easily get tangled in a butterfly, so it might be preferable to organize the yarn using a bobbin.

There are other ways to manage your weft yarn. Weavers who work on smaller frame looms use the widest variety of tools for this purpose: I've seen people use netting shuttles, small stick shuttles, yarn needles, and other small cardboard, wood, or plastic pieces to hold lengths of yarn. Many of these devices are made to hold and organize embroidery yarns.

For Picking Up the Shed

If you have a loom without a shedding device, you may need a tool to help you pick up one or both sheds. On small frame looms in particular, a small pointed shed stick is very useful. You can use the stick to pick the shed, then turn it sideways to open the shed so you can insert the weft. Sometimes people use yarn needles to pick the shed and pull the yarn through. This is functional but may be hard on the yarn. My favorite tool for picking up the shed is a shed stick that is about ½ inch wide, 7 inches long, and ⅜ inch thick, as seen on page 112.

If you're using a loom with a shedding device, the shaft/treadle assembly or leashes open the shed for you.

For Beating In the Weft

A tapestry fork or beater is essential for tapestry weaving. There are many kinds out there, and the type you choose will probably depend on the loom you're using and the way you're weaving. Tapestry forks can be simple lightweight tools. They can be made of wood, metal, or even plastic, but my favorite ones have teeth similar to the metal tools used to comb a dog's hair. The sturdy metal teeth slide easily through the warp.

The beater you use has a lot to do with the nature of the fabric you create, and tapestry weavers sometimes disagree about the optimal weight of the beater. The more you whack the fibers together, the stiffer the resulting fabric will be. I strive to create a flexible fabric, and though I want the surface of the tapestry to be firm enough that it will remain

▶ *Various kinds of tapestry forks*

structurally sound for as long as someone wants to enjoy the work, I do not want a fabric that feels like cardboard. Therefore, I use the same lightweight forks on my low-warp, high-warp, and frame looms. As long as I've chosen the right warp for the weft I'm using, a gentle tap is all that is needed to place the weft, and a heavily weighted beater is not necessary. There are tapestry weavers, however, who swear by their weighted, usually metal, beaters for really whacking the weft into place.

Tapestry forks are made with different numbers of tines or teeth per inch. I recommend getting a tapestry fork with six to eight tines per inch. When the space between the tines is too narrow, the teeth catch on the warp, which makes beating difficult or impossible. The metal-toothed beaters I favor have tines set at various widths.

If you use a tapestry bobbin to manage your yarn, you may want to use the point of the bobbin to beat in the weft. Bobbin users often use a tapestry fork to give the weft an extra tap from time to time. On high-warp looms, the warp is often picked or opened with leashes. It is efficient to use a bobbin to both hold the weft and beat it into place. With one hand you can open the shed, and with your other hand you can place the weft and tap it in with the bobbin. See page 119 for further instructions on how to weave with a tapestry bobbin.

If your loom has a beater that contains a reed, you may use that to beat in the weft occasionally or most of the time, depending on the forms you're weaving. You'll still need a tapestry fork, since no matter how you weave, you will at times build up shapes and use the fork to beat in smaller areas.

For Winding Yarn

The way yarn is packaged for sale, also called the "put up," varies. Your yarn might be wound on cones or tubes, or it might come in a skein, hank,

▲ *Yarn can come packaged in many ways.*

or ball. If the yarn you purchase is already in a ball or on a small tube, you may be able to weave with it just as it is. If you order larger amounts of yarn on a cone, you may want to divide the yarn into smaller balls or cakes.

If your yarn comes in a skein or hank, you'll have to wind it into a ball before you can use it. To do this, you'll need either an umbrella swift and ball winder or a patient helper (or an extra chair), a lot of time, and some creativity. You can have someone hold a skein open or put it around the back of a chair and then wind a round ball by hand. But you'll be able to make a nice center-pull ball of yarn (sometimes called a yarn cake) using a swift and ball winder.

SWIFT. There are different kinds of swifts available, but I use an umbrella swift, so called because it folds up sort of like an umbrella for easy storage. It opens easily to accommodate various sizes of yarn skeins, and it swivels to allow the skein to unwind as you wind your ball.

◄ Umbrella swift and ball winder

BALL WINDER. This tool takes the yarn from the swift and makes a ball from which the yarn can be taken from either the outside or the inside. Ball winders come in both hand-crank and electric versions.

For Warping a Beamed Loom

There are as many ways to warp a floor loom as there are weavers. These are the tools you should consider for this task:

WARPING BOARD. This is a four-sided board that has pegs on all four sides and is usually 1 yard wide. It is used to measure long warps for floor looms.

SLEY HOOK. This simple metal tool helps grab the yarn and pull it through the reed and perhaps the heddles on your loom. Both high- and low-warp tapestry looms can have reeds.

LEASE STICKS. These sticks hold the "cross" that you create when winding the warp (see page 83) and make sure the warp bundle doesn't get out of order. They must be wider than your weaving width and usually have holes in the end so they can be positioned parallel to one another and tied together. When putting any warp wound on a warping board onto a large loom, you'll need two lease sticks.

warping board

Common tools for warping a beamed loom. Lease sticks can consist of two sturdy dowels, as shown here, or flat sticks with holes in the ends to tie them together.

sley hook

lease sticks

Notions

- **Sharp embroidery-type scissors** are great for snipping weft yarn.

- You'll need some **tapestry needles** to sew in yarn tails and to stitch slits closed. A tapestry needle is dull on the end. I like size 18 or 20 tapestry needles.

- Use **sharp sewing needles** for finishing and mounting your tapestry.

- **T-pins** are helpful for securing broken warps. You can also use them to pin your cartoon to the tapestry in progress as you mark the next bit of the design on the warp.

- **Strong thread** is needed for sewing slits. I use Coats & Clark upholstery thread, which comes in various colors, though most often I use white. Sometimes it is advantageous to match the color of the thread to the weft used on one side of the slit.

- Keep a **permanent marker** to mark your design on the warp. Test your markers before using them on your weaving to make sure the marks will withstand high heat and water without bleeding. (See page 233.)

- Use a **measuring tape** to measure things that are round or flexible.

- A **sewing machine** is helpful but not required. I use my sewing machine to finish the hems and sew on the twill tape for hanging. All of this can also be done by hand.

3 Yearning for Yarn

Cloth is a primary human need. We have made it for tens of thousands of years to use for shelter, clothing, and other practical purposes. It's also served as decoration both for our bodies and for our buildings. Cloth is one of the fundamental building blocks of our world, and so it isn't surprising that many of us are so interested in making it for either functional reasons or decoration. For the maker, the magic of cloth lies — at least in part — in the sensuous nature of yarn. Many fiber artists and crafters are drawn strongly to this tactile, rich, textural, and pliable material.

In reality, you can weave with almost anything that is flexible and fiberlike. But not all yarns work well for tapestry. In fact, I recommend that beginners choose from a fairly small subset of yarns. You'll need a strong plain-colored yarn for the warp and multicolored yarns for the weft.

Choosing yarns for tapestry can feel a little overwhelming at the beginning. A good place to start is with one of a few basic tapestry weft yarns (see the chart on page 51) at 7 to 8 warp ends per inch (called the sett). As you understand better what is possible with tapestry weaving and what

images you want to create, you can adjust your yarn, sett, and even your tools. The yarn you start with and what you learn about it can then serve as the basis for choosing other yarns, perhaps ones with different colors, textures, fiber types, or sizes, if necessary. We'll talk more about sett in chapter 4.

Most of the yarns you'll find in your local yarn store probably aren't the best for tapestry weaving. As you learn to weave tapestry, it's helpful to understand which characteristics are important in a tapestry yarn, why they are important, and which yarns have these characteristics.

Understanding Fleece

The terms below are common ones used to refer to fleece from any animal and will help in your understanding of how tapestry yarn is made.

Micron count: A laboratory test that measures the diameter of a fiber. The larger the number, the coarser the fiber. Micron counts can vary not only within a flock but within one fleece.

Staple: The length of one lock of a fleece from cut end to tip.

Lock: A small naturally occurring group of fibers in a fleece. It is easy to grasp a lock of a fleece and pull it out to examine it, as seen below.

Color: Sheep fleeces come in a variety of colors. In recent decades, many sheep lines have been bred to produce white sheep because the industry values white fleece for dyeing. But many small flocks are still bred to produce a range of natural colors, which can be beautiful when used undyed in tapestries.

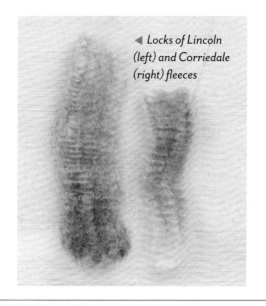

◀ *Locks of Lincoln (left) and Corriedale (right) fleeces*

Fiber Common in Tapestry Yarns

It is possible to choose just one warp and one weft yarn for all your tapestries, but exploring the wide variety of yarns available in the world can be inspiring and fun. After all, yarn is the basic material of our art form. For hundreds of years, tapestries have been made from linen, cotton, wool, and silk. These natural fibers are available in many places in the world and are good candidates for weft. Some can also be used for warp. Each of these fibers acts differently in a woven structure.

The material used most for tapestry weft today and throughout history is the protein fiber wool. As you can see in the illustration below, the outer layer of a wool fiber has scales that overlap each other, rather like shingles on a roof. These little scales grab the scales on adjacent pieces of yarn, increasing the stability of the structure. This makes wool an ideal fiber to use for tapestry weaving. If you've ever accidentally thrown a wool sweater in the washing machine with hot water, you know how firmly these fibers can grab each

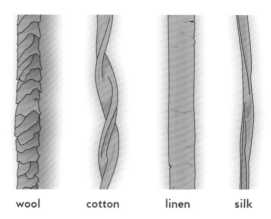

wool   cotton   linen   silk

▲ *As seen under a microscope, the structure of various fibers. Wool has tiny scales that overlap each other. Linen and cotton are plant fibers that lack scales. Silk, made by silkworms, is one continuous strand that is very smooth.*

other because you may have managed to felt your sweater into a shrunken, thick, unwearable mess.

In contrast, linen and cotton (which are cellulose fibers, meaning they come from plants) lack these scales. Linen, which comes from the flax plant, has a long fiber length, or staple, much longer than that of cotton. You won't find linen used very often for weft anymore because wool is so much easier to weave with and is available in more colors. But linen is still used occasionally for warp because it is very strong and smooth. Since linen does not stretch, however, beginning tapestry weavers may find it difficult to use as warp. Cotton comes from the seed heads of the cotton plant, which are known as bolls. The fiber length is quite short, but cotton can be made into a fantastic warp material for tapestry. Cotton also is a possible fiber for weft and is a good choice if you have a wool sensitivity.

Silk is a natural fiber that silkworms produce as one long strand into a cocoon. It is completely smooth and often has a very shiny appearance. Silk fibers are less elastic than wool, but they are very long and can make luxurious, lustrous yarn. Tapestry weavers often blend silk with wool to take advantage of both the lustrous nature of the silk and the structural tendency of the wool to grab fibers next to it.

Synthetic or manufactured fibers are also made into yarns, but I encourage you to look for the natural fibers mentioned here. Synthetic fibers are created from oil and chemicals, and more and more research indicates that we're filling our environment with these substances that do not easily degrade.

The Wonder of Wool

Wool is by far the preferred fiber for tapestry weft. Wool is a wonderful, versatile fiber, with a lot of elasticity; it also takes dye very well. There are many sheep breeds, and each breed has distinctive staple lengths, fiber thicknesses, and colors.

Because there is such a range of fleece characteristics, the resulting yarns also vary widely. Some are better than others for tapestry weaving.

The staple length from sheep within the same breed can vary slightly depending on how often they are shorn, but there can be a dramatic difference between the staple lengths of different breeds. A lock of one breed's fleece could be 1 inch long, while a lock from another breed could be 14 inches long. Merino sheep have short, low-micron-count fleeces. They produce very fine, soft wool that is great for clothing. But for tapestry weaving we often want yarn that is more lustrous (or reflective) because these shiny wools reflect light more readily and make the surface of the tapestry look less muted. Tapestry wools are frequently made from fleeces with longer locks, which have thicker (higher micron count) fibers. These longwool breeds include Wensleydale, Romney, Teeswater, Corriedale, Spelsau, and Lincoln, among others.

Thanks to the Internet, fiber lovers have access to a wide variety of wool types, often from small flocks. These marvelous yarns frequently come from small mills scattered all over the world. The breed of sheep your wool comes from may not be important to you, but you should take care to observe the way the yarn reflects light, especially in the weaving. If you like a surface that has some shine, be sure to choose a wool that has some longwool breeds in it. If you like a more matte, or less shiny, look to your tapestry surface, shorter-staple breeds are fine.

Yarns you might want in a soft garment that you'll wear next to your skin have smaller, and therefore a greater number of, scales. The smaller size and larger number of scales breaks up the light reflected off the fiber's surface, which results in yarn that is not as lustrous as yarn made from fibers with larger scales. In addition to reflecting more light and seeming shinier, these larger, courser fibers are also thicker, and the yarn doesn't feel as soft to your hand. But we can weave tapestry with wools that have larger scales because we are usually not wearing a tapestry next to our skin.

Other animal fibers such as alpaca, llama, cashmere, and mohair can be used for yarn, but most yarns for tapestry weft are made from wool. Wool is also used for warp yarns, though there are fewer choices for wool warps than cotton ones. (For more about choosing warp yarns, see page 46.)

Yarn Terminology

Many words get thrown around when we start talking about yarn. These are the most common ones used for tapestry weaving.

SINGLE. The basic building block of a piece of yarn is a thread made by twisting together fibers from a sheep fleece (or other animal or plant fiber) so that those fibers make a continuous strand. A yarn that is made up of just one strand is called a single, and you can weave (and knit and crochet) with singles.

PLY. Because yarn is used in so many different kinds of projects, it comes in many different sizes (which refers to thickness). One way to make a thicker yarn is to twist together two or more singles to make a plied yarn. The ply number refers to how many individual threads or singles make up the yarn. Many tapestry yarns are 2-ply, but they could contain more plies than that.

WEFT BUNDLE. In tapestry weaving, we have a narrow range of yarn sizes that will work with the warp sett at which we are working. Some weavers make their weft yarn the size they need it to be by grouping several smaller yarns together in a bunch called a weft bundle. We'll discuss weaving with weft bundles more on page 49. The yarns in the bundle could be singles yarns or thinner plied yarns.

Most yarns for tapestry are either a singles yarn or a 2-ply yarn. Beginners often find it easiest to start with a yarn that is thick enough to use just one strand at a time; that strand could be a single or a plied yarn. More advanced tapestry weavers often use a weft bundle because this allows them to mix colors.

SIZING TERMS. If you've been to a yarn store lately, you've probably noticed that the yarns are often categorized by sizes with names like lace weight, fingering, DK, sport, worsted, and bulky. The sizes range from lace weight, which is very thin, to bulky, which is quite thick. Each of these designations comes with a number, and you may see these symbols on the yarn packaging instead of the actual term. These terms may be helpful in talking about weft yarn sizes for tapestry, but I don't recommend using most knitting yarns for tapestry weaving. We'll talk about why later in this chapter.

▲ Yarn sizing often includes numbers like this.

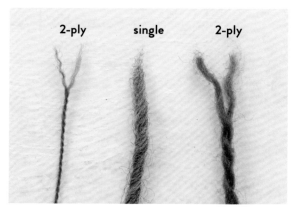

▲ Yarn thickness does not depend on the number of plies it contains. A 2-ply yarn can be thick or thin, as pictured here. Similarly, a singles yarn could be very thick, as it is in this photo, or very thin, which makes it easy to bundle with other strands.

Yarn Numbers Explained

Yarn numbering systems vary depending on the yarn's fiber content; the numbers for cotton yarns, for example, are different from those for wool or linen or silk yarns. This numbering system dates from days when a separate guild governed each type of natural fiber. (For more information on this numbering system, see Liz Gipson's book *A Weaver's Guide to Yarn*.) As you choose warp and weft yarns, it can be helpful to have a basic understanding of what the numbers mean.

Because I recommend using cotton seine twine for warp, I will explain the numbering system used for cotton. Cotton seine twine yarn comes in a wide range of sizes, which are denoted as 12/18, 12/12, 12/9, 12/6, and 20/6. The number *after* the slash refers to how many plies are in the yarn. If you unravel a piece of these yarns, you'll find there are 18, 12, 9, or 6 plies respectively.

The number *before* the slash refers to the size of each individual ply making up the yarn. The higher the number, the thinner the thread and the more yards in a pound. For example, 20/6 is thinner than 12/6 because, even though both have 6 plies, the *size* of each ply is smaller in the 20/6 yarn than in the 12/6 yarn.

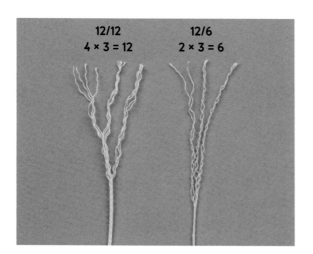

12/12
4 × 3 = 12

12/6
2 × 3 = 6

The common cotton rug warp, on the other hand, is usually denoted 8/4. This yarn has 4 plies, and the size of each ply is thicker than the size of each ply in the cotton seine twine described.

What the fraction doesn't indicate is the way the yarn is made. As you see in the image at left, the seine twine contains three separate bundles. In 12/12 seine twine, four threads are plied together, then three of those yarns are plied again. This creates a cabled yarn that is incredibly strong and resistant to abrasion — perfect for tapestry warp. The 8/4 carpet warp has 4 plies that are only twisted together one time. This results in a much weaker yarn that does not resist abrasion as well.

Many weft yarns also are denoted in fractions, such as 5/2 or 60/2. As with the cotton examples, for wool weft yarn, the number *before* the slash refers to the size of each individual thread making up the yarn and the number *after* the slash refers to the number of plies. The 5/2 yarn, then, is much thicker than the 60/2 yarn.

Most tapestry yarns are either 2-ply or singles (these would technically have a fraction with a "1" after the slash, such as 4/1, but you'll rarely see this). For example, the weaversbazaar fine yarn is denoted 18/2, as shown in the chart on page 51. It is a thin 2-ply yarn, thinner than the weaversbazaar medium yarn, which is 9.5/2. In fact, the medium yarn is approximately double the size of the fine yarn, as seen when you do the math: 9.5 × 2 = 19, which indicates a size similar to 18/2.

If figuring out what the numbers related to a particular yarn mean seems too confusing, I recommend purchasing a small amount of the yarn you're interested in and sampling it before committing to a large order.

◀ *The individual threads making up these two warps are the same size, as indicated by the "12," but the number of plies is different, as indicated by the "12" and "6."*

Good Tapestry Yarn

Don't waste your time weaving tapestry with a yarn that isn't attractive to you when you see it in the skein or on a cone or that isn't a functional yarn for tapestry weaving, as I describe in this section. Weaving tapestry is a slow process, and spending days, weeks, or months weaving a tapestry that is not pleasing because you chose poor yarns is disappointing and discouraging to your progress as a tapestry weaver. Some of the yarns that are appropriate for tapestry are relatively inexpensive, so take the time to seek them out if cost is an issue.

For the Warp

Warp is important. It needs to be strong enough to withstand the constant abrasion caused by opening the shed, passing the weft yarn through it, and beating in the weft. It also has to hold a tight tension and potentially to provide some shrinkage once the piece is off the loom. Many traditional warps were made of linen, which is a strong fiber that does not shrink or stretch. It makes a strong warp, but it is more difficult to weave on than wool or cotton. If it is on the loom for a long period of time, linen can become limp, which can cause problems with warp tension. The lack of stretch in the fiber also makes it less forgiving than cotton or wool warps, and any slight difference in the tension from one warp to the next warp can make it difficult to get an even surface. I do not recommend that beginners use linen warp.

Today, most tapestry weavers use warps of wool or cotton. Not all warps of the same material are created equal, however. As I discussed on page 45, an 8/4 cotton rug warp is an inferior tapestry warp to one of cotton seine twine because the construction of the yarn makes it less resistant to abrasion. Similarly, a single-ply wool warp is much weaker than a wool warp with 2 or more plies.

Navajo weavers traditionally use wool warps that they often spin themselves. A tightly spun or plied wool warp can be a wonderful thing to weave on, but well-made wool warps are harder to find commercially. Wool will shrink a little bit when steamed, though not as much as cotton does when it is steamed. Wool warp is similar in elasticity to cotton and can be used by beginners. Take care to test the strength of any wool warp that is a single (not plied). If you can easily break it with your hands, then it is too weak for tapestry.

Cotton warps are the easiest to find and provide an excellent ground for any tapestry. When steamed, a cotton warp will shrink a fair amount after the piece comes off the loom, so take that into consideration when planning your design (shrinkage happens in the direction of the warp). The shrinkage from steaming helps flatten and tighten up a tapestry and can get rid of slight inconsistencies in warp or weft tension. (See page 266 for more information about accommodating for shrinking warp and weft.) The cotton seine twine warps I recommend are cabled and strong, and they come in many sizes. They are most often sourced from Scandinavia, though frequently are made in Egypt. Many tapestry weavers use them throughout their careers.

How the warp feels in your hands is also important because you'll be touching it a lot as you weave. A singles wool warp is wonderful and soft, but because it can break easily, I don't trust a singles warp for large pieces. A plied wool warp is much stronger than a singles, though not quite as soft. Cotton seine twine will take a very high tension, so if you find that your cuticles are bleeding from manipulating the warp, back off on your loom tension a little bit. Your hands will get tougher as you weave, but tapestry making shouldn't include raw fingers.

The color of the warp is less important. Cotton seine twine in the 12/6 size comes in many colors, and wool warps are available in black, brown, and white. Because in tapestry weaving the warp is completely covered by the weft, most tapestry weavers just use white warp. This is the easiest to see as you work, and if the tapestry has hems at the top and bottom, the warp is not seen in the finished piece. However, if you want fringe on your work or are using a technique such as four-selvage warping (where tiny amounts of the warp will show), you might consider a colored warp.

For the Weft

A good weft is a firm yarn that packs in easily and makes a sturdy fabric. Because it doesn't have to withstand the tension of the loom, weft yarn doesn't need to be as strong as the warp. It should be well constructed, however, so that it is strong enough to withstand some light abrasion while being passed through the shed. In addition, it shouldn't fall apart while you adjust the weft tension and beat it into place.

FIRM. Wefts that are firmer hold their shape well. Remember that tapestries will most likely be hung on a wall, and you don't want squishy yarn compacting over time and sinking on the warp. Lofty yarns have a lot of air in them, which makes them lovely for knitted garments but terrible for weft-faced weaving. Lofty yarns also pack in too much, meaning you have to weave many, many passes to make progress in the weaving. Additionally, yarn with a lot of air in it will compress as you beat, making the surface of your tapestry look very flat and dull.

NOT TOO STRETCHY. Stretchiness is another quality that makes knitting yarns exceptionally difficult to weave with. You don't want your yarn to have a lot of stretch in it when you put tension on a piece of it. When a yarn wants to bounce back on itself, as a nice knitting wool will do, it

will want to do that in your weaving as well. This causes problems with weft tension and draws in your edges.

COLOR OPTIONS. Since tapestry is an art medium and we are creating images, color choice is a big consideration, especially if you don't dye your own yarn. Many commercially dyed yarns don't come in that many colors. If you are weaving something for which you want five reds in gradation, for example, most commercial yarn sources are not going to provide that. Notable exceptions are weaversbazaar, Appleton crewel, and Australian Tapestry Workshop yarns. (See chapter 5 for more on making yarn color choices.)

DURABLE COLOR. You also want your yarn to be both lightfast and colorfast, which means that the color won't fade in light or run in water. Every fabric left in direct sunshine will fade, some more quickly than others. Tapestries should never be hung in direct sunlight. Beyond that, some yarns are more resistant to light than others. Many natural dyes are not very lightfast, but you can easily test the yarn before you weave with it: Wrap the yarn around a big card and cover half of the card with another card. Place it in the sun for a few months, then remove the covered half of the card to see if fading has occurred. To test whether the dyes in your yarn will run if the textile gets wet (even if only from steam), wet the yarn before weaving with it. If you are not familiar with a yarn and you suspect it might have been hand-dyed, naturally dyed, or is not colorfast, it is best to put it through these tests before you work with it.

SIZE. The size of the yarn is critical. A wide range of sizes are used for tapestry weaving, depending on your sett and whether you bundle your weft yarns or not (see page 49). Using a yarn that is thin enough to allow multiple strands in a weft bundle gives you more color options. However, if you are new to tapestry, consider using a thicker yarn that allows you to use just one strand at a time until you learn how to manage the weft. (See page 61 for more about weft size.)

Though there are many wonderful yarns in the world, it is important to learn with just one yarn for your weft. Mixing yarns is difficult because every yarn has different characteristics in its thickness, pliability, luster, and how it reacts to heat or water. It can be frustrating for beginners to use a variety of yarns in one weaving, because when the characteristics of the weft vary, the amount of weft you need in each area also varies.

As a beginner, it's common to choose a yarn because of its color. But until you can weave a tapestry fabric that has an even surface with edges that don't pull in or push out radically, you need to keep your weft yarn consistent. Choose just one weft yarn. Once you have mastered the amount of one yarn to put into each pick of your weaving, you will be able to expand that knowledge to other yarns much more easily.

Eventually you may want to mix sizes of wool and even fiber types in the same tapestry. This is a more advanced skill, but it is not against the rules! Just keep in mind that different fibers shrink and react to heat differently. If you throw a synthetic fiber into a tapestry and then use a steamer on it, the synthetic might melt. Cotton and wool will shrink in different amounts when steamed. And weft tension will vary dramatically between different fibers while weaving. I know it is tempting to use whatever yarn you have when you begin. All those little bits of yarn from other projects are begging to be woven! But I recommend starting with just one yarn type. When you have gained more skill, you can mix yarns and fiber types if you want to.

But how do you settle on just one yarn, especially when it can be hard to find yarns appropriate for tapestry? There are very few brick-and-mortar weaving shops left, and most of the ones that still exist cater to people weaving household textiles. In most cases, you will probably have to order your tapestry yarn by mail.

Choose a yarn that has the characteristics listed at the bottom of this page and work with it for a while. Weave several tapestries or samplers with it to make sure you've mastered that yarn. If you find it lacks something you want, you can branch out and try another yarn after that. Think of this first weft yarn as your "anchor" yarn because it gives you a basic understanding of how one yarn acts in tapestry weaving. Once you understand one,

Characteristics of Good Tapestry Yarn

WARP

- Abrasion resistant
- Strong (you shouldn't be able to break it with your hands)
- Variable sizes for weaving at different setts
- Feels pleasant between your fingers
- Some shrinkage with steaming

WEFT

- Abrasion resistant
- Firm but not lofty
- Little end-to-end stretch
- Enough color choices to provide hue and value differences
- Yarn size appropriate to sett (see chapter 4)
- Lightfast and colorfast

Weft Bundling

Some tapestry yarns are large enough to use just one strand at a particular warp sett. (See page 58 to learn how to match your weft yarn to warp sett appropriately.) But many of the best options for tapestry yarn are too thin to use in one strand. To adjust for this, we bundle multiple strands of weft and use them as if they were one yarn. Weft bundling provides a great advantage when it comes to color, since available colors of yarns appropriate for tapestry can be fairly limited. By mixing colors in a weft bundle, you can create the perception of new colors.

When you're using multiple strands of yarn in a weft bundle, you want to get the bundles to be as close as possible to the same size, especially as you're learning. I suggest using all one kind of yarn as you learn the techniques, but if you do end up mixing yarns of different sizes, you can twist the yarns from each bundle together to test the size.

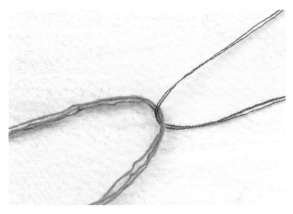

1. Loop a piece of each yarn together as shown.

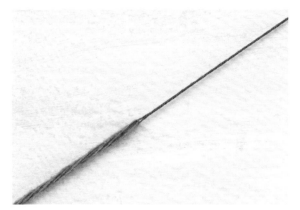

2. Twist the resulting strand of yarn. You may be able to see the difference in bundle size as shown above, or if the difference is subtle, you will be able to feel it when running your fingers from one bundle of yarn to the other.

▲ *Multiple wefts bundled together on a bobbin*

you can make better choices about future yarns by comparing them to the yarn you know. Of course, the first yarn you try might be the one you stick with.

Here are a few good possibilities for your anchor yarn. There are many other options out there, so if one of these doesn't work for you, compare the yards per pound and other characteristics in the chart on page 51 as you choose another yarn. I've chosen these four yarns because they weave up beautifully, and I believe they will continue to be manufactured for the foreseeable future.

HARRISVILLE HIGHLAND is my personal anchor yarn. It is made by Harrisville Designs, a small mill in New Hampshire. This was the yarn that my teacher James Koehler taught with, and it is the yarn that I currently use in my beginning tapestry workshops. Highland is a light worsted weight yarn, and it was originally made for weaving. It makes great blankets and also works for tapestry. The fiber for the yarn is dyed prior to spinning and then mixed in the spinning process, a process known as "dyed in the fleece." Because of this, most of the colors have a heathered appearance. Highland does have a large number of middle-value colors,

so when choosing your yarn, make sure you have some lighter and darker values for your palette.

WEAVERSBAZAAR is a yarn made in the United Kingdom. The company is run by two tapestry weavers, and their yarn is designed and produced especially for tapestry. It is a high-twist yarn made from luster longwool breeds (which means that it has a nice sheen) and is available in three sizes: fine, medium, and heavy. The yarn comes in a wide range of color gradations, and the company ships to the United States.

FRID VEVGARN is a yarn made by Hillesvåg Ullvarefabrikk, a spinnery in Norway, and is sold in the United States. This beautiful yarn is made from Spelsau and other luster longwool fleeces.

FÅRÖ is a yarn made by Bockens in Sweden. It is a single, not plied, yarn. This and its slightly fuzzy nature make it easy to use in bundles and give the face of the tapestry a slightly downy texture. Fårö is made from Scandinavian longwool sheep and has a nice sheen to it. This yarn most closely resembles Harrisville's undyed Koehler singles, which I dye myself and use in my own work. The two yarns are identical in size, and if you don't dye your own yarn, Fårö is a great choice.

Australian Tapestry Workshop

If you live in Australia and you want to work with weft bundles, you can't find a better yarn than Australian Tapestry Workshop yarn. It is not listed as an anchor yarn here because it is difficult to get in the United States.

A Comparison of Tapestry Yarns

YARN NAME	YARDS PER POUND	AMOUNT AT 8 EPI	NUMBER OF COLORS	QUALITIES	FIBER SOURCE
Harrisville Highland	900	1 strand	64	Dyed in the fleece, heathered look, 2-ply	Mixed New Zealand wool
weaversbazaar 18/2	4,900	4–6 strands (experiment with this)	200+ Comes in gradations	2-ply	Longwools from South American and New Zealand
weaversbazaar 9.5/2	2,300	3 strands	200+ Comes in gradations	2-ply	Longwools from Europe, Australia, and New Zealand
Frid Vevgarn	1,500	2 strands	108	2-ply	Scandinavia: 50% Spelsau, 50% luster longwool
Fårö	3,040	3 or 4 strands	74	single	Scandinavian longwools

This chart compares five possible anchor yarns. Notice the relationship between yards per pound and the number of strands you use at 8 epi. The fewer yards per pound (ypp), the thicker the yarn is and the fewer number of strands you would use at 8 epi. So if the ypp number is very large, it is a very thin yarn. If the ypp number is smaller, the yarn is thicker.

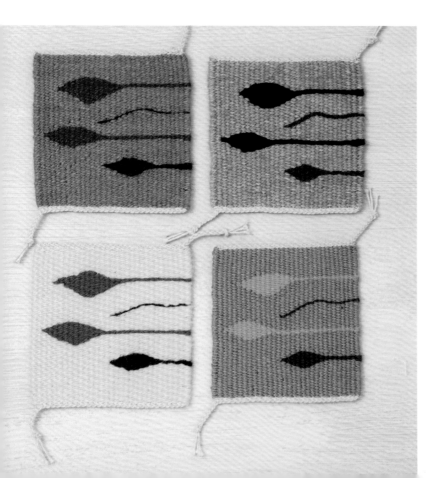

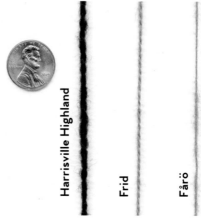

◀ *Woven samples of these four anchor yarns described on page 50. Clockwise from top: Harrisville Highland, Frid, weaversbazaar, Fårö. To see these samples in greater detail, turn to page 294.*

How Much Yarn?

Though most of us yarn lovers have no trouble justifying increasing our yarn stash, when starting your tapestry yarn collection as a new tapestry weaver, you don't know what you like yet. It stands to reason that you don't want to purchase a lot of yarn you might not like or be able to use. Here's how to estimate yarn amounts for a project.

Calculating Warp

Calculating the amount of warp you need for a project is relatively easy, but *how* you do it will vary depending on the kind of loom you're using.

UNTENSIONED FRAME LOOMS. These looms are often so small that I recommend just purchasing a cone of warp yarn and warping without measuring. One cone will last you a long time. If you want to know how much warp you need exactly, measure from bottom to top of your loom and multiply by the number of warps per inch. Add 10 percent for the warp that travels around the pegs or slots.

TENSIONED FRAME LOOMS. If you're warping continuously, measure the height of your loom and double that amount. Then multiply by the number of warps per inch. If you will double your selvage warps (see page 68), add two more warp lengths, or just add 10 percent to make sure you have enough.

BEAMED LOOMS. If you're warping a large floor loom for a big piece, doing the math is important to make sure you have enough warp. Here's how:

(Length of project in inches + loom waste★) × number of warp ends★★ = amount of warp needed in inches

Divide the amount of warp needed in inches by 12 to get the number of feet or by 36 to get the number of yards.

★There can be 36 to 72 inches of loom waste on a large beamed loom, depending on the way the loom is built. If you have the choice, it is better to waste a little bit of warp, which is fairly inexpensive, than to run out. There is no invisible way to lengthen a warp in the middle of a tapestry.

★★Number of warp ends = width of project in inches × epi + 2 if you double your selvages

NOTE: All of this can be done in metric units if you live in one of those lovely countries that uses the very logical metric system (see page 295).

Calculating Weft

How much weft yarn you need is a less precise puzzle. Amounts of weft yarn vary by sett of the tapestry, size of the piece, your style of weaving, and how many yards are in a pound. The fewer warps you have in an inch, the more yarn you'll need per square foot. A piece at 6 epi is heavier than a piece at 8 epi because there is more yarn in it. Your weft bundle needs to be bigger to fill up the wider space between the warps, and that results in a thicker tapestry and more yarn used.

A very general starting place is that at 6 ends per inch, you'll need about 6 ounces of weft yarn per square foot, and at 8 ends per inch, you'll need about 4 ounces per square foot. Please remember that there can be a large variation in these numbers! If you beat very firmly, you'll need more yarn. Always add 10 to 20 percent extra for waste and to make sure you don't run out. And if you're making tapestries smaller than a square foot, just know that the total amount of yarn you'll need at 8 epi is probably less than 4 ounces.

Other Yarn Considerations

In addition to learning the terminology of yarn and understanding what makes good warp and weft yarns, there are a few more things to consider in relation to choosing yarn.

KNITTING YARN IS (USUALLY) NOT TAPESTRY YARN. Most of us have attempted to use yarns available in knitting stores for tapestry weaving. Who can resist the gorgeous color options? But resist you should in most cases. Knitting yarns are intended to make garments. Many yarn designers use fibers that are very soft because softness sells skeins of yarn. While these yarns might be fantastic for a scarf or sweater you'll wear next to your skin, they are difficult to weave tapestry with. Tapestry weft yarns do not have to be soft, and in fact, they perform better if they are not soft to the touch.

Knitting yarns often are also very lofty. They have a lot of air in them, so when you put them in your weaving and beat them down, they disappear into a tiny dull lump. They lose all their beautiful charm in both color and texture because that charm was relying on the airiness, which would be maintained in most knitted garments.

Knitting yarns also often have a lot of end-to-end stretch. Again, this is a fabulous quality if you want to knit a sweater that continues to fit you every time you wear it. But when you're weaving tapestry, the yarn wants to pull back into itself, and that makes it difficult to get the correct amount of weft into each pass and often results in the edges of your tapestry drawing in.

Knitting yarns, especially sock yarns, are often superwash. This means that the wool has been treated with a chemical that strips the scales off. Without its scales, wool doesn't play as well in a structure like tapestry. It has lost all its "grabbiness" and becomes more difficult to manipulate.

Superwash wool also won't shrink, which is great for socks but not ideal for tapestry. You want your tapestry to shrink just a little when finishing because it makes the textile flatter and allows the yarn to bloom a bit.

I BELIEVE IN SAMPLING. It is an excellent way to learn how certain materials behave and to understand how to create various color combinations outside of an actual tapestry. Even if you're that person who never ever knits a gauge swatch for an upcoming sweater and you're totally willing to wear a garment several sizes too big, I recommend doing some sampling as you learn tapestry techniques.

▲ I weave samples for all of my large-format tapestries. Since I have used the same yarn for a decade now, I mostly sample for color and form. I keep a small loom in my studio warped at the same sett as the larger piece so that I can quickly try out combinations of colors or experiment with a particular design.

Because, of course, if you're new to the techniques, you need to practice them. If you just think of your first works as samplers, it can allow you to play with possibilities a little bit and maybe discover something interesting you wouldn't have otherwise tried. If you expect your first attempts at weaving tapestry to end up on your living room wall or win a juried show, you're asking too much of yourself. Consider allowing yourself time to make things that are not all that beautiful. The things you learn about technique, your equipment, your materials, and the woven interactions that you love will become evident only as you practice.

Sampling also applies to using tapestry yarns that are new to you. It can help you figure out how a particular weft yarn works at a certain sett given the tools you have and the way you beat in the fiber.

DYEING YOUR OWN YARN IS A JOY. Most yarns that are appropriate for tapestry weft do not come in a wide range of colors, and only a few are available with value gradations within each hue family. To solve that problem for myself, early in my tapestry career I learned to dye yarn and have dyed all the yarn for my tapestries ever since. This allows me to produce almost any color I want.

Acid wool dyes are fairly simple to use. If you have any inclination to make your own colors, I recommend exploring dyeing your own yarn. All of the yarns listed in this chapter can be purchased undyed, and they all take dye beautifully. Yes, dyeing creates a mess, but the joy of making any color you want far outweighs the time it takes to dye your own colors. I do not recommend dyeing in your kitchen if at all possible, however, because dyes can mix with food or become airborne and get inhaled by someone who is not taking necessary precautions inside a home. I have dyed yarn outside on patios, in carports, on decks, and just out in the New Mexico dirt. All you need is a heat source (such as a hot plate), a stainless steel pot,

some dye, a few small pieces of equipment, and a desire to experiment.

TRY USING HANDSPUN FOR TAPESTRY WEFT. Some of you undoubtedly know how to spin your own yarn, and tapestry weaving is an excellent opportunity to use that yarn in creative ways. When designing a handspun yarn for tapestry, consider the characteristics of a good weft yarn discussed on pages 47 and 48. Remember that you're not going to knit a sweater with this yarn, so it does not need to be bouncy or soft. Tapestry yarns do well with a worsted or semi-worsted preparation (see the definitions on page 15). Some of the best tapestry yarns I've made have been with hand-dyed, combed, lustrous longwool spun with a short forward draw. I don't think it is necessary to become fixated on making a pure worsted-spun product, but it is fun to think about how you can keep some of the air out of the yarn and best use longer staple wools. This is your opportunity to use coarser, more lustrous fibers because you won't be wearing them. For more information about spinning your own yarns, Jillian Moreno's book *Yarnitecture* is a great resource.

Spinning gives you the advantage of mixing fibers and thus colors in one yarn. Even if you don't process your own fleeces or comb or card your own wool, you can use commercially prepped roving or top to create some great tapestry yarns. Start playing with mixing colors. Can you divide the braid and spin the colors in a particular order? A variegated yarn can be stunning in a tapestry. Mixing colors in with hand cards and spinning in this way also allows you to create more complex yarns than you can when using solid immersion-dyed yarns from commercial suppliers.

When spinning for tapestry, remember these characteristics in the prep and spin:

LUSTER VS. MATTE FIBERS. Longwools will be shinier; if you don't like luster, use finer wools for less shine.

CONSISTENT SIZE. Tapestry will be much easier to weave if your yarn is a consistent diameter.

SPIN FOR YOUR SETT. You probably will have experimented with weaving some commercial yarns by this point. Make sure to match the yarn you're making to the sett at which you want to weave.

SPIN A FIRMER YARN. This probably means tend toward a worsted preparation and spinning technique.

PLIES. You can use singles or plied yarns for tapestry. I've done a lot of weaving with singles I spun for tapestry to maintain a color progression, but I've also chain plied to maintain color changes. Regular 2- or 3-ply handspun yarns work just fine for tapestry also.

AMOUNT OF TWIST. There are various schools of thought on this. Knitting singles is different from weaving singles, and I probably put more twist in my singles yarn for tapestry than a knitter might. I have found that a moderate range of twist in the singles is fine. If you're going to ply the yarn, make it a balanced yarn. If the singles are spun in a semi-worsted manner and are fairly firm, the ply twist doesn't have to be all that high.

Wool or Camelid Sensitivities

Very few people are actually allergic to wool, alpaca, or other camelid fibers, though these people do exist. Usually a sensitivity to these protein fibers has to do with chemicals used to treat the fiber during processing, lanolin still in it due to light processing, or the prickle factor that the little scales on these fibers provide. If you feel you are sensitive to wool or other protein fibers but have not explored why that might be, consider washing your yarn and testing it again.

If these fibers are not for you, there are others that will work. You do not have to use wool to be a tapestry weaver. Cotton and silk are the most frequent substitutes for wool, but you could also consider bamboo or even rayon. Many small-format tapestry weavers use cotton embroidery floss. It comes in a large color range and is readily available. When considering embroidery yarns for tapestry, please note that in Europe the word *tapestry* often refers to embroidery. Yarns labeled "tapestry wool" may not actually be appropriate for tapestry weaving, as they are very lofty and intended for embroidery on canvas.

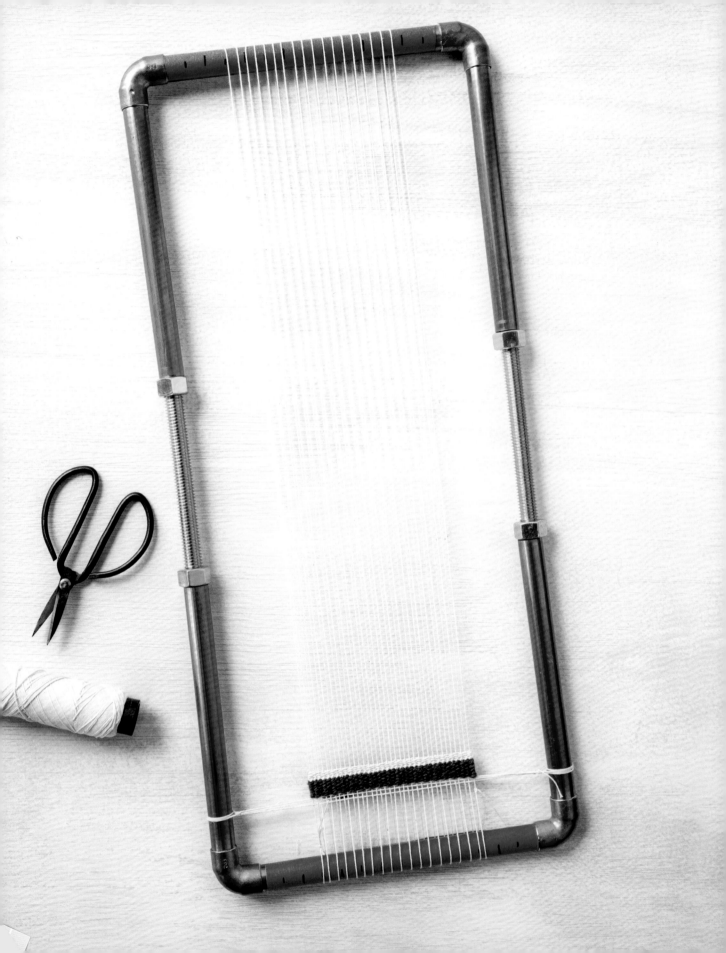

4 Only the Warped Can Weave

The warp is the foundation for your tapestry, so it is important that you spend some time carefully preparing your warp. Uneven tension or mistakes in threading will be visible in your finished weaving; many warping mistakes are impossible to fix once you've begun your tapestry.

An important concept to understand at the beginning of your tapestry practice is the relationship between the size of yarns you choose for warp and weft and the sett you use. Sett is the number of warp ends in 1 inch of warp width (denoted as *epi* or "ends per inch"). In some countries, sett is measured in centimeters (epc). If you've wondered why your warp shows through the weft or why your fabric seems so loose, you may have a mismatch between your warp and weft size and your sett. When your yarn choices match your sett, you can create a firm, stable textile while maintaining relatively straight selvages and creating the image you're interested in.

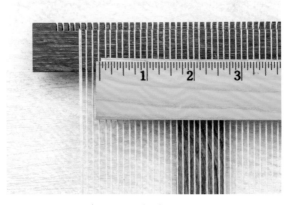

▲ *Measuring ends per inch (epi) on an untensioned frame loom. Notice that the 9th warp thread begins the 2nd inch, so this loom is warped at 8 epi.*

Why Warp Size Matters

Warp is the ground of your piece — the tightly held strings upon which your image is built. In traditional tapestry weaving, the warp is completely covered by the weft, yet it is the core of the textile's structure.

As the cross-section illustrations below show, the weft has to follow a curved path to go around each of the warps. If we could straighten one of those pieces of weft, it would be significantly longer than the width of the weaving. This fact will be important when we talk about weft tension in chapter 7. There also has to be room for the weft to fit between the warps.

If you choose a warp that is very thin, the amount of space in that little eye-shaped bubble changes, creating a lot of room for the weft to shift around, as shown in figure B. Similarly, if your warps are very large, eventually there will not be enough room for the weft to fit between them, as shown in figure C.

A quick way to gauge whether a weft yarn will work on a particular warp is to hold that weft along the warp and see if it just about fills the space between the warps, as shown at right.

▲ *If your warp sett is correct for the weft you're using, the weft should come close to visually filling the space between the warps when held in this orientation.*

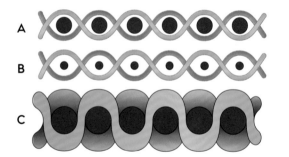

▲ *These cross sections show 6 warps (the black dots) with 2 weft picks woven. Version A illustrates a good ratio of warp to weft size, while in version B the warps are too thin, and in version C the warps are too thick.*

Warp Ribs: The Effect of Warp Size on Surface Texture

The thicker your warp threads are, the more prominent the vertical ribs in your tapestry will be. Thicker warps and more prominent warp ribs give the tapestry's surface more of a textured look, something very particular to tapestry weaving. In my own work I like less emphasis on the warp ribs, so I choose a thinner warp. It is possible to weave a stable tapestry at 8 epi on cotton seine twine warp in any of these sizes: 12/6, 12/9, or 12/12 (see page 45 for a reminder about the numbering system for tapestry yarn). However, 12/12 is approximately twice the size of 12/6 and thus provides a much more prominent warp rib. I use a 12/6 or 12/9 cotton seine twine warp at 8 epi, which makes the ribs less obvious. The weft yarn I most often use is also slightly fuzzy, which further blurs the texture of the surface and makes it look flatter.

Compare the detail of my tapestry *Emergence V* below with Suzanne Paquette's *Cordes Sensibles* (at right). Paquette's warp sett is approximately 6 epi, and because her warp ribs are quite prominent, you can see that she uses a much fatter warp than I do. How much you want the textured appearance of larger warp ribs to show in your tapestry is purely an aesthetic choice. Experimenting with different size warps can help you decide what you like best in your tapestry surface.

Suzanne Paquette,
***Cordes Sensibles*, 2015.**
Cotton, wool, and synthetic, 59" × 36".

Rebecca Mezoff, *Emergence V: The Center Place* (detail), 2011.
Wool and cotton, 45" × 45".

◀ *In this detail of my tapestry, woven at 10 epi, you can hardly see the warp ribs. See page 96 for a full image of* Emergence V.

▶ *This figure shows four samples I wove at 8 epi, with different-size warps and the same weft. The woven numbers are the warp sizes of cotton seine twine. Notice how much more pronounced the rib is for the 12/15 warp than for the 20/6. The warps coming out of the weaving help you see the large difference in warp size.*

How Weft Size Influences Your Textile

Thicker or thinner wefts can affect the structure, appearance, and weaving time of your work.

WARP COVERAGE. Both too-thick wefts and too-thick warps may result in the weft's inability to cover the warp. The resulting spots where the warp peeks through are called lice.

In figure C on page 58, the weft would likely not cover the warp at all. Each pick of weft is too fat to allow the next one to slide over and cover the other side of the warp. This effect is visible in the photograph at right, where the weft is too thick for this sett. Warp lice show up as little flecks of white throughout the weaving where the warp is showing. We shouldn't see the warp at all.

If you use a very thin weft, it will always cover the warp. But you will have a textile that is not as structurally sound as one where the warp and weft match well. When the weft is very thin for the sett, there is too much room for the fibers to move on each other and you get a fabric that feels loose. I call this sleazy cloth. The weft moves on the warp, and in a very large textile, this can cause structural problems when it hangs.

APPEARANCE. All four samples at right were woven on the same warp: 12/6 cotton seine twine with a sett of 8 epi. I used a singles yarn for each sample, but I changed the number of strands of yarn used at one time so that I could compare the effects of fatter and thinner wefts. The horizontal lines were made with 2 rows of whichever number of wefts I was using for that section. Notice the thickness of the lines in each sample. The top example (A) was woven with one strand of yarn, the next sample (B) was woven with two strands, the third sample (C) with three strands, and the bottom sample (D) with four strands. Each example has exactly the same number of passes.

▲ *Lice are visible because the weft is too thick for this warp sett.*

◀ *Weaving at 8 epi with four different weft thicknesses*

A

B

C

D

An Ideal Plan for Your First Tapestry

Let's make this practical. Say you want to weave at 8 epi, an excellent choice of sett if you're just starting out in tapestry and your loom will accommodate it. Your newly clumsy fingers can find the shed, and the individual warps are spaced widely enough that you can manipulate them especially if you don't have a shedding mechanism. But the sett is also fine enough that you can get some detail in your images.

The weft you have to work with is a worsted weight 2-ply yarn of about 900 yards per pound (see page 51). You decide that you like a more prominent rib in your fabric, so you choose a 12/9 cotton seine twine for your warp. This combination of warp, sett, and weft will work well, your tapestry will be structurally sound, and the warp will be covered.

Remember, if you decrease the size of the weft considerably, your warp will be covered but the fabric will be sleazy, and you'll have to weave many rows to complete your tapestry. If you increase the size of the weft, you'll see warp lice because the weft won't cover the warp.

If you could feel these samples, your hands would understand the difference between the fabric with a thicker or thinner weft. The examples with one and two strands of yarn (A and B) are thin and flexible. The sample with two strands (B) feels stable enough for a larger textile. In the version with only one strand (A), the weft moves around on the warp noticeably. The examples with three and four strands (C and D) feel very stable. The cloth is much thicker and the weft doesn't move at all.

In addition to the way these samples feel, there are large differences in how they look. Imagine how this translates to an image. With a thinner weft, lines are more delicate, and it's possible to get much greater detail, especially in the horizontal direction. You could make very smooth low angles and curves with a thin weft like this.

TIME TO WEAVE. The sample with one strand (A) took a long time to weave because so many rows were woven in an inch. This one-strand example is ⅞ inch high. The example at the bottom with four strands of yarn (D) is 3¼ inches high. Both samples have the exact same number of weft rows. It takes about four times as long to weave the same distance with the thinnest weft as the thickest.

Tapestry Sett Examples

The three examples on the opposite page were woven at three different setts: 4 epi, 8 epi, and 12 epi. Even with a simple striped pattern, the differences are quite clear: 4 epi creates large warp ribs and a much chunkier look than the weaving at 12 epi. The warp sizes were changed for each of these weavings. The fattest warp was used for 4 epi, and it is important to increase the size of the warp at wider setts to fill up some of that space inside the little eye-shaped areas we saw in figure B on page 58.

4 epi   **8 epi**   **12 epi**

I used a yarn wrap (see the tip on the next page) to plan the stripes because I wanted to follow the same sequence of colors and size of stripes for each sample, even though the yarns I used for each one were different weights. Once I had the sequence I wanted, I followed that as closely as I could for each piece. With the finest yarn, it was easy to get the stripes the width I wanted them to be. With the fattest yarn, each pick covered a longer vertical distance on the warp, and I had to compromise on the width of some of the stripes.

As you can see from both the photo and the chart, the wider the sett, the larger the weft bundle you need. In the piece woven at 4 epi with a very fat weft bundle, the weaving has a lot of texture and the horizontal lines are quite wavy. In the piece woven at 8 epi, the weaving has less texture and the horizontal lines are less wavy. In the piece woven at 12 epi, the detail is quite fine and the horizontal lines are very straight.

▲ *These 3" × 3" tapestries were woven at three setts with three different warp and weft sizes. The image demonstrates the differences in the look of the weaving when these three variables are changed.*

Warp and Weft Combinations for Samples			
Sett	4 epi	8 epi	12 epi
Strands of singles	6	3	1
Warp used	12/15	12/6	20/6

I used cotton seine twine for the warp and a thin singles for the weft. The chart describes each combination for the samples shown in the photo above.

Yarn Wraps for Color and Design Planning

A yarn wrap is a quick way to plan a design. Simply cut a length of cardboard or stiff paper 1½ inches wide × 5 to 6 inches long, and wrap your yarns around it as shown. You can easily change the widths of the stripes as well as the sequence of colors. I often make multiple yarn-wrap cards with different combinations of colors or patterns as a quick way to figure out whether I like a certain color palette. (See chapter 5 for more about choosing colors.) I find it helpful to tape the ends on the back so that the yarn doesn't come off the card.

Sett Affects Image

Weaving is a gridded structure. The images we make have to fit onto the grid formed by the warp and weft. Because the structure so easily forms squares, it is more challenging to make other shapes in tapestry weaving. But we do want to weave something besides squares.

Consider the two diagrams below. Pretend that each square along the top indicates 1 warp thread. When building a shape like a circle, we have to make little steps. With only 8 warp ends in an inch, those steps are quite noticeable. Each warp thread is represented by one column, but each row must include several weft passes.

Now, what if we doubled the number of warp ends in an inch? The steps are now much smaller. The more warps you have in an inch, the smaller those little steps can be. This fact is the most important thing to understand when you're choosing a sett for your tapestry design. Horizontal lines are easy to make in tapestry weaving. Vertical lines are always stepped to some extent, and the fewer warps you have in an inch, the larger those steps will be. There are some technical tricks we'll learn in chapter 11 to minimize the look of those steps, but for now remember that the nature of tapestry is to have these steps in the vertical direction.

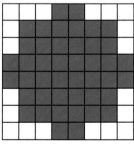

▲ *Steps created to make a shape at 4 epi*

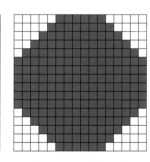

▲ *Steps created to make a shape at 8 epi*

Tips for Warping Success

There are so many different kinds of tapestry looms that I can't cover how to warp each of them in this book. Instead, I'll give you general tips that are relevant for all looms and teach you to warp most frame looms. Please refer to one of the many books on warping beamed looms for specific instructions on how to warp them.

EVEN WARP SPACING IS VITAL. When you start weaving, the warp spacing will be a clue about whether you are putting in enough weft or using the right weft tension, and whether your piece will tend to draw in or push outward in shape. When your loom is completely warped and ready to weave, you should see that all the warps are the same distance apart. Different looms have different mechanisms to even out spacing, including reeds, coils, twining, and manual adjustment against marks on the loom. For more information about these methods, see page 18.

EVEN TENSION ON EACH WARP THREAD creates a nice, flat fabric. If adjacent warps are looser or tighter than their neighbor, or if the warp tension varies in sections across a warp, it will be difficult to make the areas of differing tension look the same on the surface of the tapestry. Not only is it more difficult to manage the amount of weft you put into each pick when the warp tension isn't even, but the effects of uneven tension will show when the piece comes off the loom. Getting the tension even is easier to accomplish on some looms than others; for more information, see pages 74 and 77.

Remember that if your loom has a mechanism that lets you increase the tension on the warp, your warping doesn't have to produce a tight tension because the loom can do that for you. You just have to get the warp on evenly.

TECH TALK

The Usefulness of Experimentation

As we've seen, the relationships between warp size, weft size, and sett are important and a little complex. For now, just know that the size or spacing of each variable will affect what you can achieve in your finished tapestry. Sometimes changing one variable, such as sett, means that you also have to change another variable, such as weft size.

All the variables matter. As you experiment and change warp size, warp sett, or weft size, you are influencing the options available to you in the finished work. They affect the following:

- **The character of the image:** very fine lines and steps versus chunkier forms
- **The character of the fabric:** stiff, thick, sleazy, or flowing
- **The structure of the fabric:** sleazy (caused by weft moving on warp) versus a textile that will last a long time
- **The speed of weaving:** the size of the weft

When you first start out in tapestry weaving, I recommend using one of the anchor yarns from page 51, at 8 epi. As you learn more techniques and decide on the sorts of images you'd like to weave, you can experiment with weft, warp, and sett combinations to achieve your goals.

Some tapestry looms, such as simple peg or slot looms, do not have the ability to have the warp tension changed. If you do have a loom with a tensioning device, such as a screw or threaded rod, make sure to leave enough room in the device before you start warping so that it can be extended after the loom is warped. Remember that in order to increase the tension, you make the loom longer so that more pressure is put against the warp.

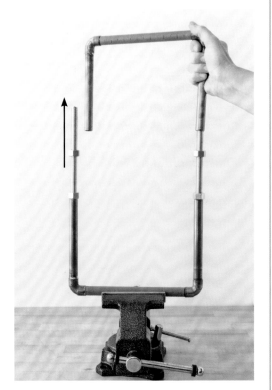

▲ *You'll need to expand the loom, using up some of that space to tighten the warp. In this photo, the left side of the loom is disconnected for illustration purposes.*

FIRM TENSION ON THE WARP AS A WHOLE makes it easier to manage the amount of weft that needs to go into each pick and to maintain the structure of the textile as the woven forms change. Your warp shouldn't be so tight that your cuticles bleed when you weave, but it should be firm enough that it feels tight when you press your flat hand against it. If your loom has adjustable tension, play with how tight the loom tension can be after you get your first warp on. Tighten the tension a lot and feel what that is like, then loosen it a lot and feel that. You're looking for a comfortable middle range where the warps can be easily picked up but the warp is still quite tight.

Warp Length

How long your warp needs to be will depend on what kind of loom you are using, how much loom waste that loom produces (see page 52), and how large the project is. If you don't have enough warp, it is impossible to add more in the middle of a tapestry. In chapter 3 you learned how to calculate the amount of warp you'll need for a project. As you make your calculations, add in at least 2 inches of unwoven warp on each end of your piece so that you can tie the knots required in the finishing process; I like to leave 3 to 4 inches to make tying those final knots even easier.

The more unwoven warp available above your fell line, the easier it is to manipulate the warps to insert the weft, which makes the weaving process feel easier. The biggest drawback to small untensioned frame looms is that the weaving gets more difficult the closer to the end of the piece you get. This is because there isn't much open warp available above the tapestry, which makes the shed very difficult to open. A longer loom that has more unwoven warp above the project makes the weaving process more pleasurable because the shed is easier to open. I recommend leaving 8 to 12 inches of unwoven warp above your project, if your loom will accommodate it.

UNTENSIONED FRAME LOOMS. Because most of these looms don't offer much warp length, you may not have 2 inches on each end of your weaving for loom waste. Instead, you can use a different sort of header that lets you leave out the waste yarn and leave less of the warp unwoven. (See Making a Double Half-Hitch Header on page 127.)

TENSIONED FRAME LOOMS. These looms usually provide more weaving length than untensioned frame looms, and you may be able to weave more than one piece on one warp if the loom is extended quite far. If you're using a loom with a continuous warp, you can turn the warp around the loom, making sure to leave 2 to 4 inches of free warp for each piece (4 to 8 inches total between the pieces). Rotate the warp and then start the new piece with exactly the same steps you used to start the first one. Put in an ordering cord (see page 78), a little waste, then your header.

If your loom also has a shedding device, this gives you another 8 inches or more that you can't weave on your warp due to the room the shedding device needs to operate.

BEAMED LOOMS. If you're using a floor loom with a warp beam and a cloth beam, you have the advantage of being able to warp one time and then cut off each piece as you finish it and retie the warp to the front beam for the next piece. I recommend cutting off pieces that will be woven sequentially on these sorts of looms to avoid the tapestry being wrapped on the front beam for long periods of time. This does mean more loom waste, as you'll have to tie new knots on the cloth beam.

Warping Procedures

It is time to warp your loom. In the following sections I explain how to warp each of three kinds of tapestry looms: untensioned frame looms, tensioned frame looms, and beamed looms.

Untensioned Frame Looms

There are numerous small pegged or slotted tapestry looms on the market these days. Many are made by small companies or individual woodworkers, and some are amazingly beautiful. Warping these looms is simple and fast, making them attractive to tapestry weavers.

It is difficult to adjust the warp tension later on these looms, especially if you've warped with more than 1 thread in some slots. Therefore, you should warp untensioned framed looms with as even a tension as possible. Using a cotton seine twine warp can be helpful because it is slightly stretchy, which makes some unevenness less noticeable.

Doubled Selvage

I recommend using 2 warp threads at each side of the warp and treating them as a single thread as you weave, a technique known as doubled selvage. This works well if you're using the fairly thin warps I recommend at setts close to 8 epi. Putting 2 warp threads at each selvage gives a little extra thickness to the edge and makes getting straight selvages a little easier. If you are using a thicker warp (such as 12/12 cotton seine twine or thicker), the doubled selvage isn't necessary.

- **On an untensioned frame loom** you can wind on the warp in a way that doubles the edge warp.

- **On a continuous warp on a tensioned frame loom,** treat the 2 edge warps on each side as 1 warp. On looms with devices to help you space the warp, put 2 warps in one slot or coil, as shown below. If you are using some kind of heddle or leashes, treat the 2 warps as one.

- **Using a figure-8 warping style,** you won't be able to double your selvage warp if you're using the top of the loom as the open shed rod.

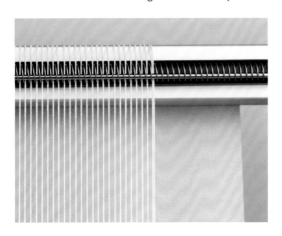

◀ *Example of a doubled selvage on a tensioned frame loom*

Warping a Pegged or Slotted Loom

You can start your warp either at the top or the bottom of the loom. I prefer to keep my knots at the bottom, where I will start the piece, because I want as clean a shed as possible at the top. I also don't want those knots to get in the way of my weaving, especially if I'm going to weave over most of the face of the loom.

1. **CENTER YOUR WARP ON THE LOOM.** Decide how wide your warp will be and identify where the center of it will be on the loom. From there, find the edge of the warp by measuring across half the width of the piece.

2. With a slip knot or a square knot (see page 282 or 283, respectively), tie the end of the warp to the first peg.

3. Carry the warp up to the corresponding peg at the top of the loom, wrap it around the top of that peg, and bring it back down to the bottom.

4. Determine what warping pattern you need to follow to get the approximate number of warps you need in 1". See page 73 for examples and descriptions of warping patterns.

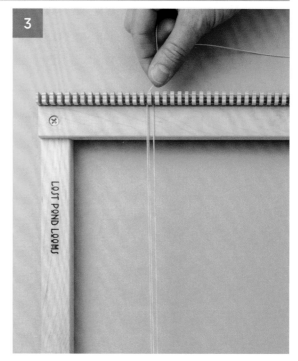

▲ *Since I like a doubled selvage warp, I wrap around that first peg again to get 2 warps on the outside edge.*

5. When you get the whole warp on, secure the warp to the bottom of the loom. On most peg looms you can wrap around a few pegs to hold the tension, then cut the warp and use a needle to secure the tail with a double half-hitch knot (see page 279). This gives you an even number of warps, so if you are weaving a design for which you want one warp right in the center, you'll need to end your warping pattern on the opposite side of the loom from where you started.

6. If you warped the loom with multiple warps in any of the slots, put a line of twining across the bottom, and potentially across the top, of your warp to even out the spacing, as described on the next page.

Evening Out the Warp Spacing with Twining

When you look at your warp, you should see that each individual warp is the same distance apart. Some peg or slotted looms may be manufactured so that winding around the peg or slot one time each creates an evenly spaced warp. But not all of these looms are made with this even spacing, and if you have warped the loom with multiple warps in some or all of the slots, you will need to even the spacing out before starting to weave your tapestry.

It is possible to even out the spacing by weaving 1 to 2 inches with waste yarn, and if you have a loom large enough to do this, it is a good solution. However, I find on very small looms there isn't enough extra warp length to put in sufficient waste to space the warp evenly. In these cases, you can instead use twining along the bottom and top of the loom to space the warps more evenly.

Twining is a method of twisting two strands of warp so that they cross between each warp thread. It does not create a woven structure and should be done on a neutral shed. If you twine with a thicker warp than you're using for your piece, it can be a great spacer to even out the warp. In addition, twining is frequently used as part of a hemmed header. For step-by-step photographs, see Making a Hemmed Header on page 122.

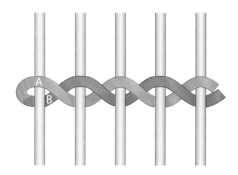

1. Cut a piece of warp three to four times the width of your warp. Fold it in half. You can start the twining with a lark's head knot (see page 282) at one selvage, or you can just put a tail on each side with the fold at the selvage, as shown in the diagram above.

2. We'll call the thread in front of the warp "A" and the thread behind the warp "B." Cross A over B and bring A behind the 2nd warp.

3. Pass the B thread under the 3rd warp. You should see the 2 twining threads form a twist between the warps.

4. Continue alternating which thread crosses under the next warp until you reach the other edge.

5. When twining just to even out warp spacing, you can tie a square knot (see page 283) and trim the tails close. This twining is not part of your weaving in any way and can be slid to the bottom of the loom.

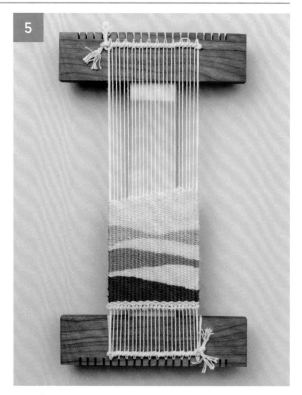

▲ *I often repeat the entire twining process at the top of the loom so the warp spacing is even over the entire warp.*

VARIATION

Warping a Slotted Loom

Looms with slots instead of pegs or nails are warped in a very similar way to pegged looms. The warp will wrap around the back of a slot in the loom instead of around a peg that sticks out from the loom, but the patterns you use to warp the loom are the same.

When warping these looms, it is tempting to think you should wrap the warp around the back of the loom, but you should not. In all of these simple looms, the warp only travels on the front side of the loom. It will go through a slot and turn around and come back through the next slot.

▲ Wrap the warp around the edge of the loom a couple times to secure it before starting your warping pattern.

as seen from the back

▲ Warping patterns vary for these looms depending on how many warps you want in each slot. It doesn't matter how you wrap the warp around the slots as long as the warp ends up on the front of the loom and you get as many warps as you need in each slot.

Warping Patterns for Untensioned Frame Looms with Pegs or Slots

Looms that have pegs or slots to hold the warp dictate to some extent the number of warps you can have per inch. Most of these looms usually vary between 4 and 8 warps per inch. You can change the number of warps per inch by warping with multiple strands in some slots and then evening out the spacing using twining (see page 71). Try using weft or other material thicker than your weaving warp; I use a thicker warp thread for this spacing twining so that the warps are evenly spaced.

For example, if your loom has six slots per inch but you want a warp sett that is closer, you could warp the loom with 2 warps in the first slot, 1 in the second, 2 in the next, and so on. This 2, 1, 2, 1, 2, 1 pattern will give you 9 warp ends in each inch. The first time you warp your peg or slot loom, you may need to experiment a little bit to get the sett you want.

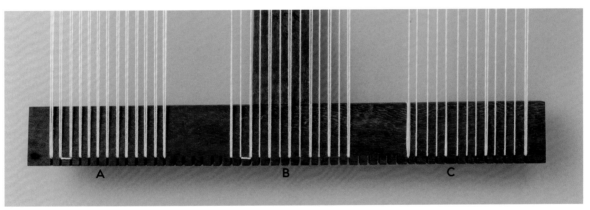

▲ Version A shows a 2-2-2-2 warp pattern; version B shows a 2-1-2-1-2-1 warp pattern; and version C shows a 2-1-1-1 warp pattern. Version A on this 6-dent loom results in a sett of 12 epi. Version B gives you 9 epi, and version C gives you 7.5 epi.

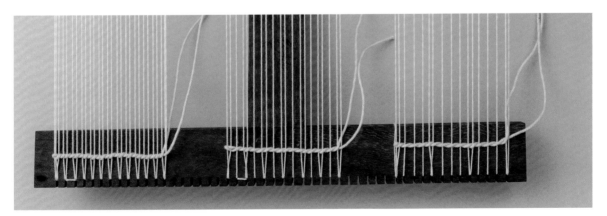

▲ You can use twining to spread out the warps evenly. In this example, the tapestry warp is 12/6 seine twine, but the twining was done with 12/12 seine twine.

Tensioned Frame Looms

Whether you are using a commercially made tensioned frame loom or have constructed your own, the warping concepts will be the same. I'll cover two different ways of warping frame looms: continuous warping and figure-8 warping. You almost always will use these methods on some kind of tensioned frame loom. If you are using a wooden frame without any tensioning ability, I recommend using the figure-8 method.

Spacing your warps. Some tensioned frame looms, like the Mirrix and Schacht Arras, have a coil at the top (and sometimes at the bottom) to help you space the warp. But many other frame looms, including those you build yourself, do not have any kind of spacing device. If you're warping this type of loom, you must space the warps by hand. I recommend putting a piece of blue painter's tape along the bottom and top of the loom with inches and half inches marked on it. Simply space the warps so that the number you need falls between those marks. For an example of this on a copper pipe loom, see page 80.

If your loom is too small to accommodate a large warp spool or you are warping it from edge to edge and the spool won't fit between the last warp and the edge of the loom, try winding some warp onto a smaller spool. The best way to do this is to use a bobbin meant for boat shuttles. These plastic bobbins can hold enough warp for a medium-size frame loom, but they have a profile small enough to fit in tight spaces. If you have a bobbin winder for these sorts of bobbins, the process will be faster, but you could also wind them by hand.

It is best to complete your warping all in one sitting. If you can't do this, use blue painter's tape (see the tip above) to hold the finished warps in place and hold your tension steady when you step away.

Putting the heddles on a continuously warped loom is tricky. Usually this has to do with the visual confusion of the second layer of warp or the struggle to just see which warp thread needs to be picked up next. It can help to use a thin ruler or stick to pick up and hold every other warp thread. Put a heddle on each of those threads on one side of the warping bar before removing the ruler, then turn the warping bar and finish the second set of heddles in the same manner. Make sure that the second set of heddles is applied to the alternate warps rather than the first set.

Some small tensioned frame looms have leash bars. Often handmade galvanized or black pipe looms have them. Leashes are long heddles that are tied between the leash bar and the back layer of warp. They allow you to find the second weaving shed quickly by pulling it forward with the leashes. Leashes are also common on large beamed high-warp tapestry looms. See page 284 for information on how to tie and use leashes.

Continuous Warping

Continuous warping is a way of warping a frame loom so that the warp can be turned around the loom as you weave, allowing you to weave tapestries that are longer than your loom. This method also keeps the area you are working on near the bottom of the loom, which is easier for your body. This method is only used on looms that can be tensioned because the tension has to be loosened to allow the warp to slide around the loom. The warp is applied with the use of a warping bar as seen on page 76. One disadvantage of a continuous warp is that, because it creates two layers of warp, it is difficult to see or access the side of the weaving facing away from the weaver.

1. Secure the warping bar with clips or another mechanism provided by the manufacturer.

2. Figure out where you'll need to start warping to center your warp in the middle of your loom. For example, if the weaving area at the bottom of your loom is 12" wide and you want to weave a piece 5" wide, the unwoven distance on your loom will be 12 − 5 = 7". Divide that number in half (3½") to know how far from one side of the loom to start warping.

3. Tie your warp to one side of the warping bar with a double half hitch or square knot (see page 279 or 283, respectively).

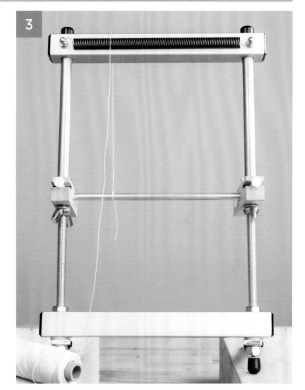

▲ Make sure to tie the knot in a position that allows you to bring the warp over the top of the loom the same distance from the side of your weaving area that you determined in step 2.

4. Bring the spool of warp up the back of the loom where the warping bar is, down the front side, and back up to the warping bar.

▶ *A couple of commercial looms, including Mirrix, use warping bars and have mechanisms to hold them. This loom comes with clips that hold the warping bar in place as you warp.*

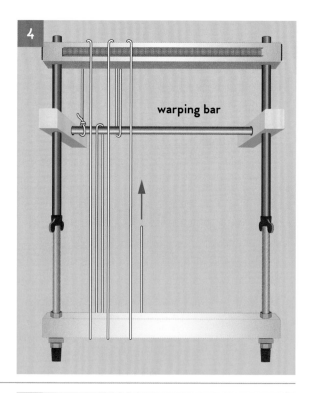

warping bar

5. Take the warp spool around the warping bar and return in the direction you just came from. When you get back to the warping bar in that direction, wrap the warp around it and reverse again.

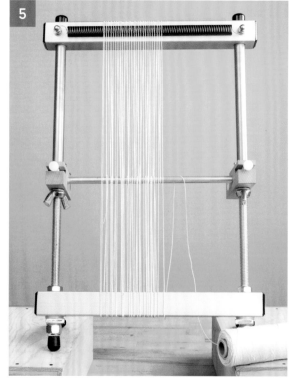

6. Continue to wrap the warp around the loom, reversing every time you come to the warping bar, until you have the number of warps you want. Remember to double the selvage warps by putting 2 warps in the edge dents.

7. When you get to the end of the warp, tie it off to the warping bar with a double half hitch. This knot is adjustable, and you should tighten it to make sure your selvage warp is firm.

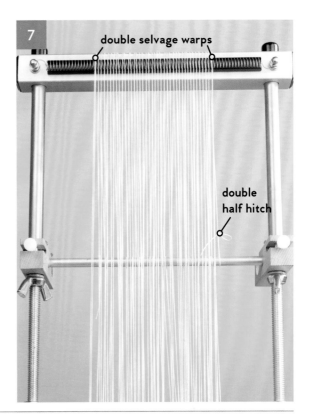

8. With your hand held flat, run it along the warp and feel for any softer spots in warp tension. You can adjust the tension by tightening each warp in order all the way to the end. Retie or tighten the double half hitch you made in step 7.

▲ *I go through an entire warp and tighten it slightly in this way after it is on the loom. If your warp is wider than about 6", you may want to use this technique to even out the tension partway through warping.*

9. MOVE THE WARPING BAR TO THE BOTTOM OF THE LOOM. When the tension has been evened out, loosen the warp tension just a little bit and push evenly downward on the warping bar. You want it to slide all the way to the bottom of the loom. Once positioned, tighten the tension on the loom again with whatever tensioning device your loom uses, usually some kind of nut on a threaded rod.

10. ATTACH THE HEDDLES. If you are using a loom with heddles, apply them now according to the man-ufacturer's instructions. When putting the heddles on, take care that you position them in the correct sequence or your shedding will be incorrect. If you have a bottom spring on your loom, your warps should be very evenly spaced and you can skip steps 11–13.

11. ATTACH THE ORDERING CORD. Cut a piece of warp five to six times the width of your loom. You need it to go across your loom four times plus have enough extra to wrap around the upright pipe of the loom. Tie one end to one side of the loom with a square knot. If you have a shedding device, open one of the sheds. Bring the thread through the open warp and tie it firmly to the other side of the loom.

12. Shift the shed and bring the ordering cord back to the other side of the loom. Wind it around the first upright, shift the shed, and bring it back again. You want the cord to travel across the loom four times. Tie it firmly to the loom upright after the fourth time across.

13. If your loom does not have a bottom spring, spend a little time spacing the warps evenly with the point of a bobbin or other strong pointed object.

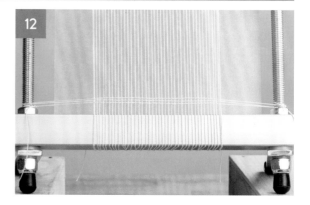

Figure-8 Warping

This method of warping a frame loom is a little easier to put on than a continuous warp, but you won't be able to advance a figure-8 warp for longer pieces. The length of the weaving is determined by the space between the top and bottom of the loom minus loom waste and any extra warp you want to provide to make shedding easier. In general, I only use this kind of warping on copper pipe looms and for smaller pieces. This technique creates one layer of warp. It is handy if you're working on something where you need to see both sides of the weaving easily or even weave from either side of the loom.

Because there is only one layer of warp, the number of wraps you put around the loom will be half the number of warp threads in your warp. For example, if you're weaving at 8 epi and you have a piece 4" wide, you'll need 4 warps per inch × 4" wide, or 16 warp wraps. This will result in 32 warp threads (8 per inch for 4 inches). With this method of warping it is not possible to double the selvage warps and maintain the open shed using the top of the loom.

If you have a vise, securing a corner of the loom in it can make this warping process easier. Otherwise you can support the edge of the loom on a table with one hand as you warp with the other hand.

1. Figure out where to start the warp so the tapestry is centered in the loom. See page 75, step 2.

2. Using a double half hitch or square knot (see page 279 or 283, respectively), tie your warp to the bottom of the loom at your starting point.

3. Bring your spool of warp upward and around the back of the top bar of the loom.

Start with a knot.

FIGURE-8 WARPING

4. Bring the spool down the front, through the center of the loom, and around the back of the bottom bar.

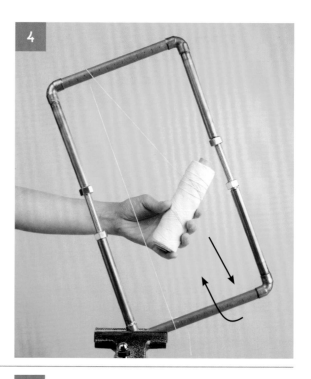

5. Continue this pattern: upward around the back of the top bar, down through the center of the loom to wrap around the bottom bar back to the front. This pattern creates a figure-8 shape in the center of the loom where the warps cross.

Bottom and top bars of the loom

6. As you wind the warp on, with your free hand space the warps according to the inch marks you've made on the tape at the bottom and top of your loom.

FIGURE-8 WARPING

7. When you have the necessary number of warp threads on the loom, tie the last warp to the bottom of the loom with a double half hitch. Slide the knot up the last warp as described on page 279 so the last warp is tight.

8. Test the tension on the warp. You'll most likely want to tighten the loom tension a little bit.

9. ATTACH THE ORDERING CORD. Cut a piece of warp five to six times the width of your loom. You need it to go across your loom four times plus have enough extra to wrap around the upright pipe of the loom. Tie one end to one side of the loom with a square knot and bring the warp through the space between the two layers of warp above the place the warp crossed. If you bring it through the warp near the top of the loom, you will have it in the correct place.

FIGURE-8 WARPING

10. Pull the ordering cord down toward the bottom of the loom. This will pull the place where the warps crossed down to the bottom of the loom (10a). Wrap the string around the far side of the loom from where you tied it on a few times. Your warp will now create one long narrow V when viewed from the side (10b), with the ordering cord at the bottom.

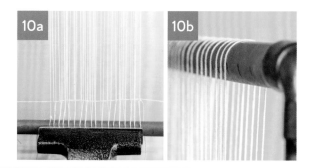

11. Using a shed stick or your fingers, pick up the warps that are in the back layer and put the ordering cord through this other shed. You either want to pick them all up with a shed stick or pick up about an inch of them at a time and put the ordering cord through, completing successive inches one at a time.

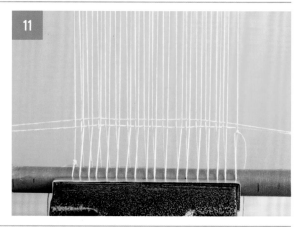

12. Complete 1 or 2 more picks with this stretcher string, winding it around the side of the loom each time. You'll have three or four strings going from side to side on your loom. Tie the warp firmly to the loom frame.

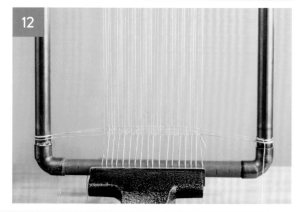

13. Use the point of a bobbin or other strong tool to space the warps evenly. The ordering cord will hold them in place for the time being.

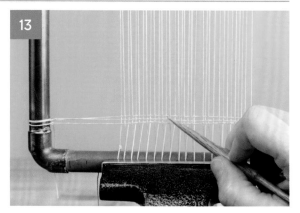

Warping Beamed Looms

Many beamed looms work very well for tapestry weaving (see pages 26–28 in chapter 2 for a reminder of which ones). Warping beamed looms is a procedure that is beyond the scope of this book, however, and if you have such a loom and are new to warping it, I recommend referring to the manufacturer's instructions, along with one of many excellent weaving manuals available today. Here are a few tips particular to warping these looms for tapestry.

For looms that use a reed, I recommend purchasing the reed at the sett you want to weave. If you love 8 epi, get an 8 epi reed. If you're going to use the reed to beat your weft in at least some of the time and the reed does not have the same dents as the sett you want, you'll see that discrepancy in the fabric. A reed that isn't at the same sett as your warp will also put excess stress on the warp as you beat.

When warping my 4-shaft countermarche low-warp loom for tapestry, I thread the heddles 1, 2, 3, 4, and tie shafts 1 and 3 to one treadle and 2 and 4 to the other treadle. Using all 4 shafts spreads out the tension on the loom and is easier on your equipment. You only need 2 shafts for tapestry weaving, so if you have a 2-shaft counterbalance loom, you would simply thread half the warps on one shaft and half on the other.

I often have the same tie-up on two sets of treadles on each side of the loom. If your loom is wide enough that you have to move your body to work on another section of the tapestry, this can help keep your hips from protesting by reaching too far for the treadles with your feet.

If you have a high-warp tapestry loom that has a leash bar instead of treadled shedding, please see page 284 for two ways to make leashes.

To double the selvage threads on a beamed loom, put 2 warp threads in the edge dents in the reed and then put both of those warp threads through the same heddle. They should act as 1 warp thread.

5 Learning to See Color

You most likely have chosen tapestry out of all the methods of weaving because you want to express an idea visually using fiber. Knowing some basic color theory can help you communicate your ideas both about color and about the subject you're working with more effectively. In fact, one of the most important aspects of design in art is color use. Knowing how to manipulate color is a powerful tool in an artist's design toolbox.

Have you ever stopped to think that the color of the blue-violet crocus that just popped its head through the snow in your garden is not the same blue-violet your best friend sees, even if you are standing next to each other and looking at the very same flower? How would you ever know if her blue-violet is the same as yours? Color is relative: it changes depending on your individual physiology and what other colors are present. That can make the concepts of color theory seem confusing. But they don't have to be.

Yarn is a wonderfully rich material when it comes to color. In tapestry weaving, all the color we see in the finished textile is contributed by the weft because the warp is completely hidden. The complexity of color in our weft yarns can vary depending on how they are made: yarn that is immersion dyed creates one solid color, while painted yarn changes color throughout one strand of yarn. In addition, fiber can be dyed in fleece form and then spun, or it can be spun before it is dyed. When the yarn is dyed after spinning, the color is more uniform throughout than when the fleece is dyed and final colors are made by combining different colors of fleece.

Even when yarn is dyed all one color by immersion, it has a depth of color that can't be created with flat materials such as paint because the light bounces around inside the fibers a little bit. People interested in tapestry weaving are often first attracted by the rich color possibilities presented by yarn.

You're Not "Bad" at Color

As a teacher of tapestry weaving, I often hear students say they are "bad" at color. This self-judgment is seldom helpful. Whether someone told your childhood self that you couldn't wear pink if you were a redhead, even though pink was your favorite color, or that lime green should never be a fashion choice, even though you always chose it with your pink sweater, those early color wounds stick with us in unexpected ways. It is time to let them go. Pretend you are 5 years old again, when all colors were marvelous and could go together in any combination and before adults told you that tree trunks are not purple and you started coloring them all brown. Because some tree trunks are indeed purple.

While it is true that some people seem to have a natural ability to put colors together in harmonious ways, doing so is a skill that anyone can cultivate with practice. Learning about and practicing color theory concepts is the best way to lose your fear of color. Start by dropping all judgments about how good or bad you are at using it. Your color choices provide a starting point for learning, so go ahead and make some "bad choices" and see what happens!

Practicing color theory concepts as you choose yarn for the tapestry exercises in this book will start to train your eye to see how colors are interacting. This process takes a lot of repetition, so don't expect that all of your color combinations will please you. As you practice, observe which colors you like together and which you don't. Then, using the concepts from this chapter, see if you can figure out why some combinations aren't as pleasing to you. Some of this is simply a matter of preference; your best friend may adore the palette you dislike. At the end of this chapter you'll practice building a color palette for your woven sampler(s).

Colorful Language

HUE: The name of a color; for example, red or yellow-green.

SATURATION: How pure a color is; a fully saturated color does not have any black, white, or other hue added to it.

SHADE: Black added to a pure hue.

TINT: White added to a pure hue.

TONE: Gray added to a pure hue.

VALUE: How dark or light a color is when compared to the range of grays from black to white; tints, shades, and tones all change the value of a hue.

COMPLEMENT: The color directly across the color wheel from any hue.

TEMPERATURE: How warm or cool a color feels.

Hue and the Color Wheel

When choosing yarn, it helps to understand the four basic properties of color: hue, value, saturation, and temperature. Hue is simply the name for a color and its lighter and darker versions. Red is a hue that includes a range of values: light red, a color we might call pink, and dark red, a color we might call maroon.

Perhaps the easiest way to organize color in your mind is to think of a color wheel. This tool arranges a number of hues in the visual spectrum in a circle. This arrangement allows us to understand the relationship between adjacent colors on the wheel as well as colors across the wheel from each other. In this book I use the 12-color wheel.

The 12-color wheel is divided into primary, secondary, and tertiary colors. The primaries — red, yellow, and blue — are the foundation of all other colors and cannot be made by mixing any other combination of colors. Secondaries are formed by mixing two primaries. For example, green is made by mixing yellow and blue. Tertiaries are made by mixing a primary and a secondary color. For example, yellow-green is made by mixing yellow (a primary color) and green (a secondary color).

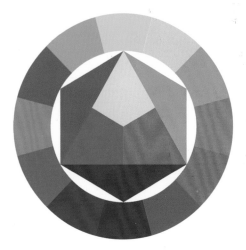

▲ *12-color wheel in yarn*

▲ This gradation of grayscale yarns, from white to black, illustrates how value works.

Joan Baxter, *The White Boat of Winter*, 2011.
Wool, linen, silk, and cotton rags, 28" × 100".

▲ *Parts of Baxter's tapestries often have a particularly misty feel, in part due to the closely related values she uses in those areas.*

Value

Value is the relative lightness or darkness of a hue. Think of it as a continuum of gray from white to black: if hue is removed from a color, it will fall somewhere on that continuum.

Many people think the hues you choose are the most important consideration in a design, but value is the first thing the human eye perceives from a distance. You notice areas of light and dark before your eye can pick up specific colors. As a result, the way your design uses value can influence the viewer's perception of light and depth of space. For example, maybe you only have one green yarn in your stash, and you decide to use it for the grass in your design. But if the green is the same value as the blue you've chosen for the sky, the grass will not stand out as a separate form, especially from a distance. Your composition will look fairly dull because adjacent colors with the same value tend to merge. To ensure that the viewer sees the grass and sky in your picture as separate, make sure that the green is a different value from the bottom of the sky. On the other hand, you can also use the fact that hues of similar value will blend together to your advantage.

TIP

Practicing with Value

One of the easiest ways to discern the value of yarns you're considering is to take a black-and-white photo. Most smartphones have a black-and-white filter in the camera app, and on some phones or cameras you don't even have to take the photo to view the value. Alternatively, you could take a photo and turn it to black and white with simple software available online for free or with a paid program like Photoshop.

Pat Williams, *The Last Grasp*, 2007.
Cotton and wool, 18½" × 47⅜".
▲ *Pat Williams often uses a wide range of values in her work. This helps the piece feel lively and emphasizes her expressive style.*

You can create smooth gradations, color shifts, and entirely new colors by mixing yarns of similar values.

Whatever values you choose, make sure they are consistent with what you want to express thematically. An exciting or cheerful piece might have a wide range of values. If the feeling you're trying to express is more subdued or quiet, you might choose values that are very similar.

Saturation

Saturation refers to the pureness of a color. Think of it as how bright or dull a color is. For example, a fully saturated red is the absolute reddest red you can experience. It doesn't have any other color added to it. By adding white, black, or some other color such as gray or a complement to a hue, the color becomes less saturated.

- Adding white **tints** the color, making it lighter.

- Adding black **shades** the color, making it darker.

- Adding gray creates a **tone**.

- Adding a color's complement creates a **chromatic neutral**, which can have varying degrees of color in it and is not a pure black.

When a color is fully saturated, it can be difficult to tell what its value is, which might make working with highly saturated colors more challenging. Any hue can exist in high saturation, but some hues seem brighter than others because their values are lighter at full saturation. (For more information, see Values of Complementary Hues on page 97.) Fully saturated colors are great for exciting, eye-popping designs or for elements that you really want to be visible. These elements will have more presence in your weaving if they are surrounded by duller colors.

▶ *The teal blue yarn at the top of this image is highly saturated. The lighter and darker versions in the grouping below have white and black added to them and are not fully saturated. Variations of the teal blue include the chromatic neutral at the bottom of the photograph.*

Lialia Kuchma, *BluRose*, 2010.
Cotton and wool, 64" × 71".
▲ *This tapestry uses lots of fully saturated color, especially in the yellow lines in the center of the piece and the brilliant blue behind them.*

Temperature

Colors also have temperature. We intuitively feel that some colors exude warmth and others feel cold: orange is the warmest color and blue is the coldest. The color wheel is divided in half as indicated below, with warm colors on the orange side and cool colors on the blue side.

Because no dye-based primary color is completely pure, there are subtle tendencies in each color that make it feel warmer or cooler. These tendencies are called undertones. For example, red with a violet undertone can feel quite cool, while red with an orange undertone may feel much warmer. Any color can be made to feel warmer or cooler depending on its undertones and the color(s) surrounding it. The colors at the edges of the warm-cool divide are especially easy to make warmer or cooler.

The property of temperature can help add the feeling of depth to your tapestry, so considering a color's temperature can be an important design element. Warmer colors feel like they are coming forward toward the viewer. Cool colors feel like they are receding or moving away.

As you weave samples, notice whether the colors you choose are warm or cool and if that affects how the weaving feels. When you start designing your own tapestries, consider the intent of the design. Do you want it to feel very warm? Should it have a glowing, cheerful quality? Or do you want it to feel more icy or cooling? Perhaps you're working with particular colors and one of the yarns you're using feels too hot or pops too much for what you want to express. You might try using it with a cooler temperature color or choosing another version of that hue that has a bluer undertone to it.

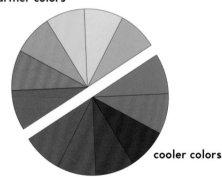

▲ Division of warm and cool colors on the color wheel. Warmer colors are on the orange side, cooler colors on the blue side.

◀ These red yarns are divided into two groups, with warmer undertones on the right and cooler undertones on the left.

Variations in Dyes

Dyes do not follow the neat categories we like to make when we talk about color theory. We may recognize a color as "green," but in practice that hue is a range of experience we label as *green*. All dyes have impurities, and colors of dyes differ between brands and types of dye. One particular version of "green" may contain more yellow pigment than another version of "green" that contains much more blue. The yellower green feels warmer and the bluer green feels cooler. But we call them both green. This difference can be very subtle, and it takes a lot of practice and experimenting with yarns to see the undertones present.

Most serious dyers will use two versions of each of the primaries: a warmer and a cooler one. This allows a full range of colors to be produced. Though the world of color would be simpler if the dyes we used followed the rules we've made up about color theory, in practice all of it is relative.

Additive versus Subtractive Color Systems

There are many theories of color and thus many different color wheels. Isaac Newton's conclusion when he passed light through a prism was that all the colors mix to create white. But if you mix yellow, blue, and red dye or paint, you don't get white. Newton was playing with light in what is called the additive color system. It is the system that computer monitors and stage lighting employ. This color system uses red, green, and blue as primary colors; you may recognize it as the RGB system your computer uses. When these primaries are added together in the form of light beams, white light results.

When the materials used are based on dyes and pigments as they are in yarn and paint, the subtractive color system is used. This system has to do with color perceived as light bouncing off of objects. Red, yellow, and blue are the primaries, and if you mix them you will theoretically get black. In reality, though, you'll likely get some version of brown by mixing paint or dye in these colors.

There is a related subtractive system in which the primaries are yellow, cyan, and magenta. Cyan is a turquoise version of blue, and magenta a hot-pink version of red. You may recognize this color system as CMYK from photographic applications. It is also the color scheme your printer uses. (The K refers to black.) Printing processes mix tiny dots of these four colors in varying amounts to produce colored images. The CMYK version can be a useful alternative when mixing pigments or dyes. If your elementary school teacher ever provided you with red and blue paint and told you to mix them to get purple, you were sorely disappointed by the resulting brown. She should have given you cyan and magenta to make violet.

Because most color theory is written from the perspective of the yellow, red, and blue primary system, I use it here to talk about color theory. But if you dye your own yarn, you might consider experimenting with turquoise and magenta dyes as primary colors.

Color Harmonies

Color harmonies are relationships between colors that can assist you in choosing hues that work well together for a sampler or tapestry. These ways of organizing colors can be thought of as hue families.

A **monochromatic harmony** uses only one hue in varying values or saturations. This color harmony could contain many tints, shades, or tones of that color, but overall the piece would contain just one color. Because there is only one color present, there aren't other hues to challenge or interact with that color, and the resulting image can be very calming. James Koehler's *Harmonic Oscillations* tapestries are a good example of this color harmony.

An **analogous harmony** uses two or three hues that are next to each other on the color wheel. Orange and red are an example of an analogous harmony, which is a little broader than a monochromatic harmony, but still doesn't contain colors from across the color wheel. A piece that is either monochromatic or analogous tends to feel either warm or cool because all the colors are from one section of the color wheel. A red and orange piece would feel very warm.

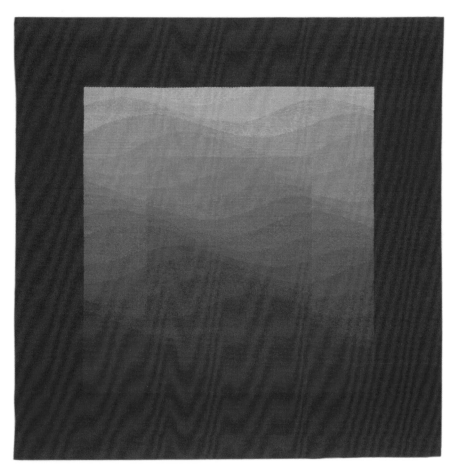

James Koehler, *Harmonic Oscillations XL*, 2006.
Wool and cotton, 40" × 40".

Sarah Warren, *Mountain Waves VI*, 2018.
Cotton and wool, 20½" × 47".

When colors in a design are analogous or monochromatic, there aren't any other contrasts. The colors don't excite or play against each other to any great extent, so the main contrast in such a design is that of value. The lightness or darkness of the examples of that hue is what creates interest for the viewer. Sarah Warren's *Mountain Waves VI* is an example of mostly analogous colors in blue-green and blue-violet. In addition, she has thrown in hints of an orange complement.

A **complementary harmony** involves the two colors directly across the color wheel from each other. Theoretically, if pigments of complements are mixed, a neutral gray-black is produced. In practice this rarely happens because of the variations in pigments or dyes. A complementary pair contains all the primaries. For example, yellow and violet are direct complements. Violet is created by mixing blue and red, so this pair contains all three primaries: yellow, blue, and red. When complementary colors are next to each other, they make each color look more intense. To reduce the intensity, you can separate the complementary colors with a neutral color or outline.

There is a lot of tension in a complementary color scheme, so I like to use a **split complementary harmony** in my work. My tapestry *Emergence V: The Center Place* (on the next page) has a predominantly analogous color harmony with yarns chosen from the blue to violet section of the color wheel. The accent colors in the floating rock forms in front are complements in orange. These bits of orange give some excitement to what otherwise would be a very calm composition.

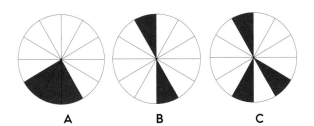

A   B   C

◀ *Examples of where analogous (A), complementary (B), and split complementary (C) harmonies would be positioned on the color wheel.*

Rebecca Mezoff, *Emergence V: The Center Place*, 2011.
Wool and cotton, 40" × 40".

▲ *The color harmony used in this tapestry is split complementary.*

Values of Complementary Hues

Each color on the color wheel has a different value. Yellow is the lightest of the hues, and violet is the darkest. If you attempt to make yellow darker by adding black, it becomes a dull greenish color. There is no such thing as a pure yellow that has a dark value. The warmer colors have lighter values overall than the cool colors. Saturated yellow always has a light value. Orange has a lighter value than blue, while red and green are fairly similar in value. Violet in its pure hue is always dark in value.

Use of complementary colors is common in art, and understanding how the values of complementary pairs influence each other is helpful. Let's look at three complementary pairs.

YELLOW AND VIOLET have the largest difference in value when fully saturated. Yellow has the lightest value and violet the darkest. This means it is important to balance the amounts of these colors carefully. The wider the variety of values present in a design, the more excitement the piece tends to have.

RED AND GREEN have the same value when fully saturated. This complementary pair is the easiest to work with because red and green are neither the warmest nor coolest colors, and the values of the hues don't fight with each other. But because their values are similar, red and green tend to blend together in a composition. When using a red-green color scheme, therefore, be careful to add some variation in value.

ORANGE AND BLUE have different values when fully saturated. Orange is lighter than blue, but the difference in value is not extreme. Still, this pair presents the largest warm/cool difference. When designing with this color harmony, decide whether you want the piece to feel warmer or cooler, then adjust the undertones or amounts of the colors to achieve this.

▲ *Look at the complementary pairs across the circle from each other. Notice how much lighter in value yellow is than violet.*

▲ *Compare the full-color photographs to the black and white, and notice how the values shift in each pair.*

When you're learning a new skill, being able to clearly see what is happening during the process is invaluable to your understanding. Weft yarns with lighter values are easier to see when you're weaving tapestry. Dark values make it difficult to see how the yarns are interacting with each other and with the warp. Some dark values are important for interest, but if all your yarns are dark, you'll struggle to see what you're doing. Similarly, it's easier to use white warp when you're a beginner. You can purchase colored warps, but a dark warp is much more difficult to work on because you'll struggle to see what is happening in your weaving.

Creating Color for Tapestry Weaving

Many of us are drawn to creating art with yarn because fiber expresses color so richly. When weaving cloth where both the warp and the weft are visible, the colors of those threads interact to create new colors for the viewer. In tapestry, however, the weft yarns contribute the color because they are all the viewer sees; the warp color does not influence perceived color. There are several ways in tapestry weaving that you can manipulate color and create additional perceived colors for the viewer that don't actually exist in the individual yarns used.

NOTE: I want you to appreciate that the range of color effects available to tapestry weavers can be greatly expanded by weft bundling, traditional tapestry techniques, and dye variations. However, I suggest that beginning tapestry weavers start with one strand of solid-colored yarn to learn the techniques. Once you master the basic techniques, you can start to experiment with these other concepts.

Optical Mixing

The structure of tapestry, along with its primary material, yarn, creates tiny bits of color that the viewer's eye and brain mix together. This tendency for the human eye and brain to mix colors is called optical mixing. It's what happens when we look at a Pointillist painting; tiny dots of color mix together to create what looks like solid colors from a distance. Your printer and computer screen work the same way: dots of four distinct colors in the CMYK subtractive color system are mixed together on a tiny scale, as seen in the image below, and we see a solid color.

▲ *Dots in four colors — cyan, magenta, yellow, and black — are combined to create the images we see on our computer screens and in our printed documents.*

You can achieve optical mixing in tapestry by using multiple colors of yarn in one area. Usually this is done by weaving with a weft bundle, a collection of thinner yarns held together on a bobbin and used together in one strand as if they were one solid piece of yarn. All of the colors in the bundle interact to create a different perceived color for the viewer. This effectively increases the number of colors a tapestry weaver has at their disposal, as seen in the images at right.

Optical mixing is practical for tapestry weaving because it decreases the number of colored yarns we need to get particular color effects. If, for example, we need 10 colors for a composition and we are using a single strand of yarn for each color, we need 10 colors of yarn. If we use thinner yarns that are bundled together and used as one weft, we might be able to combine yarns to create a color that doesn't exist by itself. Perhaps we'd only need yarns in six or seven colors to get the same effect.

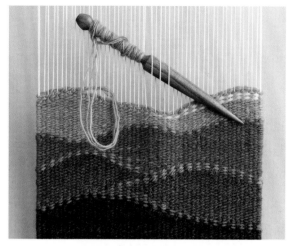

▲ *Thin strands of yarn held together in a weft bundle and woven as one strand allow for lots of color variation in tapestry.*

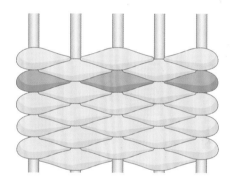

▲ *The structure of tapestry creates tiny rice-shaped bits of color with each pick. These bits of color blend together in the eye and brain of the viewer to create perceived colors.*

Archie Brennan, *The Ravens — An Omen* (from the *Dersu Uzala* series), 1997.
Cotton and wool, 36½" × 24".
▲ *Archie Brennan's weavings are very graphic in nature, in part because he rarely mixed colors in a weft bundle.*

Sarah C. Swett, *Back Alley Blues*, 2014.
Wool, 31" × 40".
▲ *Sarah Swett uses multiple colors in one weft bundle, which often gives her work rich depths of color.*

Tapestry Techniques

Most of the standard techniques we use in tapestry weaving can also help you blend color in some way. You can blend colors vertically up your warp using techniques like pick and pick (see page 205), and you can blend colors horizontally using some form of hatching (see chapter 8). As you practice the techniques throughout the rest of this book, consider how the hues and values you choose influence how the form or technique is perceived.

TIP

Endless Color Possibilities

You can produce further color effects through dye and spinning techniques not covered in this book, including:

- Purposefully dying yarn unevenly or even overdying it in places.
- Tying and painting yarns to change colors in a specific pattern, as in ikat.
- Dying and carding fleece in a variety of ways, and plying your handspun yarn with other colors to create all sorts of colors and effects.

Ways to Mix Color in Tapestry Weaving

There are several ways to create color areas when weaving tapestry. You often will use two or three of these approaches at once to create images.

- **Purchase or dye solid yarns,** one color for each color area. If you are using just one strand of yarn at a time, every new color in your tapestry will require a separate dyed yarn.

- **Use thinner yarns and bundle** more than one together. By changing one strand in the bundle, you can shift the look of the bundle overall. See chapter 3 for more about weft bundling.

- **Blend colors using tapestry techniques** such as pick and pick (see page 205), weft bundling (see page 49), and hatching (see page 161).

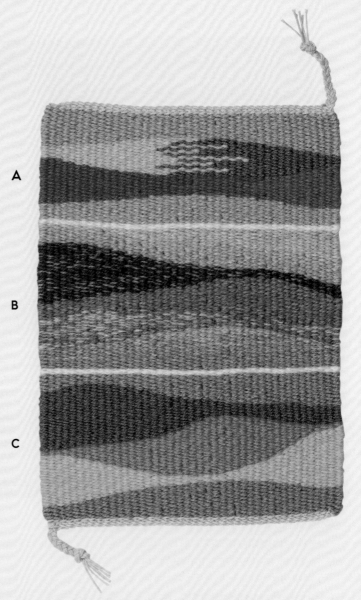

▲ *Examples of color use in tapestry: (A) hatching used to create a different perceived color where the two weft yarns overlap; (B) weft bundling with multiple colors of yarn used at once; (C) solidly dyed yarns used in distinct areas*

▶ A photograph may serve as a starting point for color explorations. I isolated some of the colors in this photo using paint chips and then chose some potential yarns for a related colorway, testing them with a yarn wrap.

Creating Your Own Color Palette

If you're new to color theory concepts, becoming a systematic observer of color can teach you a lot about color use. You can start by noticing which colors are your favorites. What colors do you wear? What colors do you use in your home, when you buy yarn, or when you're just choosing office supplies?

The culture we come from influences our ideas around color in ways we may not even recognize. The color red in North America can mean passion, love, or anger, but to people in some parts of Africa, it may signify death. Do particular colors have personal or cultural associations for you? And how can you use that knowledge when designing a tapestry that is a visual expression of something meaningful to you?

Think of yourself as an adventurer who is searching for clues about how the world works based on perceptions of color. Watch the world around you and collect impressions of the colors and values that fill your daily experience. Notice the grayish lavender shawl of the woman sitting next to you on the subway. Take a moment to watch the shifting light across the Great Sand Dunes or the Empire State Building. Watch how the green of the pine tree in your front yard changes over the course of a day and a year. Notice what colors surround that perfect blue you saw in a billboard on your way to work.

Then consider documenting these observations somehow. You could take photographs and print them out. Glue them in a journal and make some notes about the impact those colors had on you. This kind of color journal can also include swatches of yarn, paint chips, or cut paper exercises.

You can experiment with color quickly using materials like Color-aid paper or paint chips from the hardware store. Keep in mind, however, that yarn reflects light differently than paint and paper do. Once you have some color combinations you'd like to use in a tapestry, making yarn wraps is a helpful and quick exercise (see page 64). Play with various color harmonies and amounts of colors in your cards. Try many combinations, including holding two colors of yarn together as you wrap.

Wrapping colors together in this way can help you see some of the effects you can get with techniques like hatching and pick and pick, which I cover in chapters 8 and 11, respectively.

Eventually doing a woven sample is the only way to really tell how colored yarns will interact when woven. When working on a large tapestry, I keep a sample loom warped so I can test yarn combinations before committing to them in a large work. On smaller pieces sometimes I experiment in the waste section before starting my header.

Choosing Colors for Your Samplers

Buying your first tapestry yarn can feel overwhelming. I suggest starting with a yarn that you can use in one strand. If you're choosing from a website page, the colors you see on the screen will likely not be completely accurate. Some yarn manufacturers make color cards with actual yarn samples, and for a yarn you're likely to use for a long time, it's worth purchasing these cards.

I usually recommend you start with a hue you love. Choose one to three values of that color or closely analogous colors. For example, if you love blue, choose a medium, light, and dark value of blue. Then add a color or two on each side of the color wheel — maybe a blue-green and a violet. For some excitement and contrast, look across the color wheel at complementary colors. Choose a few examples in the orange range.

You'll need five to eight colors total for your sampler; of course, you can use more if you want. Make sure that the final choices represent a range of values.

PART 2
MÄKING

6 Let the Weaving Begin

The woven structure of tapestry is a simple over/under pattern that alternates between 2 picks. In the first pick, the weft travels over and under sequential warps. In the next pick, the weft goes under the warps it went over (and over the warps it went under) in the previous pick. If you look at the most recent pick of weaving, you can tell which warps the next pick needs to go over and under because it is the opposite of the previous pick. This 2-pick sequence is repeated over and over again.

Parts of a Tapestry

All tapestries are constructed similarly, regardless of the equipment on which they are woven. Once a tapestry is taken off the loom, you cannot tell what kind of loom it was woven on or whether it was woven from the front or the back. There are, however, variations in how you start and end the tapestry depending on how you warp and how you want the finished piece to be used or displayed. Nonetheless, the following components are usually present.

ORDERING CORD. This cord stretches between the sides of the loom three or four times, in alternate sheds, to create a firm foundation against which subsequent weft is packed and to allow the weaver to adjust the spacing of the warp before the weaving starts. Not all looms, such as I-shaped looms or beamed looms, use this device at the bottom of a tapestry, but it is a helpful addition on a frame loom.

WASTE. A small amount of waste yarn is woven in before the actual tapestry is started and after it is finished. This provides spacing and holds the tapestry together during the finishing process (see page 266).

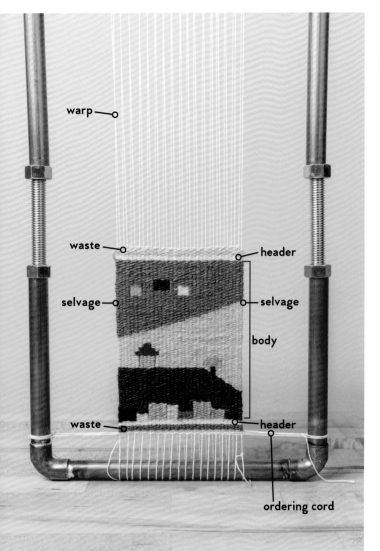

warp

waste — header

selvage — selvage

body

waste — header

ordering cord

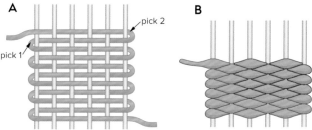

pick 1 | pick 2

▲ *The structure of tapestry before (A) and after (B) beating in the weft.*

HEADER. While there are many different ways to make a header, you should always include a header on the bottom and on the top of your tapestry. Headers provide structural stability at the beginning and end of the tapestry, making it possible to finish and hang the piece.

BODY. This is the part of the tapestry that is visible when everything is finished. It's what you have been wanting to make.

SELVAGE. The woven edge of the tapestry. Beginning tapestry weavers will spend considerable effort learning to make selvages even and straight.

EXTRA WARP. Some headers and finishing methods leave fringe in the finished work. You have to plan for this when starting your tapestry.

Picky Terms

There are four tapestry weaving terms that some books and some teachers use to mean different things. This is how I use them in this book.

PICK: A weft that travels in one direction across either a portion or the whole width of the warp

HALF-PASS: The same thing as a pick

PASS: A weft thread that travels across either a portion or the whole width of the warp and returns over that same distance; a sequence of 2 picks

SEQUENCE: The same thing as a pass

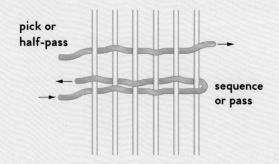

pick or half-pass

sequence or pass

Using Shedding Devices

No matter what kind of loom you use when weaving tapestry, there are only two sheds. There are also two sets of warp threads. You raise a set of warp threads in one shed while you lower the set of warp threads that form the other shed, and vice versa. The sheds alternate. To understand how this works, imagine numbering every warp thread across your warp. You will create the first shed by raising the odd-numbered warps and keeping the even-numbered warps lowered. You create the next shed by then raising the even-numbered warps and lowering the odd-numbered warps.

While there are only two sheds in tapestry weaving, how you make the two sheds differs from loom to loom. A loom with a shedding device that holds the shed open makes it easier to see how the woven structure works than when you look at a flat or closed shed. However, you do not have

to use a shedding device at all to weave tapestry. Some people prefer to pick up every shed with their fingers, a needle, or a shed stick. In addition, the entire shed does not need to be opened at once. Often tapestry is woven in small sections (see Weaving One Shape at a Time on page 235).

There are many kinds of shedding devices on looms used for tapestry; see tools for picking up the shed on page 36 for a refresher. On the next three pages I explain how to use an open shed rod and a shed stick, leashes, and rotating bars with heddles to help open the two weaving sheds on both tensioned and untensioned frame looms. Tapestry looms with beams have more complicated shedding mechanisms that use shafts and treadles. To understand how these mechanisms work, see Looms with Beams on page 26. For further information, check out Deborah Chandler's classic weaving book for beginners, *Learning to Weave*.

Making Sheds

Sheds can be made in many ways depending on the kind of loom you're using. On untensioned frame looms, you often use a tool to open the shed one warp at a time. Tensioned frame looms and beamed looms can make use of leashes and a variety of shedding mechanisms to speed up the weaving and make it easier to open the sheds.

Open Shed Rod and Shed Stick

Simple pegged or slotted looms produce a warp that is flat. There generally is no mechanism to open the shed on these types of looms. However, you can identify and open one of the two sheds much more quickly by inserting a thin shed rod at the top of the loom and leaving it there throughout the weaving process (A). Additionally, a shed stick is useful to widen a shed as you weave: quickly insert the shed stick in the opening (B), turn it sideways, and pass the weft through.

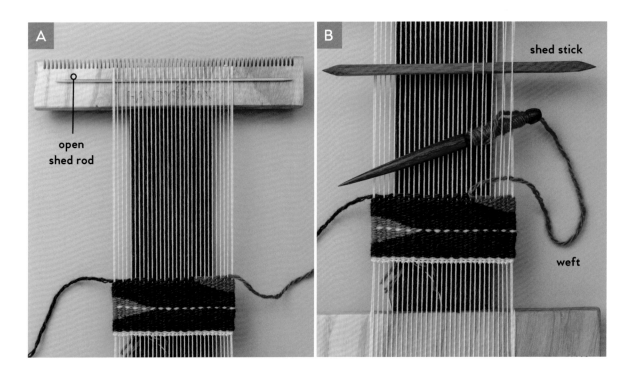

A — open shed rod

B — shed stick — weft

If there is no shedding device or if a shedding mechanism does not automatically cause a layer of warp to move forward and open a shed, you have a more labor-intensive job: you must "pick" the shed by hand, pulling forward each of the warps before passing the weft under. Sometimes weavers pull forward a few warps at once with one hand and pass the weft behind them with the other, putting the weft through the warp in sections about an inch wide. Other weavers pull those warps forward with a shed stick, inserting the stick through the entire section they are working on, and turn the shed stick sideways to pass the weft through.

On small looms, a double-pointed knitting needle of U.S. size 1–3 (2.25–3.25 mm) may work as the open shed rod. On wider looms, a thin metal or wooden rod or dowel may be used as a shed rod. These are available at a hardware or craft store.

On simple rectangular pipe looms, the top pipe of the loom is often used as the open shed rod, and you pick the other shed with your fingers or a shed stick. An open shed that is larger than ½" can start to cause problems with ridging (see page 155) in the weaving, especially on a small loom. If your loom is made of pipe larger than ½", insert a thinner rod into the warp in the opposite shed and tie it to the top of the loom.

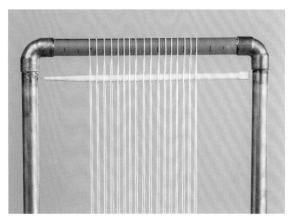

▲ You can use a secondary rod at the top of a pipe loom to make the open shed a little smaller if your loom is made of pipe larger than ½". The loom pictured here is made of ½" pipe and shows the wooden rod for demonstration purposes only.

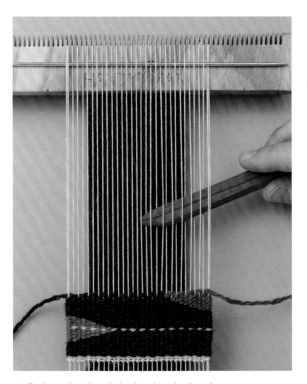

▲ Picking the closed shed with a shed stick

Leashes

Leashes are long heddles that are attached to the back layer of warp (also called the closed shed) to pull it forward instead of picking it. The first shed is held open by a shed rod or by the top bar of the loom, as shown on the previous page. Leashes make opening the second shed quicker and easier. Pipe looms, which frequently are made with legs to sit on a table or on the floor, often have leash bars. In addition, some high-warp beamed tapestry looms have leash bars instead of sliding shafts. See pages 284–288 to learn how to tie and weave with leashes.

Other Kinds of Shedding Mechanisms

Some tensioned frame looms, such as the Mirrix and the Schacht Arras tapestry looms, have a rotating shedding bar that can hold the shed open while you insert the weft. On the Mirrix, this bar has a handle that hooks around the side of the loom to hold the shed open, while the Schacht loom has an internal tensioning mechanism that keeps the shedding bar in place.

Looms with beams change the shed with shaft and treadle mechanisms, as described in chapter 2. The shed is held open by maintaining pressure on the treadle or by using locking treadles, which hold the treadles down without having to maintain pressure on them with your feet. There are many books about how to warp and tie up beamed looms, so I don't cover it in detail here.

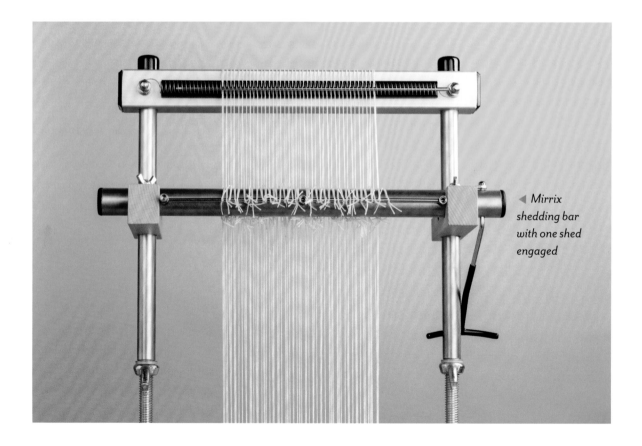

◀ *Mirrix shedding bar with one shed engaged*

Butterflies and Bobbins

Butterflies, or finger skeins, are a simple way to organize your weft yarn and do not require any tools. They work well for single strands of yarn or bundles of weft yarn with only two strands. Bundles of yarn with more than two weft threads will tangle quickly if wound in a butterfly. If you are using bundles of weft with three or more strands that are not plied together, a tapestry bobbin is a better choice to keep it organized.

▲ *Butterflies and tapestry bobbins will both keep your weft yarn organized.*

Making a Butterfly

1. Lay a long tail up the center of your nondominant palm and around the top of your thumb.

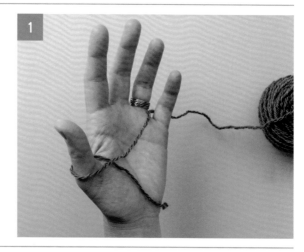

▶ *Leave an 8"–10" tail at the start. This is the end that you will start weaving with, and you do not want to confuse it with the tail at the other end.*

2. Wrap the yarn around your thumb and pinky finger in a figure-8 pattern. The yarn needs to cross the last wrap each time it travels from thumb to pinky. This keeps the layers of yarn separated and in order. Without the cross, the yarn will get hopelessly tangled.

3. As you wind the figure 8, stack the yarn up the outside of your thumb and pinky finger. Do not wrap the new yarn on top of what is already on the outside of your fingers or this will tangle when you use the butterfly. You want a smooth row of yarn up the outside of your thumb and pinky fingers.

stacked weft

4. Wind 10–15 wraps, leave a tail about 10" long, and then cut your yarn.

5. Grasp the center of the butterfly, where the cross occurred, and pull the butterfly off your hand. Hold this center portion of the butterfly firmly.

6. Firmly wind the last tail around the center of the butterfly 5–10 times.

7. Use your index finger to make a space so you can pull the loop through. Tuck the tail you just wrapped around the butterfly under the last wrap and pull tightly to secure it (A). If you leave that last tail with a loop instead of pulling it all the way through, you can avoid the resulting knot at the end of your butterfly (B).

Weaving with a Butterfly

Start weaving with the end from which you started winding the butterfly. This tail should pull out of the center of the finger skein easily. Butterflies will fall apart as the center amount of yarn is used, much like a center-pull yarn ball will. This is just the reality of using them, and there is no way to make butterflies in which this will not happen. When your butterfly falls apart, simply rewind it by starting the butterfly with the yarn close to your weaving, then progressing to the free tail.

Winding a Tapestry Bobbin

A bobbin winder is a tool used for winding boat shuttle bobbins in fabric weaving. Some bobbin winders can be modified to hold a special attachment to wind tapestry bobbins. While the specifics differ depending on the bobbin winder, in general the bobbin winder rotates the tapestry bobbin and winds on the weft yarn as it turns. Most people wind their tapestry bobbins by hand.

1. Lay the tail end of the yarn along the bobbin shaft, with the tail toward the point.

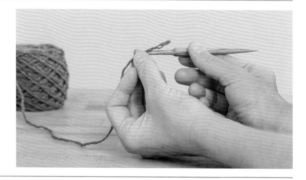

2. Wrap the weft around the bobbin, starting near the bulb end. Turn the bobbin with the bulb end facing you so you can see whether you are wrapping clockwise or counterclockwise. It does not matter which way you wrap; just choose a direction you like and stick with it, because your hands will come to expect the weft to roll off the bobbin in the same way every time.

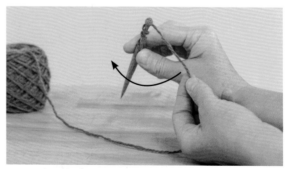

▲ *I like to wrap my bobbins clockwise.*

3. Wrap the weft around the bobbin, spreading it evenly up and down the shaft until either you have enough yarn on it for your project or the bobbin is full. Cut the weft yarn. You will weave with this tail.

After starting the winding, rotate the bobbin in your dominant hand and pinch the weft thread lightly in your other hand. This provides a little tension and ensures there will be no loops in any of the yarns as you wind them together onto the bobbin. You can use the same process when winding multiple strands of a weft bundle onto the bobbin.

4. As you begin weaving, make a hitch around the end of the bobbin by twisting the yarn over itself once to keep it from unrolling (A). Many bobbin users allow the bobbins to hang down the front of the weaving when the bobbins are not in use. In this case, the hitch around the end keeps the yarn from unrolling with the pull of gravity. If you make the hitch correctly and if your yarn is fairly smooth, you do not have to undo the hitch to work with the yarn. The yarn will unroll with the hitch in place (B).

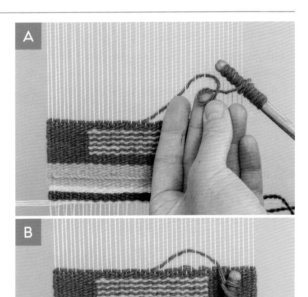

Weaving with a Bobbin

New tapestry weavers often try to put the point of the bobbin through their shed first. This is incorrect. Either the bulb end of the bobbin passes through the weft first (A) or the bobbin is passed in a vertical orientation, tip up (B). The point of the bobbin is used for tapping the weft into place (C). Passing the bobbin vertically with the tip up provides the quickest passage through the weft.

Bobbin users traditionally weave on high-warp, or vertically oriented, tapestry looms. Often these looms have open shed rods and leashes to manage the shedding. Bobbins are an efficient tool for these kinds

of looms because the weaver can manage the warp with one hand and the bobbin with the other. Since the bobbin both holds the weft and beats it in, the weaver does not have to put tools down between picks.

Bobbin weavers also manage bubbling and weft tension in a particular way. The weft is most often put into the shed in small bits, about 1" wide, in just one bubble. Bobbin weavers do not have the longer waves of bubbles that are typical of weaving on a loom with a shed that stays open or of using other tools to manage your weft. I will address these concepts further in chapter 7.

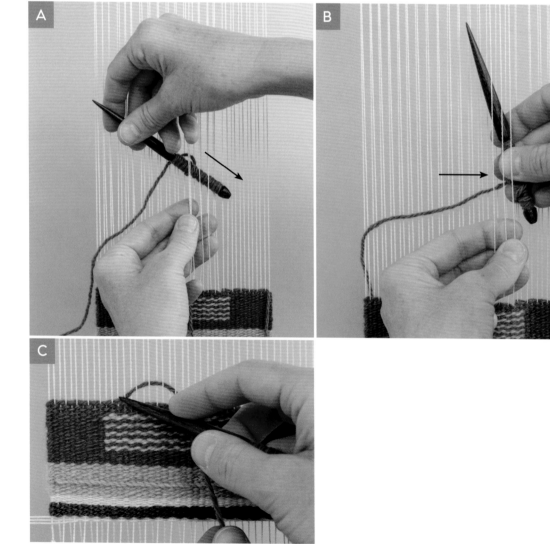

Headers

At this point, your loom is warped, you've prepared your weft, you have an idea how to use your loom, and you understand the parts of a tapestry. You are almost ready to start weaving! But before you start weaving the body of your tapestry, you need to put in some waste yarn and weave a header.

The header gives the tapestry a stable beginning and end as well as provides the structure for finishing and hanging the completed piece. It is important to create your beginning header carefully, since it is the foundation for the rest of the piece. In your hurry to finish a piece you're excited about, it is easy to forget to weave a second header at the end. But the ending header is also important, because the tapestry hanger typically attaches to it.

Think of headers as bumpers or bookends: after weaving the body of your tapestry, you will put another header at the top. Usually this finishing header is a mirror image of the header you did at the beginning; your final header will be a reverse of the steps you followed at the beginning of the piece. And just as you started the weaving with some waste yarn, you'll add some waste yarn after the top header to keep the work from unraveling in the finishing process. If you do not make your headers carefully, they can cause the top and bottom of the piece to be narrower than the body. This cannot be fixed after the tapestry is taken off the loom.

There are as many ways to make headers as there are tapestry weavers. I find that hemmed headers and headers using the double half-hitch knot (see pages 122 and 127, respectively) meet most of my needs, regardless of the size of the tapestry. As you become more comfortable with the techniques in this book, you may want to experiment with different headers that meet your personal artistic needs.

If you are using a tensioned frame loom, such as a pipe loom or Mirrix, you already should have tied on ordering cords and spaced your warp as evenly as possible. If you missed these steps, refer to page 78 for details.

Start with Waste

Prior to weaving one of the headers described on the following pages, you need to weave some waste yarn. This helps you ensure the warps are evenly spaced and holds the tapestry together as you do the finishing process.

This initial weaving is called waste because it will be cut out or unraveled as you complete the finishing process when the tapestry is off the loom. The waste will not be part of your finished tapestry, but it is extremely important nevertheless. You should use the same weft yarn in the waste that you plan to use in the body of your tapestry, because weft wants to follow what comes before, and it is very good at bossing the warp around. You want your warp to accept the weft from the beginning.

The term *waste* is unfortunately misleading. It is common for fabric weavers making household textiles to use scrap yarn for the waste to get their warps spaced evenly before beginning their weaving. I have seen people use all kinds of things for this, including strips of fabric, cut-up plastic bags, and toilet paper. I strongly discourage you from making this mistake in tapestry weaving. A waste section of toilet paper will make the warp anticipate that more toilet paper is to come, and if you follow toilet paper with a beautiful wool tapestry yarn, the warp will treat your yarn like toilet paper for an inch or two before settling into the new weft.

If you are concerned about the loss of the waste yarn after the finishing processes, simply unravel the "waste" and use it again at the beginning of the next tapestry. Otherwise, chalk it up to the cost of ensuring even warp spacing and weft tension.

If you use a beamed loom, you will have triangles of warp where you tied the warp to the front beam. You will need to weave enough waste so that the warp spacing becomes perfectly even. This often takes about 3 inches of weaving at 8 epi, but it will vary depending on your loom and how many warps you tied in each bundle.

On frame looms, you may have fairly even warp spacing right from the beginning. In this case, weave ½ inch of waste to hold the tapestry together once it comes off the loom. If you do not have enough space on your loom to do this, use the double half-hitch header described on page 127.

Remember that the width of your header will be equal to the width of your weaving. It is important that the waste and header are not narrower than you want the tapestry to be, because you can't make it wider later.

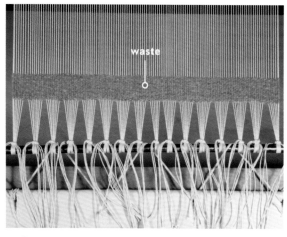

▲ *Tying warp to the front of a beamed loom results in warp-spacing problems that must be evened out with woven waste.*

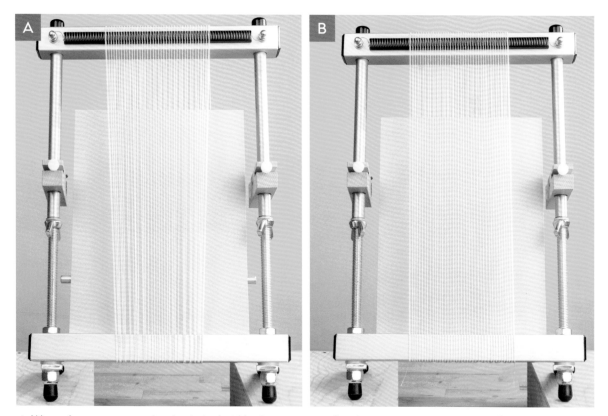

▲ *Warps that are not spaced to the desired width when warping will make your tapestry narrower at the beginning (A). As you warp the loom, space the warps as wide as you want the finished piece to be (B).*

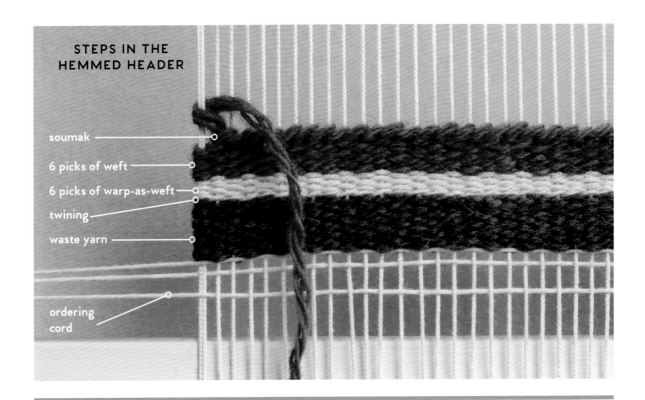

STEPS IN THE
HEMMED HEADER

- soumak
- 6 picks of weft
- 6 picks of warp-as-weft
- twining
- waste yarn
- ordering cord

Making a Hemmed Header

The hemmed header produces a clean edge, without any fringe or warp showing. This header ends with a single row of a textural outline stitch called soumak, which makes a subtle ridge where the tapestry will fold in the finishing process. This row of soumak gives the edge a crisp appearance.

Waste Yarn

Weave some waste yarn as discussed on page 120.

Twining

Before putting in a line of twining, disengage any shedding mechanisms so the warp is lying flat (that is, neither shed is open). Twining creates a twist between each warp thread as seen in the diagram at right.

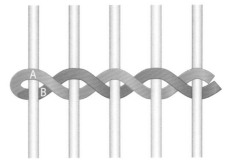

1. Cut a piece of warp thread three to four times the width of your warp. Fold it in half. You can start the twining with a lark's head knot (see page 282) at one selvage or you can just put a tail on each side with the fold at the selvage as shown at right.

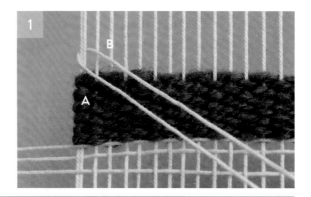

2. We'll call the thread in front of the warp "A" and the thread behind the warp "B." Cross A over B and bring A behind the 2nd warp.

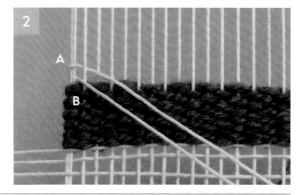

3. Pass the "B" thread under the 3rd warp. You should see a twist between the 2 twining threads between the warps.

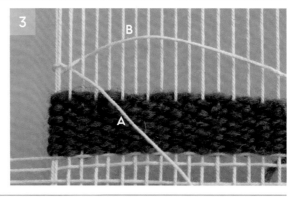

4. Continue alternating which thread crosses under the next warp until you reach the other side.

5. These tails can be worked into the next section of warp-as-weft as described on page 126. They may also be left to hang and then worked with a needle back into the tapestry when it comes off the loom.

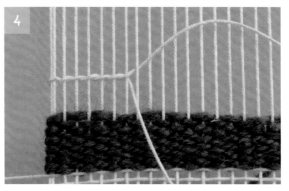

Weave 6 Picks of Warp-as-Weft

Cut a piece of warp at least eight times the width of your piece and use it to weave 6 picks. This fiber can be difficult to get in neatly. The warp woven as weft is not as flexible as the regular weft yarn, and it may be tricky to get the warp-as-weft section to look right. If you see big loops of warp thread poking out of your weaving, put in less warp-as-weft. If you get a tight line across, put in a little more as described in the section on bubbling on page 145. Remember that this part will be folded into a hem and no one will ever see it. Therefore, it is more important to create a firm, narrow bit of weaving to which you can sew the finishing materials than it is to make it look pretty. You also want to be careful that this section is as wide as you want the beginning of your tapestry to be: having too much warp-as-weft (and causing tiny bubbles in the weave) is better than having too little warp-as-weft, which can draw your weaving in.

Weave 6 Picks of Weft Yarn

For these 6 picks, use the colors of weft yarn with which you will start the piece. If you have planned a tapestry with many colors at the beginning, you do not have to match them in this part. Just choose one color that will blend in, especially at the selvages.

Soumak

The last piece of your header is 1 row of soumak. Once you complete this, you'll be ready to start the body of your tapestry. Soumak creates a small float that goes over 2 warp threads. This float needs to be on the front side of the tapestry. If you are weaving from the back, you'll need to reverse the soumak row so that the float occurs on what will be the front of the tapestry.

1. Begin with a closed or neutral shed just as you did for the twining. You can do the soumak with the same butterfly you used to weave the 6 picks of weft.

2. If the butterfly you will use for the soumak row is exiting the previous pick behind the edge warp thread (A), you can start the 2-warp float pattern immediately. Wrap the weft around the 2nd warp from the edge.

   If the butterfly you will use for the soumak row is exiting the previous pick in front of the edge warp (B), you have to fudge the first stitch a little bit. Wrap the weft around the edge warp and back to the front of the tapestry (C). Then wrap it around the front of the 2nd warp from the edge, beginning the soumak pattern (D).

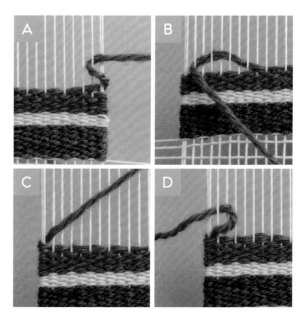

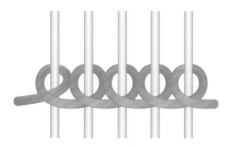

◀ *Soumak as it should look on the front of the tapestry.*

3. The soumak is now set up and you can progress across the warp. Your weft yarn will be coming toward you between 2 warp threads. The next wrap will go over the 2 adjacent warps, then around the next warp. This will create a short float that goes over 2 warp threads.

4. Continue wrapping each warp until you get to the other side. Because the soumak will show in the final tapestry, if your design changes color at the bottom of the tapestry, you may want to change the color of the soumak. To do this, simply leave a tail of one color and continue with the next as if there were no break.

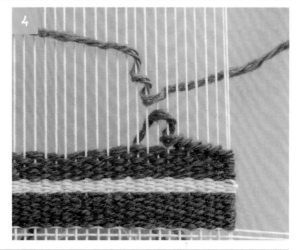

Finishing Your Piece with a Hemmed Header

When you get to the end of your piece, don't forget to finish it with a second hemmed header. After finishing the body of the work, follow the header steps in reverse order, like this:

1. Soumak

2. 6 picks of weft

3. 6 picks of warp-as-weft

4. Twining

5. Waste yarn

Hemmed Header Problem Solving

Soumak

Starting the soumak row can be tricky if you are doing it with a new piece of yarn. Hold the tail in your palm and start the soumak, completing several stitches as shown in the diagram on page 124. After looping 5 or 6 warps to anchor the yarn, go back to the tail at the start. Unravel it from the first warp, bring the tail to the back of the tapestry, and complete a pigtail as shown on page 142.

The soumak will produce tails. You will learn ways to avoid some of them in the section Meet and Separate (see page 132). For now, just leave those tails hanging at the edges of your work, or start weaving with whatever was left of your butterfly at the end of the soumak row.

Soumak causes your yarn to untwist or twist more, depending on which direction it was twisted when it was made and which side of the warp you started the soumak row. Just add more twist to the yarn as you go, or allow your butterfly to untwist if you get a twist buildup.

1. Cut a piece of warp thread six times the width of your piece.

2. Splice the twining tail to the new piece of warp.

3. Weave the 6 picks of warp-as-weft and, as you do, carry the second twining tail under the selvage wraps.

4. At the end of the 6 picks, do not bring the last pick all the way to the selvage. Instead, bring the twining tail into the shed to meet the last pick and make a second splice, which will join the two tails together.

This technique is the *only* time I ever allow a weft to travel in the selvage. Carrying weft threads up the selvage and weaving over them is not a good practice in tapestry weaving because it distorts the edge and makes it difficult to keep the selvage straight and firm. In this particular instance, the warp-as-weft section will be hidden in the fold of the hem.

Dealing with the Tails of the Twining and Warp-as-Weft

When working the hemmed header, it is possible to splice the ends of the twining and the warp-as-weft thread together to get rid of the tails completely by the time you finish those two sections. Splicing cotton seine twine warp is fairly difficult because the threads are spun so tightly that they don't easily tease apart. Later in this chapter, you will practice splicing the weft (see page 140), which is much easier because the weft is usually thicker and more loosely plied. When you finish your twining, begin weaving the warp-as-weft section with one of the twining tails, following the directions below.

NOTE: This procedure is a little fiddly, and I recommend you return to this description for your second tapestry if it does not make sense right now.

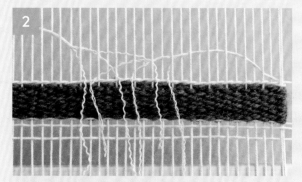

▲ *The tails from these splices can be trimmed off after you have woven an inch or so on top of them.*

Making a Double Half-Hitch Header

The double half hitch (see page 279) is a very useful knot that holds firmly if you tie it tightly. It can be used as the header at the beginning and end of a tapestry if you want to leave fringe showing. Note that the knot looks different on the front and the back. You can tie it so that you see a tiny diagonal line in each knot (A) or two horizontal lines (B).

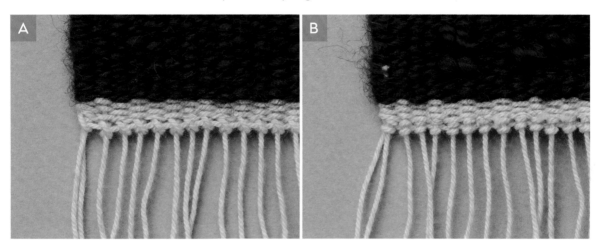

▲ *These two images are the front and back of the same piece. The knots can be tied to make either example show up on the front of your finished tapestry.*

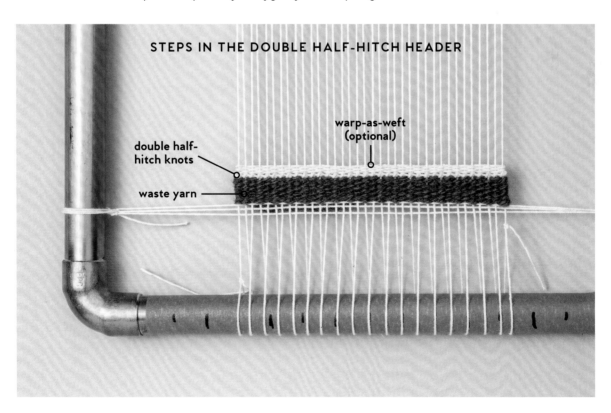

STEPS IN THE DOUBLE HALF-HITCH HEADER

warp-as-weft (optional)

double half-hitch knots

waste yarn

Waste Yarn

Weave some waste yarn as discussed on page 120.

Double Half Hitches

1. Cut a piece of warp thread six times longer than the width of your warp.

2. Begin the row of double half hitches by wrapping the new length of thread around the first warp and underneath the tail.

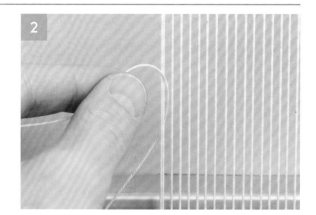

3. Wrap the working thread around the same warp again. You're forming a loop that looks like the bump on a lowercase letter *d*.

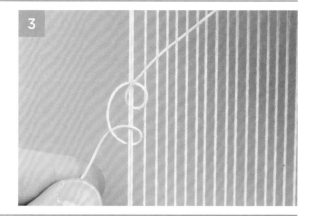

4. Pull the knot tight. This method of tying the knot results in a diagonal line on the front of each knot. For diagrams showing how to make the knot with the other side facing the front, see page 280. Let the initial warp tail hang until the piece comes off the loom.

5. Repeat steps 2–4 to continue making this knot all the way across your warp. Make sure to keep the spacing even between the warps as you tie the knot. Do not let the knots pull the warp threads closer together.

Optional Decorative Edges

In the images at the top of page 127, I wove a few sequences of warp-as-weft for a decorative edge. This is not functionally necessary, and after the single line of double half hitches you can start the body of your tapestry.

There are many variations of the double half-hitch header. You could make the knots with a colored warp thread, or you could do a row of these knots with a thin, strong upholstery thread and then make a row of soumak or another row of the knots with the weft yarn to hide that thread. The thread will anchor the bottom and top of the weaving, but the knots made of thread will become invisible.

▲ *If you make the half-hitch knots with a thin thread to anchor your weaving, you can cover the knots with weft.*

Finishing Your Piece with a Double Half-Hitch Header

When you get to the end of your piece, don't forget to finish it with a second double half-hitch header. After finishing the body of the work, follow the header steps in reverse order, like this:

1. Row of double half-hitch knots with the same fiber you used at the beginning of the piece (warp, thread, or weft)

2. Waste

When the tapestry comes off the loom, finish the tails this way: Using a needle, thread the warp ends from the double half-hitch row and work them back into the weaving. When the warp ends are secure, trim them off.

Weaving the Tapestry Body

Now that your beginning header is woven, you're ready to start the body of your tapestry. Weaving some simple stripes at the beginning lets you get used to manipulating the weft yarn and practice the very important concept of meet and separate before you start weaving more complicated forms. Be sure to spend some time on these important sections even if they seem simple at first glance.

Getting Started

Stripes

Start by weaving some stripes to get the feeling for opening the sheds and putting the weft through.

1. Wind one butterfly or bobbin. Leaving the tail at one of the selvages, weave 1 pick across the warp. The important concepts of bubbling and weft tension are covered in more depth in chapter 7. For now, however, it is enough to know that you need to put in some extra weft so there is enough to go over and under all of those warps. We call this bubbling, and it looks something like the wavy row of working yarn at the top of the image at right.

2. Put the weft yarn through the shed and adjust the bubbles. (See page 145 for more information on how to make bubbles.)

3. Change the shed, then beat the weft in with your tapestry fork. Weave back and forth with this butterfly to get a feel for changing the sheds and beating.

4. When you get tired of one color, cut your weft and start another butterfly of a different color. You will have tails at the selvages as you do this. Soon you'll learn a technique called meet and separate, which lets you keep tails in the center of the weaving. For now, remember that you can use a needle and sew the ends along a warp rib once the piece is off the loom. As you practice on your sampler, I recommend just leaving them.

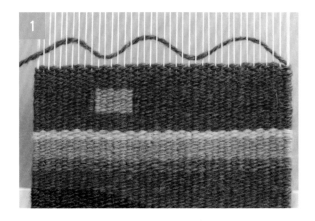

NOTE: Never run your tapestry weft up the selvage wrapped under the new weaving. This distorts the selvages and makes it difficult to get a clean edge.

Beating with a Tapestry Fork

Beating, or packing in, the weft locks it into place and allows it to slide down against the fell line without shifting. There are a few different pieces of equipment — and several approaches you can use — for beating the weft. Whether you use a tapestry fork to beat in every pick or only occasionally to firm up the weaving depends on your weaving style and equipment: some weavers use the fork to do all of their beating, on every pick, while others use a tapestry bobbin most of the time but pack everything in a little more firmly with a fork on occasion. Some use the reed of a floor loom but employ the tapestry fork when weaving eccentrically (see page 251), and still other tapestry weavers push the weft in with their fingers for many picks and then give it a tap with a fork from time to time to even up the packing. Regardless of which method you prefer, you likely will use a tapestry fork from time to time.

All that is necessary is a light flick of the wrist, which taps the tines of the fork against the fell line. Repeat this motion across the woven area. Take care to not beat using a lot of force; instead use a consistent, gentle tapping. Beating with force compacts the weft a great deal and results in a very stiff tapestry fabric. This not only changes the surface of the weaving but also the way the yarn reflects light and, therefore, color.

Beat on either a neutral shed or change the shed before beating, depending on the kind of loom you are using. If you beat on a neutral or shifted shed, it does not matter whether you beat in any particular pattern — such as from one selvage to the other or from the center to the edges. It's best *not* to beat in your weft with the shed of that weft open. If you beat with the shed open and the weft loose within it, the weft can shift around and make it more difficult to get the correct amount of weft into each pick.

The weft likely will not completely cover the warp for a full sequence or more. Seeing little bits of warp near the fell line is okay. As long as there are not any other problems with weft tension (see page 145) or with

weft that is too thick for your sett (see page 154), these bits of warp will be covered as you continue to weave and pack the weft together more tightly.

▲ *The tapestry forks I like to use are lightweight, and I beat from one side of the woven area to the other. I use a similar wrist motion whether I'm weaving on a high-warp or a low-warp loom. However, some low-warp loom users use a tool called a grattoir, or they grasp a specially shaped tapestry fork (called an Aubusson beater) in their fist to pull it toward them.*

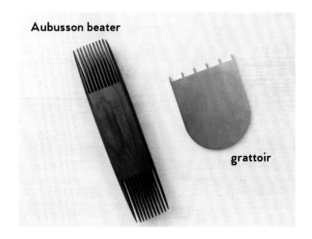

Aubusson beater

grattoir

Meet and Separate

You are ready to weave with more than one butterfly, which is the key to making shapes. To move butterflies to new positions in order to create those shapes, the butterflies must travel in opposite directions in the same shed. This is called meet and separate. Neighboring wefts are either moving away from each other or toward each other in the same shed. Weavers use various phrases to remember this, but I like "head to head and tail to tail."

NOTE: From now on I will mostly use the term *butterfly* to indicate one weft strand. Realize that no matter how you package your weft, whether you use a butterfly, bobbin, needle, or long loose pieces of yarn, I'm talking about the same thing. When weaving a wide area with a solid color, you will often use multiple butterflies of the same color to avoid drawing in the selvages.

In the diagram at right, notice that the tails start together and the butterflies move away from each

▲ *This image should help you remember the principles of meet and separate: head-to-head and tail-to-tail.*

other in the 1st pick. In the 2nd pick in the other shed, the butterflies move toward each other. This process is meet and separate.

Almost without exception, when weaving tapestry, your butterflies will travel in opposition to each other. The tails of the butterflies will be next to each other and the heads of the butterflies (or your tapestry bobbins) will be next to each other. If you have this set up correctly, on the surface of the tapestry you will see pairs of wefts lined up, and all the butterflies will be in the same shed.

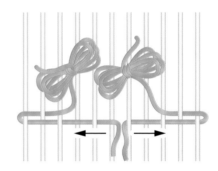

▲ *Meet and separate is demonstrated here with the tails starting together in the center and the butterflies moving apart, or separating. In the next shed, the butterflies are moving toward each other and will meet somewhere in the center of the warp.*

"In the Same Shed"

When you're new to tapestry weaving, even knowing what shed you're "in" can be confusing. To make this easier to visualize, use either heddles or a shed stick to find one shed all the way across your loom. Try opening the whole shed and fill in all the butterflies you need in that pick all the way across. Leave the bubbles up (do not beat) during this process to ensure the whole shed is full.

This method, called weaving line by line (see page 32), ensures that you fill the whole shed before you move on to the next one and decreases problems with some wefts being in the other shed.

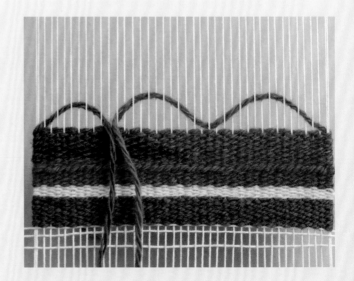

Meet-and-Separate Practice

Continue weaving stripes, now using meet and separate. You may notice that one of the first advantages of using two butterflies instead of one is that you can start your tails in the center of the warp instead of at one edge. When I talk about splicing a little later in this chapter, you will learn to splice those two tails together so they disappear completely.

1. Make two butterflies of the same color. Start them in the center of your warp, both weaving outward toward the selvage.

2. Change your shed and beat. If you are weaving from the front, tuck the tails to the back.

3. Weave the butterflies in the next shed toward each other. Make the butterflies meet in a different spot on the warp than where you started. When using meet and separate, the butterflies can meet again anywhere on the warp.

4. Shift the shed, beat, and weave back to the edges with both butterflies.

5. Bring the butterflies together again, but this time, have them meet in another different spot.

6. Continue to weave this color until your stripe is as wide as you like. When you want to switch colors, bring both butterflies together in the middle of the warp and cut them, leaving a 2"–3" tail.

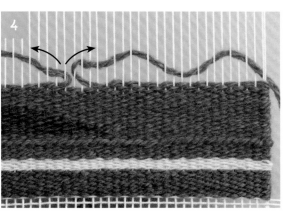

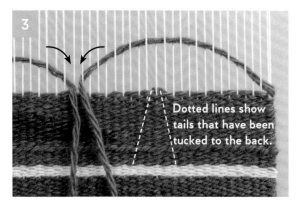

Dotted lines show tails that have been tucked to the back.

7. Add more stripes as you like. When you do, start each new pair of butterflies in a different spot on the warp.

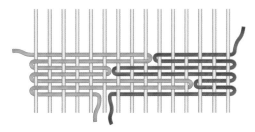

▲ *This diagram shows how the relays (the point where the weft turns back) do not line up. If they did, it would create a slit. For clarity, the diagram shows two different colors, but you will weave with two butterflies of the same color when making stripes.*

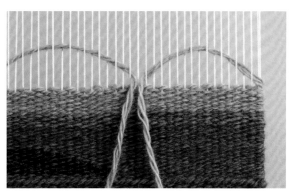

▲ *Notice how you wove all the wefts without putting two wefts in the same shed. What you just did is meet and separate.*

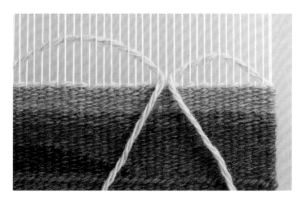

▲ *As you weave the butterflies toward each other, they will exit the shed through the same hole between two raised warps.*

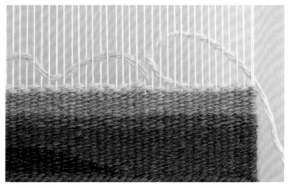

▲ *When you change the shed, an uncovered warp thread comes forward. This warp must be covered by one of the two butterflies. The one that covers it will wrap around that warp and return to the selvage, the other butterfly will simply return.*

Stripes Practice

By continuing to weave stripes, you will practice making your butterflies come together and move apart. You will also be working on bubbling and getting the correct amount of weft into your warp. Stripe variations can be astoundingly beautiful, so take a moment to study the rest of the information in this chapter, as well as advice about weft tension and bubbling in the next chapter. If you get bored, vary the width and color of the stripes as you play.

Adding and Subtracting Butterflies in Pairs

Now that you have practiced with two butterflies, let's add one more. When you add a new butterfly at the selvage, your meet and separate will remain intact as long as you keep adjacent butterflies moving in opposition to each other (see diagram at top, right). Remember: head to head and tail to tail.

But if you want to add a butterfly in the center of your weaving, you will add one butterfly between two moving in meet and separate, causing you to lose the head-to-head, tail-to-tail orientation on one side, as shown in the second illustration from the top.

The weaving system works best when *pairs* of wefts are added or removed. If you add two butterflies rather than one, your meet and separate is maintained, and you can continue weaving without changing the original butterflies. Adding a pair of butterflies works well if you have enough room in your weaving to accommodate two more butterflies. But if you do not have enough warps to add two butterflies weaving back and forth, you will need to change the direction of some of your wefts. This is described in Correcting Wefts Moving in the Wrong Direction on page 136.

▶ *The same principle applies to removing butterflies. If you drop just one butterfly, the remaining two will be traveling in the same direction in the same shed, and you'll need to correct this problem.*

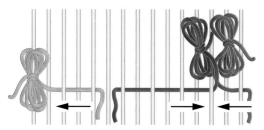

▲ *The red butterfly was added at the selvage. Meet and separate is maintained.*

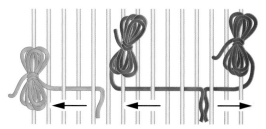

▲ *Adding one butterfly between two destroys meet and separate. In this example, the red butterfly has been added between the outer butterflies, which were in a meet-and-separate pattern.*

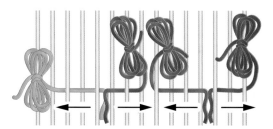

▲ *Adding pairs of butterflies maintains the existing meet-and-separate pattern.*

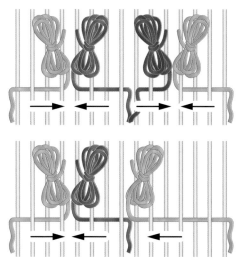

Correcting Wefts Moving in the Wrong Direction

When adjacent wefts are not moving in meet and separate in the same shed, you will not be able to weave one weft over another and maintain the structure. To describe this, sometimes weavers say that your "sheds are wrong" or that your "butterfly is in the wrong shed." Each of these statements means the same thing. But how do you know if one or more of your butterflies is moving in the wrong direction?

Image A shows what happens when you attempt to weave one shape over another with the wefts moving in the same direction in the same shed. Notice that where the weaving started, the butterflies were both moving left to right. In image B, the wefts are set up to move in opposing directions. In this case, they started on the outside edges of the weaving, but they could have both started in the center, tails together.

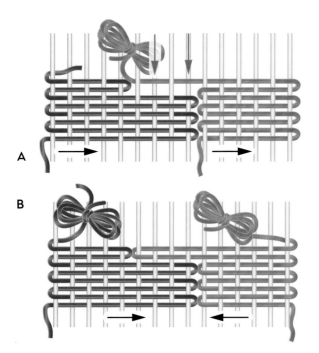

When the orange weft moves over the blue weft in image A, there are two wefts in the same shed, as indicated by the red arrows. When two wefts are woven

in the same shed, there is twice as much yarn in that shed and it is impossible for the weft to cover the warp because the weft buddle is too large to allow the next pick to slide over and cover it. As a result, you will see little dots of warp, called lice, peeking through. See Two Wefts in the Same Shed on page 154 for information about how to address this problem.

Image B demonstrates what happens when you use meet and separate to set up your weft directions. The butterflies are moving in opposition to each other in the same shed, and thus either butterfly can move on top of the other one at any point and maintain the weave structure.

There are three basic ways to correct shedding problems such as butterflies that are not traveling in the correct direction: resetting your butterflies, adding another butterfly, or using a half-pass to shift the shed.

RESETTING THE BUTTERFLY means that you cut the butterfly and start it traveling in the opposite direction within the same shed. This will immediately fix your shedding problem. If the distance it has to travel is not great and you don't mind floats on the back of your work, you can loop the butterfly across the back and enter it in the shed in the other direction. Because I like a clean back, I do not work this way, but many tapestry weavers do. If the shedding problem is in the middle of a group of multiple butterflies, you may need to reset the butterflies all the way to the selvage on one side of the weaving to regain correct shedding.

ADDING ANOTHER BUTTERFLY means that between two butterflies moving in the same direction you introduce one butterfly moving in the opposite direction. This regains meet and separate.

USING A HALF-PASS TO SHIFT THE SHED changes the shed, which allows your butterfly to continue weaving. The half-pass can be done with the same size of yarn you have been using, but you could also use a thinner piece of yarn. This approach avoids adding more weft, which may interfere with precise expression of your design. If you are using weft bundles to weave (see page 49), you could use just one of the strands to make this shift.

Wefts Moving in Wrong Direction

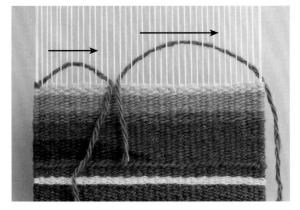

▲ *Butterflies moving in the same direction in the same shed. If you try to weave with butterflies in this orientation, you won't be able to shift them over without putting two wefts in the same shed.*

Resetting the Butterfly

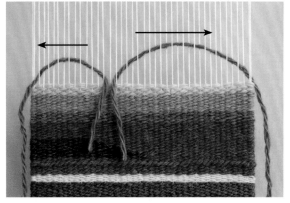

▲ *Cutting a butterfly and restarting it traveling in the opposite direction allows you to weave in meet and separate again. When in the same shed, all your butterflies should have heads together or tails together.*

Adding Another Butterfly

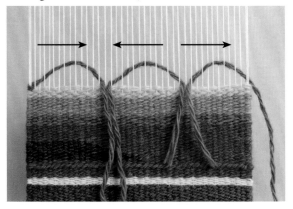

▲ *Instead of cutting or resetting one of the butterflies and making it travel in the opposite direction, you can add another butterfly between the two.*

Using a Half-Pass

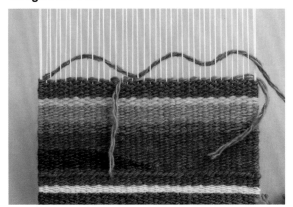

▲ *When using a half-pass to shift the shed in an area, use the same color yarn that you are weaving with. This half-pass is shown in gold for demonstration purposes only. To make the correction blend into the weaving, you would work the half-pass in red.*

Cornelia Theimer Gardella, *Abiquiu Lines I*, 2007.
Cotton and wool, 39" × 39".
▲ *Cornelia Theimer Gardella has made a body of tapestry work using stripes. This piece creates beautifully rich colors using only stripes.*

Hill and Valley Threads

The shedding challenges I have been talking about are directly related to whether a weft travels over or under a warp thread. The woven sequence of over/under, over/under continues in the next pick, but where a weft went *under* the warp before, now it goes *over*.

Every time a weft travels in front of a warp thread, it makes a little rise, or hill. When it travels behind the next warp, it creates a little dip, or valley. The hill threads cover the warp, and the valleys leave a little warp exposed. But in the next pick, that valley will be covered by a hill, which fills in the dip.

If the hills and valleys do not alternate in each subsequent pick, you will be weaving two wefts into the same shed: the hills can't sink down into the valleys, and the warp will show. This is what's happening where the double weft is created in image A on page 136.

I cover hill and valley threads in more detail in chapters 10 and 13 because they affect how smoothly you can make lines, curves, and angles. For right now, just get in the habit of looking at your weaving and recognizing when the weft creates a tiny hill and when it forms a valley. Remember, a valley thread on the side of the weaving facing you is a hill thread on the side facing away from you.

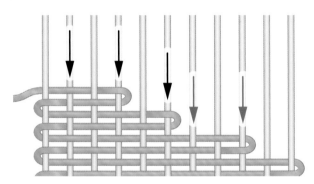

◀ *The black arrows indicate hill threads, and the red arrows indicate valley threads.*

Managing Tails

Because you change weft colors a lot in tapestry weaving, tails are created wherever the wefts start and stop. There are a variety of ways to deal with these tails, including splicing or feathering weft ends, working in the ends with a needle when the piece comes off the loom, or leaving tails on the back of the piece and tying them together into small bundles during the finishing process.

When you're deciding which way to manage your tails, keep in mind that not all yarns act the same way. A fuzzier wool weft will grab onto its neighboring wefts and create a cohesive textile. The cut weft ends of these kinds of yarn are less likely to work to the front of the tapestry. If you use a smoother wool yarn or a smooth fiber like silk or cotton, cut tails close to the surface of the work can work out over time and show on the front.

Splicing

Splicing is a method of overlapping two pieces of yarn in such a way that the total amount of weft in an area remains constant. Splices done with slightly fuzzy wool yarn will hold firmly, and the tails can be cut next to the fabric during the finishing process, which saves time by avoiding working in those ends with a needle.

Any time I run out of yarn in my butterfly, I splice a new length of yarn to it and keep weaving. Think of splicing as just extending the yarn that was too short so you can finish the area you are weaving. In larger areas, I frequently use more than one butterfly of the same color moving in meet and separate and splice the two butter- flies together at the beginning and sometimes at the end of these spots to cut down on the number of tails.

NOTE: Avoid splicing yarns that are not the same color. If the two colors are different enough in value or saturation, you will see dots of each color where they were spliced together. If you need a clean join between color areas, it is best to leave the tails hanging, poten- tially with the use of a pigtail (see page 142).

1. Separate the plies of the yarn that you have been weaving with (the brown yarn here). If you're using a weft bundle, treat each strand like 1 ply in this exam- ple. Leave a tail about 3" long.

2. Bring 1 ply out of the warp and continue weaving the other under 1 or 2 more raised warps.

3. Separate the plies of the yarn you will begin weaving with (the turquoise yarn in the image).

4. Insert the new piece of yarn into the shed moving in the same direction as the piece you just ended. Bring each unplied tail of the new yarn out of the same space between two raised warps that the old yarn come out.

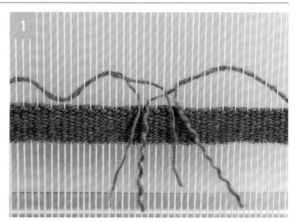

▲ *Normally these yarns would be the same color, but they are different here so you can see what is happening.*

5. If you are weaving from the back, your splice is now complete and you can continue to step 6. If you are weaving from the front, you'll need to tuck the tails of the splices to the back. Eventually you'll get good enough at visualizing where the tails go that you can tuck them behind as you place the yarns. As you're learning, complete the splice first and then tuck the tails to the back as shown here.

6. Leave the tails on the back of the work until you take it off the loom. At that point you can trim the splices flush with the fabric. If you're weaving from the back, you can trim them off after weaving about ½" of weft above them.

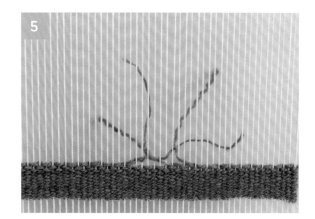

VARIATION

Feathering

The splicing procedure described on these two pages works with 2- or 3-ply yarns or with a weft bundle if you treat individual yarns the same way you would the plies of a 2-ply yarn. If you use handspun or one single at a time, there is another way to splice yarns. This is also the way I've seen Diné weavers splice; it keeps the back of their tapestries clean. With this method you'll thin out the weft at the end of the old piece of yarn and at the beginning of the new piece of yarn, a process called feathering. You will then overlap those two thinner pieces in the tapestry where one piece of yarn ends and a new one begins.

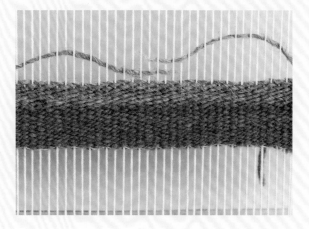

1. Slightly shred the end of the yarn with your fingertips, scissors, or by breaking the weft instead of cutting it.

2. Weave the first weft all the way into the shed. Feather the end of the new piece of yarn as described in step 1, and lay it on top of the first weft.

Pigtailing

Pigtailing is a way of making an extra wrap at the beginning or end of a piece of weft to make it more secure in the weaving. A pigtail helps secure the weft in place and keeps little puffs of weft from working to the front of the weaving over time. Pigtails are also useful in areas with many different wefts. The weaving in these places tends to get looser because of all the small gaps between the color areas, and a pigtail can help keep the weft more firmly anchored. When doing a pigtail, in half the cases you will be adding an extra wrap around a warp, so there will be one extra weft traveling in front of that warp and showing on the front. You will not notice this little bit of extra weft in most techniques.

Pigtails are also used to accentuate the corner of a shape. For example, if you want to really sharpen the corner of a rectangle, use a pigtail, which puts an extra wrap on the corner warp. This relates to hill and valley threads: if a valley thread ends up at the corner of a shape, it will sink and the corner of the shape will not be as crisp as it would if a hill thread were there. You can use the tail at the end of the shape to pigtail that corner and define it more, as seen below.

You want the weft tail to end up on the back of the tapestry when making a pigtail. If your weft comes out of the shed behind the warp to be pigtailed, as in the images directly below, simply wrap the tail around the selvage warp to secure your pigtail. This directs the tail to the back of the weaving.

When the weft comes out in front of the warp to be pigtailed, if you simply wrap it to form the pigtail, the tail would end up on the front of the tapestry (A). To create the pigtail in this case, make a small float on the back (B), then complete the pigtail (C).

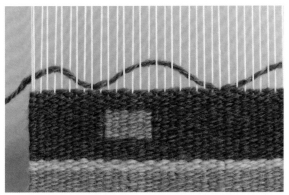

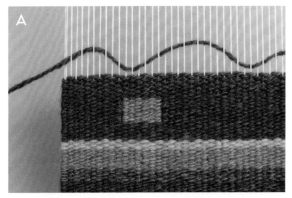

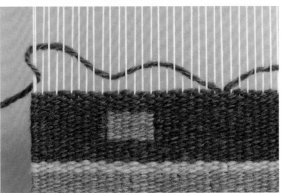

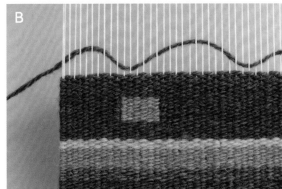

▲ These images show making a pigtail when the weft comes out of the shed behind the warp to be pigtailed.

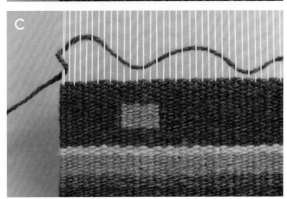

▲ Notice that every other warp is covered with a hill thread after the pigtail is completed.

7 Heading Off Trouble

The most common challenge for all tapestry weavers throughout their weaving careers is managing weft tension, a term used to describe how much weft goes into any particular area of the weaving. Managing it takes practice and experience, and though it does eventually become second nature to adjust for it, weft tension issues never entirely go away. You manage weft tension in a process called bubbling. In this chapter you will learn all about bubbling, weft tension, and other common challenges for new tapestry weavers.

Bubbling's Effect on Weft Tension

Before weaving one more pick, stop to think about weft tension.

Most weavers think that a firm warp tension will keep the warps evenly spaced as they weave. But the weft is really the boss of the system, and the weft tension can pull the warp spacing into all kinds of uneven configurations quite readily. Think of weft tension as the amount of weft that goes into any one portion of a tapestry. Recall this diagram from chapter 4 illustrating a cross section of the warp. The curved lines are 2 picks of weft and the dots are the warp ends.

▲ *Warp cross section with two picks of weft*

In a functional woven textile such as a tea towel, usually one weft thread travels all the way across the warp and back. The whole textile is woven with that weft, and because the warp and weft act the same way throughout the weaving process, the towel ends up being rectangular. It is a uniform fabric and the selvages neither push out nor draw in.

Now imagine you are weaving a textile that is full of tiny holes. The size and frequency of those holes change throughout the weaving. Sometimes one weft travels a long way through the warp without creating any holes, and sometimes many butterflies are used to complete 1 pick of weaving across the warp, which creates a tiny gap everywhere the colors change. Both of these scenarios occur in tapestry weaving. Every time you change colors, you create a small, usually invisible hole. Sometimes where the holes get larger, they create slits, which must be closed up by sewing or with joins. (I will cover this in chapter 9.) Wherever there are holes, more spaces are created in the textile, and the weave becomes a little bit looser. Conversely, where one weft travels longer distances, there are no holes and the fabric is a little tighter, like the tea towel.

This variation in how much or how little weft there is in any one part of the tapestry is known as weft tension, and it has an effect on the density and pliability of the fabric. The warp tension is largely a function of your loom and stays pretty constant throughout a tapestry, especially if your loom has a tensioning mechanism. But the weft tension changes all the time: you move the weft through the structure as you weave, and you therefore alter the weft tension with the forms you create and how well you manage the amount of weft in any one area by bubbling.

In tapestry weaving the weft yarns must be long enough to travel over and under each of the warps. This over/under path of the weft requires more yarn than it would if you just stretched the weft straight through the shed. If you were to put the weft straight across, the spaces between the warps would necessarily become narrower and narrower as the fabric tries to adjust for the lack of weft. This causes the weaving to get narrower, or to draw in, as the weft pulls the warps closer and closer together in that area.

Tapestry weavers introduce this necessary extra amount of weft by bubbling. These "bubbles" look like gentle waves in the weft thread and are placed with your finger before shifting the shed and beating in the weft. The necessary amount of bubbling depends on variables such as warp and weft size, sett, and even the type of equipment you use. It will take some experimenting to find the right amount of bubbling for your particular tapestry.

▲ *Bubbles at the fell line*

The height and length of your bubbles will vary depending on what and how you are weaving. For example, if you are weaving a design that has many butterflies next to each other, you may not need to bubble at all because the slits created between the colors will provide enough room to prevent draw-in. In larger areas that are covered with one butterfly, however, your bubbles may be a couple of inches wide.

How the Loom and Beating Affect Your Selvages

Often new tapestry weavers are very fixated on creating perfect selvages. This is a worthy goal. But there are many factors that contribute to neat selvages, and learning them all takes some practice. Among other factors, the equipment you are using affects the way you weave. The selvages on the tapestries I have woven on my Harrisville rug loom are, for the most part, extremely straight. The Harrisville is a low-warp, countermarche loom with a beater that holds a reed through which the warp is threaded. When weaving tapestry on a loom with a reed and beater, you can watch the placement of each weft in the dents on the reed and know immediately if the tapestry is drawing in or getting wider. This type of loom is unique in providing a constant and immediate indication as to how effectively you manage weft tension. Tapestry weavers such as Michael Rohde, Susan Iverson, and James Koehler, who produce work that is extremely square and flat, do this in part by using the beater on the loom. Of course, they're also all excellent technicians with decades of experience as weavers.

On frame looms or other looms without attached beaters and reeds, you will use a tapestry fork or bobbin to beat in the weft. There is a lot of variability in how weft gets packed with these tools. This is okay because the weft tension tends to even out over the course of the tapestry. But you may find that if you weave when you are angry or tired, your beating will change and so, too, will the nature of the fabric and selvages. The force with which you beat can also vary if you're using the beater that's often present on beamed looms, but it is far easier to get a consistent beat in tapestry weaving on those looms.

For some people, entering small amounts of weft and beating it in immediately with the bobbin is the best way to effectively manage weft tension. This gradual approach helps ensure you are putting the right amount of weft into any area of a weaving. Weaving with bobbins in this way is almost always done on high-warp tensioned looms that use leashes or finger picking to make the shed. This method of adjusting weft tension is not as effective if you are using a loom on which the shed stays open, such as a Mirrix or beamed loom with treadles.

Susan Iverson, *Lingering*, 2015.
Wool, linen, and silk, 29" × 101½".

▲ *Susan Iverson's tapestries have extremely straight edges partly due to the kind of loom she uses. She wove* Lingering *sideways, so the selvages are the long edges of the tapestry.*

Fixing Weft Tension Problems

Learning how to manage weft tension is one of the first challenges for a beginning tapestry weaver. While dealing with weft tension never goes away no matter how much weaving experience you have, adjusting your weft tension will eventually become second nature.

These are the most common weft tension problems:

- Warps get closer together.
- Warps move farther apart.
- The width of your tapestry changes by more than ⅛"–¼".
- Lice are apparent and the fell line rises up.
- Waves appear in the surface of your tapestry.

If there is not enough weft in sections of your weaving to allow it to travel over and under all those warps, the warps will have no option but to draw closer together. The first clue that you are not putting enough weft into one area of your weaving is that the spaces between the warps will get narrower, as seen toward the left-hand selvage of the weaving below. As the warps get closer together, there is not room between them to allow the weft to slide down and completely cover the warp, causing little dots of warp, called lice, to appear. Over time you will learn to prevent these problems by watching your warp spacing and making larger or smaller bubbles as you place the weft.

The spacing between warps becoming wider and narrower can absolutely happen on different parts of the same warp. When warps spread apart due to too much weft, they can cause warps in other places to bunch up. The weft will sink into the places where the warp spacing is wider, which makes the hills created in places where the warps are too close together more prominent.

Weft tension is the number one frustration I see new tapestry weavers struggle with. Remember that many things contribute to weft tension challenges, and learning to avoid those problems can take a lot of practice. The more aware you are of your warp spacing and the width of your tapestry, the easier it will be to spot problems before they get too extensive. Also remember that you are creating a textile, not a rigid structure, and sometimes the warps will not be evenly spaced. With some techniques, such as joins (see chapter 9), more widely spaced warps are unavoidable. This is okay: the warps shift around as you manipulate the weft. The overall goal is to keep the warps somewhere near even spacing most of the time.

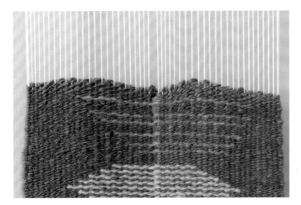

▲ *Uneven warp spacing is the easiest place to spot weft tension problems.*

Warps Getting Closer Together

There are two things you should do when you see your warps starting to bunch up in areas of your weaving.

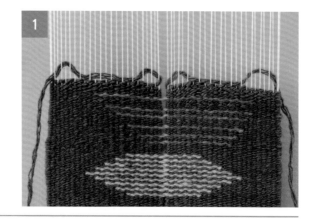

1. **Put more weft into that area.** Make your bubbles bigger where the warps are closer together. This extra weft forces the warps apart and helps regain an even warp spacing.

2. **If you are using a strong warp** such as cotton seine twine, pull the warps apart to encourage them to spread out. You must do this on every single pick for it to be effective.

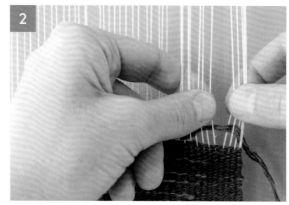

Warps Getting Farther Apart

When your warps are farther apart than they were at the beginning of your weaving, you should make your bubbles much lower or stop using them altogether. Bring your weft straight across the wide spots to encourage the warps to move closer together.

You may not even realize that your warps are spreading apart if you have been very consistent in your bubbling. The warps can spread apart very evenly and quite slowly. Measure the width of your work every ½" to make sure it is not getting wider or drawing in. Notice that where the warps are farther apart in the image at the top of the page, there is no bubbling of the weft.

Four Pointers to Keep You on Track

Over my years of teaching thousands of tapestry students both online and in person, four things consistently cause new weavers the most trouble. I identify them here and explain how to avoid them in your own weaving.

WAIT FOR THE POPPED-UP WARP. Especially when weaving on looms where the sheds stay open (like a Mirrix or a beamed loom with treadles), when two wefts come together in the shed (A), there is a warp between them that seems like it isn't covered by weft, and beginners want to "fix" it so that it is covered. That warp is actually in the other shed; it will be covered when you weave your next pick. Wait for the next shed and then wrap one of those two wefts around that warp before it returns (B).

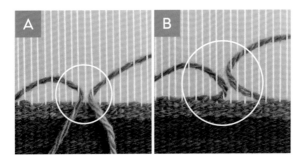

FINISH YOUR SEQUENCE. New students frequently get frustrated because they want a weft to move some-where, and it does not seem possible. Remember, moving wefts to new locations generally requires a full sequence, or 2 picks. If you feel stuck, it may mean you just have to do one more pick to finish the current sequence. Then you will find in the following pick you can move that weft wherever you want. This all works only in meet and sepa-rate, of course! You will practice this a lot more in the next chapter when I introduce you to hatching.

USE MEET AND SEPARATE. It is easy to forget that meet and separate is the basic structure that creates the weft-faced fabric we strive for in tapestry weaving. Often if things just do not seem to be working at all, it is because your butterflies are not moving in meet and separate. To check for this, unweave until everything is in the same shed. Hold that shed open with your shedding device or a shed stick turned sideways. Are all of the wefts either coming together or moving apart? If not, refer to Correcting Wefts Moving in the Wrong Direction on page 136.

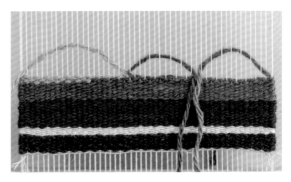

BUBBLE MORE THAN YOU THINK YOU SHOULD. Novice tapestry weavers often do not put enough weft into their warp and consequently have difficulties with draw-in, lice, and other things I address in this chapter. Unless you see your weaving getting wider or waves appearing on the surface of it, make your bubbles a little bigger.

Troubleshooting

As you learn various techniques, you're bound to encounter some common problems. Do not worry about avoiding these issues from the beginning. Instead, refer to this section to practice fixing them when they occur. These problems happen to all tapestry weavers at some point, and you will learn a lot from managing them as they happen.

Fixing the Problem

Top and Bottom Are Narrower than the Center

This common problem related to weft tension is noticeable only after the piece comes off the loom. Often tapestry designs include an area of one color or have a simpler design at the top and/or bottom of the piece. It is difficult to keep the weft tension even when going from a section of one color woven with one weft to a section with multiple colored wefts creating a design. The best way to introduce more weft into the less complicated one-color areas is to break up solid-colored sections with multiple butterflies. You will weave the multiple butterflies in meet and separate, using either cutbacks (see page 202) or irregular hatching (see page 164).

Smoothing Out Weft Turns

In tapestry weaving, wefts usually do not travel the whole distance across the warp. The point where a weft turns back on itself is called a relay. New weavers often find that they get little bubbles of yarn sticking out of the weaving at the end of every relay.

Managing this turn of the weft is an important skill. Placing too much weft in the turn will leave a bump of yarn; not enough weft will cause the warps to draw apart and create a hole. While some tapestry artists use the bumps and holes artistically, if you are striving for a flat textile with unnoticeable weft relays, you will need to practice.

▲ Too much weft results in little bubbles sticking out at the end of every relay.

At the point where two butterflies meet and turn back, you want just enough weft in the turns to fill the space between the warps — but not so little weft that it pulls the warps apart or leaves a hole there.

It is common to leave too much weft in the turns at the selvages, but these turns should be handled the same way as interior relays. Unconsciously, you may not want to pull the edge relay too tightly because you do not want the piece to get narrower. But if you do not pull it tightly enough, the edge warps will actually start to move outward. Where one warp goes, the rest will follow and your piece will start to widen.

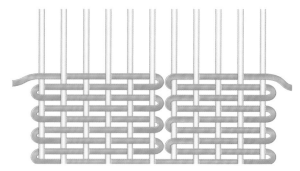

▲ *The weft turns should just fill the space between the warps.*

⬡ TECH TALK

Weaving Multiple Tapestries on the Same Warp

On many looms, it is possible to weave more than one piece sequentially on the same warp. It is important to finish the first piece completely (including your top header and some waste yarn) before advancing your warp to start the next piece. Then make sure you have at least 5" between each of the tapestries to do the finishing (see chapter 15).

On a frame loom with a continuous warp, rotate the finished piece so that it is in the back of the loom, and make sure you have at least 5" of empty warp. Then start your new piece as though it were a new warp and put in the ordering cord/stretcher string, waste, and header.

On a beamed loom, roll the finished tapestry forward, leaving at least 5"–8" between pieces. Then start again with waste and the header.

On an untensioned frame loom, the loom is probably too small to allow you to do more than one piece at a time, and you will need to rewarp the loom for each tapestry.

▲ *I often push my index finger all the way through the warp and manually adjust the relay. I use butterflies for my yarns, and my finger is the most efficient tool I have readily available.*

▲ *If you use bobbins, the point is very handy for making those weft turns nice and crisp but not too tight.*

Floats

A weft float is formed when you miss one or more warps as you are placing your weft. Floats can occur on either the front or the back of the tapestry, but you are less likely to see them if they occur on the side facing away from you. In this case, you often will not see the float(s) until you take the tapestry off the loom. Do not despair. Most floats are fixable.

1. Snip the float right in the center with a sharp pair of scissors.

2. Gently push apart the weft and unweave the cut weft back 1"–2" in each direction.

3. Thread a needle with the same color weft. Use it to replicate the over/under pattern of the weaving in the spaces where you took the cut weft out of the weaving.

4. You will now have four tails, but the weaving should look regular again. You can needle these ends back in during the finishing process.

Lice

The kind of lice you get in tapestry weaving is not the same lice you might get if you tried on all the winter hats in a kindergarten classroom. Tapestry lice do not look like bugs, but if you are using a white warp, they will be little white specks. They can occur over large sections of the weaving (as seen on page 61), in one or two spots, or more randomly throughout the piece. Lice occur when the weft does not completely cover the warp. There are many reasons full coverage of the warp may not happen. Here are a few common ones.

Your weft tension is not correct. If you do not put enough weft in to allow it to travel over and under all the warps, the weft will not cover the warp completely. This can be an intermittent and infrequent problem. But if your warps are drawing together because you are having serious weft tension problems — if the weft cannot pack down at all, for example — you will see large areas of lice as you do on page 61.

You inadvertently put two wefts in one shed. This can happen for 1 warp if you created a float. When you miss a warp thread, the weft will float around it, and the remaining two wefts will be in the same shed. This causes the warp to show. You can also get two wefts in one shed due to shedding errors (see Two Wefts in the Same Shed, on this page).

Your weft bundle is too large for your sett. As discussed in chapter 4, the relationship between warp and weft size and sett is important. If your weft is too large for your sett (see page 61), you will see lice.

Two Wefts in the Same Shed

Weaving two wefts in the same shed will, in most cases, cause an even line of warp lice. This is because there is too much weft in that area to allow the weft to sink down and cover the warp. Many fabric weavers on floor looms tuck their tails back into the shed as they start a new weft. Unfortunately, if you do this in tapestry weaving, you will cause an even line of warp lice for as long as there are two wefts in the same shed.

This problem is also common if you are using a loom with a shedding device that holds the shed open. You may finish a section, shift the shed, beat, then when you go to insert the new weft in a different color, shift the shed again. Since the shed was shifted twice, the new weft is now in the same shed as the previous one.

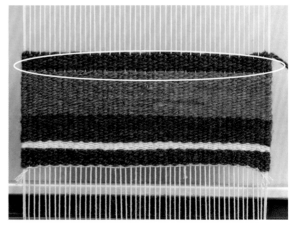

▲ *Lice created from putting two wefts in the same shed*

You can usually fix having two wefts in the same shed, even if you see the problem after you have woven more or when the piece is off the loom. To make that row of lice disappear, follow these steps:

1. Locate the problem and push apart the weaving a little bit between the two wefts that are in the same shed.

2. Put a length of that color weft yarn on a needle.

3. Weave the yarn into the shed opposite the original two wefts. Leave some extra weft in there so that the new weft has room to move over and under the warps.

4. Gently pull the weaving back together with the point of your needle or bobbin.

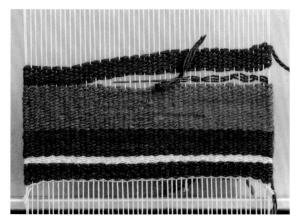

▲ *You may notice the remedy for two wefts in the same shed resembles the fix for a float (see page 153). In both cases, you must do a little surgical removal and repair.*

Ridging

Ridging occurs when every other warp thread pops forward. This is common near the selvages, but it can also happen across wider areas of the weaving. It happens because 1 pick in your sequence has less weft in it than the pick that follows. The tighter pick pushes the warp threads forward.

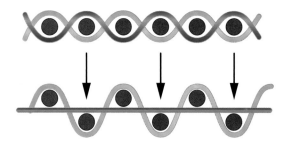

▲ *When the blue weft pick is not bubbled enough, as seen in the second diagram above, it forces every other warp to pop forward, creating a ridge along the warp. The top diagram is a cross section of a balanced fabric without ridging.*

▲ *Ridging as seen on the face of a woven tapestry*

Most of us have a dominant hand and are probably better at managing the weft with that hand. This can mean you place the weft in 1 pick with more skill than in the other pick. If you consistently put more weft into 1 pick than the next one, some amount of ridging will occur. This also frequently happens at the selvages as you attempt to make a clean turn. When the weft returns around the selvage, the temptation is to pull the return pick harder and thus introduce less weft into that area. This causes the kind of ridging seen on page 155. The other reason this can happen at a selvage is that some people tend to leave too much weft in the turn. This extra slack will eventually cause the edge warps to walk outward, and it may also create a ridging problem since the first pick is tight and the second one is loose.

To fix ridging problems over the long term, you have to learn to put the same amount of weft into both picks in your sequence. If you start to see a ridging problem, you can stop it fairly quickly. Take your thumbnail and dig it into one of the raised warps. Wiggle your thumb side to side while you push that warp backward. This redistributes the weft more evenly and allows the next picks to follow a more balanced path. Repeat this procedure every sequence, while at the same time evening out your bubbling in both picks.

▲ *Fixing a ridge by encouraging it to recede with your thumbnail*

Ridging may also happen if you weave too close to a shedding mechanism or if your loom is small and you don't have much unwoven warp between the body of your tapestry and the top of the loom. Having a longer loom — and thus a longer warp — can help avoid ridging. Using a loom that lets you advance the weaving farther away from the shedding mechanism can also help avoid this problem. If your loom is small, you can decrease ridging by making sure, when you only have a few inches of warp remaining, that you don't force the sheds open all the way by turning a shed stick sideways.

Waves in the Surface of Your Weaving

You are weaving along happily, your warps seem evenly spaced, your selvages are pretty straight, and you are having fun. Then you notice gentle waves in the fabric that run vertically in columns across your weaving. Students often think this is due to uneven warp tension, but usually it is because you are introducing too much weft into the warp.

If you could spread out those waves, it is likely that the tapestry would measure a bit wider than it did at the beginning because you are creating extra fabric side to side. Your warp spacing might look perfectly even, and if that is the case, you have probably bubbled very consistently but made the bubbles just a little too big, adding too much yarn. The solution for this is to decrease your bubbles until the waves go away. Measure the width of your tapestry frequently — at least every ½" — and adjust your bubbling if you see the tapestry gradually getting wider. If the waves are small, they will usually steam out in the finishing process, especially if you use cotton seine twine warp.

◀ *Waves in the surface of the weaving due to too much weft*

Fixing a Broken Warp

Sometimes bad things happen to good weavers. Your favorite 3-year-old is practicing scissor skills and thought your tapestry warp would be a great place to start. Your cat decides cotton seine twine is a great thing to chew on. The yarn has manufacturing flaws. Eventually one of your warps will break in the middle of a project. Though a broken warp is a little tricky to fix, on most looms it is not the end of your tapestry.

On beamed looms, simply insert a T-pin into the weaving, with the insertion point over the broken warp and several inches down into the portion already woven. Leave the broken piece of warp hanging on the back of the tapestry until you take the piece off the loom. At that point it will be stitched into the body of the tapestry and will disappear.

Cut a new piece of warp that is long enough to drape over the back beam of the loom and use for the rest of your project. Wrap this piece of warp around the T-pin four or five times. Do this so that the long end of the warp comes out the side of the pin and is lined up with the broken warp.

Thread the warp through the reed and heddles (if you have them), then drape it over the back beam of your loom. You will need to weight this warp to keep tension on it; fishing weights or a plastic bottle with some pebbles or liquid in it works well. Tie your weighted object to the warp so that it is hanging free over the top or back of the loom. Continue weaving. When the piece comes off the loom, needle the 2 warp ends into the fabric for a few inches, then trim.

On a frame loom that is continuously warped, fixing a broken warp is a little trickier because the warp is all one piece. Remember that, if possible, you do not want knots in your weaving. If your loom was warped with a warping bar and you have enough warp, tie a double half hitch (see page 279) around that bar to keep one of the two cut ends secure. With the other end, add a new piece as described in the beamed loom section above: insert a T-pin, wind the warp around it, bring it through any shedding mechanisms and over the top of the loom, and add a weight.

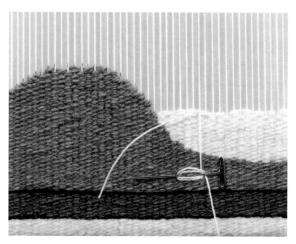

▲ *Using a strong pin as an anchor point for a new warp on either a beamed or continuously warped frame loom*

On an untensioned frame loom or a loom that doesn't have a warping bar, use T-pins in the fabric to secure new warps. With a peg or slot loom, a broken warp in one spot affects the warp next to it also. To fix this you can use one pin and wrap the warp around the pin, up around the peg or top of the loom, then back to the same pin to secure it. Adjust the tension on the warp as you do this so it is the same as the other warps.

If just 1 ply of the cotton seine twine breaks, the warp is probably still strong enough to continue weaving on as is, but I find that smoothing the frayed ply with glue is helpful. Put a little bit of white glue or school glue on your index finger and work it into the warp over the broken ply. Allow it to dry and then keep weaving.

If you notice a knot or flawed part in your warp while you are warping the loom, make sure that you put that part of the warp near the warping bar or near a peg or slot. This gets it out of the way so that you are not weaving over it. You may have to cut the warp and tie a new knot that is positioned out of the way of your weaving.

Fixing Uneven Warp Tension

Sometimes you find a thread or two much looser than the rest of the warp. If you weave on a beamed loom, it is likely that as you advance the warp you will find a few warps that were wound on with a looser tension. The looser warps come forward as you turn the back beam, and you will feel them as you weave.

To tighten individual warp threads on a beamed loom, pull the loose warp out of the fabric in a small loop and use a T-pin to pin it firmly to the fabric. The warp loops created by doing this can be pulled out of the fabric from either warp end when the piece is off the loom. Use this same procedure if the tension on one warp is particularly loose on a frame loom.

On almost any tapestry loom, you can put a thin piece of material under a loose warp to tighten it. Any kind of evenly shaped material will work: a wooden skewer, a ruler, or smooth dowels of some kind. Loosen the tension a little bit, put the shim under the looser warps at the top of the loom, and retighten the tension.

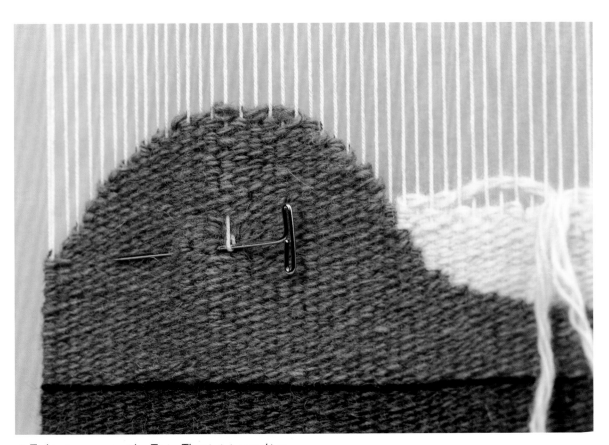

▲ *Tightening a warp with a T-pin. The pin is inserted into the side of the tapestry facing the weaver regardless of whether you're weaving from the front or from the back.*

8 Color Blending Magic

As you practice tapestry weaving techniques, it will be important to periodically review the information about color in chapter 5. In this chapter you will learn to mix colors in adjacent wefts through a technique called hatching.

Hatching is a common tapestry technique in which two adjacent colors are woven over each other in alternating sequences to create an area between them where the colors are blended. Hatching, like almost all tapestry techniques, is created by two colors coming together or moving apart in the same shed in meet and separate. What often happens in hatched areas is optical mixing (see page 98): our eyes and brains blend the alternating colors together to create a new perceived color.

When hatching is done without a specific line where the relays line up, it is called irregular hatching. This type of hatching is used most often solely as a way to blend two colors together. When the relays do line up to create a defined form or effect, it is called regular hatching. A more formalized form of hatching called hachure was perfected by medieval weavers in Europe and is still used by some artists today. Hachures blend two adjacent colors by forming elongated triangles stacked on top of each other instead of alternating colors in every sequence as regular and irregular hatching do. Because adjacent colors weave over each other sequentially, all of these techniques have to be woven line by line in the areas in which they occur.

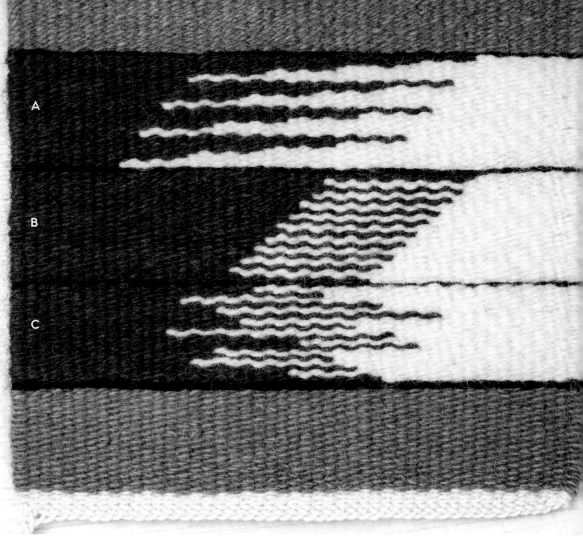

▶ *Notice how the three kinds of hatching differ. Irregular hatching (C) is fairly random and doesn't create defined shapes. Regular hatching (B) uses the same weaving patterns to make shapes that are defined. Hachure (A) takes regular hatching one step further and adds a triangular shape to interlace the colors.*

How Hatching Relates to Meet and Separate

Irregular hatching is often equated to meet and separate using two different colors. This isn't entirely correct.

Meet and separate is a weaving technique that you will use almost all the time regardless of what color butterfly you hold in your hand. If you're weaving randomly in meet and separate with two different-colored yarns, irregular hatching does happen. But hatching creates a striped interaction between two colors, while meet and separate does not necessarily do this. In other words, irregular hatching is always woven using meet and separate. But meet and separate does not always look like hatching.

Creating Color Illusions with Irregular Hatching

Irregular hatching is a technique used frequently in tapestry, especially when the artist wants to create blended colors. It is possible to weave an entire tapestry without any hatching, and the resulting piece may be quite graphic in nature as the forms will be sharply distinct. With various forms of hatching you can create gradation, transitions, transparencies, and illusions. Tapestries made with irregular hatching may be full of subtle effects, dimension, and color shifts. Compare the tapestry of Susan Martin Maffei (right) and that of Julia Mitchell (below). Maffei's work tends to be graphic, with solid forms and few instances of hatching. Mitchell's work is full of subtle color shifts, illusions, and transparency, and it has a softer feeling; she uses a lot of weft bundling and hatching to achieve this.

Hatching allows you to create the illusion that other colored yarns are present without actually using yarn of that color. This is helpful for tapestry weavers, as multiplying the number of yarns in a project can become expensive.

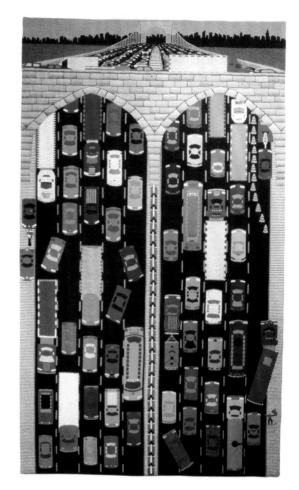

Susan Martin Maffei, *Traffic*, 2001.
Cotton, wool, linen, and silk, 80" × 48".

Julia Mitchell, *Cave Weaving 3*, 2016.
Wool, silk, and linen, 42" × 96".

Irregular Hatching Practice

Weaving irregular hatching can feel very freeing. As you start practicing this technique, enjoy moving weft sequences back and forth across your weaving. It is a good technique for playing with different hue and value combinations. After you understand how irregular hatching works, try some variations with different colors, and observe how you can make subtle shifts between colors or create different color harmonies (see page 94) in the hatched area.

When using irregular hatching, you must set up everything in meet and separate. You can move the colors where you want them to go only once in a sequence. On one of the 2 picks in a sequence, you'll be able to move a particular butterfly, and on the other pick it will only be able to return. If you think you're stuck, do one more pick and you'll be able to weave the yarn where you want it to go. For other problems with meet and separate, see Correcting Wefts Moving in the Wrong Direction on page 136.

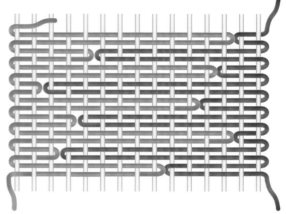

▲ *Diagram showing the structure of irregular hatching*

1. Choose two dissimilar colors — one light and one dark — to work with so you can see what you're doing. It does not matter as much what the hue actually is.

2. Set up your two butterflies or bobbins in meet and separate. Start both tails at opposite selvages for now.

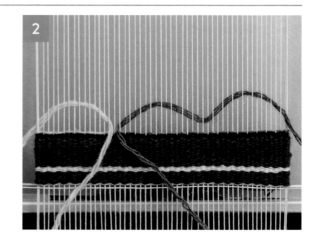

3. Bring the butterflies together somewhere near the center of the weaving and then shift the shed and return them both to the selvages. You've woven 1 sequence.

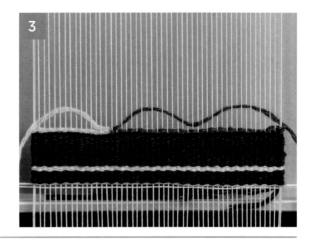

4. On the next pick, decide which color will travel on top of the other color and for how far. Bring your chosen color across and on top of the second color. Bring the second color in to meet it. Shift the shed and return both butterflies to the selvages.

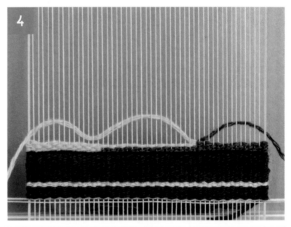

5. Continue to practice irregular hatching using two different colors (A). Vary the place at which the points shift (the relay). The colors can overlap for just an inch or two or for many inches, depending on how much room you have on your warp.

▶ *The values of the two colors you choose to hatch together impacts how distinct they remain. Regardless of the hues, if the values are very similar, as in B, they may blend together subtly enough to create a gradation horizontally across your weaving, as seen in B and C. (See chapter 5 for more about hue and value.)*

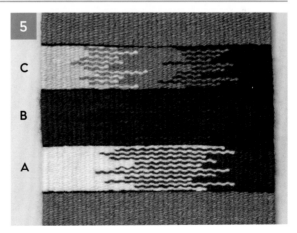

VARIATION

Further Practice

A. Choose three to five yarns of one hue in different values, and make one butterfly of each. In example A, I've used light to medium blues. Set these butterflies up in meet and separate and weave an inch or more with irregular hatching. Are you able to create a gradation in value from light to dark across your warp?

B. Now choose three to five yarns that are similar values but different hues. In example B, I've used a mustard color, two shades of violet, and a blue. Can you arrange the colors so that they blend from one to the other across your warp? Notice which values blend together and which values stay more distinct when woven in irregular hatching. Do you see how you might be able to create a gradation from one hue to another by keeping the values of the hatched yarns similar?

▲ *Many tapestry weavers use irregular hatching for blending and shading. Continue practicing this technique until it feels natural and you've experienced the effects of using different hues and values.*

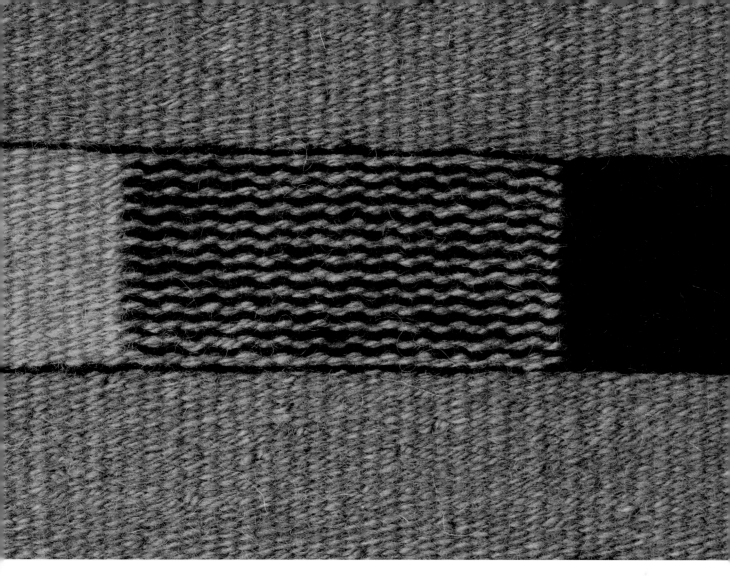

Creating Forms with Stripes

Regular hatching is one way to create shading, transparency, or a geometric design using only two colors. In this technique, the position where each relay ends is more carefully controlled than it is in irregular hatching. One full sequence in one color alternates with a full sequence in another color. This creates a striped effect, and you can control how much of these sequences overlap to define shapes. The blending of the two overlapping colors will make the viewer believe there is a different-colored shape between them.

▲ *Regular hatching mixing a deep gold on the left and a dark violet on the right to form a third color area in the center*

Regular Hatching Practice

By mixing two colors in a regular way between solid portions of the colors, you will create a square or rectangle. The butterflies alternate complete sequences in a defined area between them. This creates a third color area. To start, choose two butterflies, one light and one dark, so you can see what is happening.

▶ *This diagram shows the structure of regular hatching.*

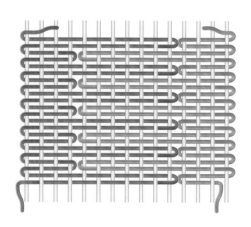

1. Decide how large your square or rectangle will be. The area where the two colors overlap should be at least 4 warps wide and could be almost the whole width of your warp. You will need a solid area of each color on the edges at least 1" wide. You may want to mark the warps at the edges of your square with a permanent marker.

2. You can start your two butterflies either with tails at one of the edges of your square or rectangular form or at the selvages. If you choose to start the butterflies at the edge of your rectangle, move them out to the selvages, back into the center where you started, then back to the selvages again for 3 total picks. If you start creating your regular hatching pattern with just 1 pick at the base (instead of a full sequence), it will show up as a dotted line where the colors overlap.

3. Both butterflies are now at the selvages or the outer edges of your regular hatching section. Bring them to meet at one side of the shape you're going to create, shift the shed, and return them to the outside edges. You've done 1 full sequence.

4. Bring both butterflies to meet at the other side of your shape. Return them to the outside edges. You should now have a solid stripe of each color in the center section.

5. Continue to alternate steps 3 and 4 until you have created the entire shape as seen below.

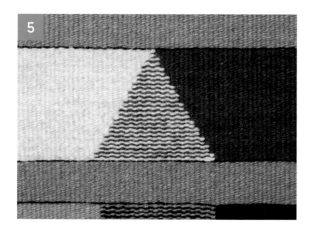

▲ *Regular hatching can be used to make many different shapes, including the triangle shown above. For further examples of how regular hatching can be used, see the tapestries of Rebecca Mezoff on page 169 and Ulrikka Mokdad on page 175.*

Regular Hatching for Transparency

Using a color that only appears every other sequence creates illusions of transparency or forms that look like they are floating on top of a background. I used this technique frequently in my *Emergence* series of tapestries. Notice that the spiral colors are, for the most part, lighter than the background colors. If the hatched form and the background are the same value, they'll blend together. This is a good way to get some subtle shapes and color mixing, but your form will not look transparent.

This technique uses full sequences in one color for the transparent shape you're creating and a second sequence in a background color between the shape sequences. You'll be creating small vertical floats on the back of the weaving as the shape butterflies jump over the background sequence. It is possible to splice each of the sequences to keep the back free of these small vertical floats if you prefer it (which means each sequence would be a floating bar as described on page 173), but I use hatching so much that it takes too much time to splice every sequence.

In the illustration at right, notice how the relays for the background color vary widely over the surface of the tapestry. This ensures that you're not creating a slit anywhere. The jump-overs (vertical floats) also vary in their placement. If the jump-overs were all lined up, you'd see an area where the weaving looks looser. The fabric in that area will also be weaker, because only the top of the sequence would be a full pick.

This technique is easiest to do when weaving from the back. It is much simpler to keep track of the butterflies that need to jump over every other sequence when the back of the tapestry is facing you. However, if you are weaving from the front, you can tuck the hatching butterflies to the back after they finish their sequence and fish them out again when it is time to use them.

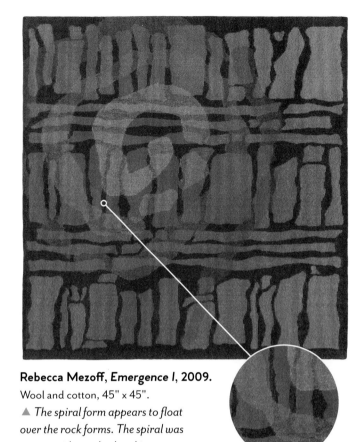

Rebecca Mezoff, *Emergence I*, 2009.
Wool and cotton, 45" x 45".
▲ *The spiral form appears to float over the rock forms. The spiral was woven with regular hatching.*

▶ *In this detail of* Emergence I, *you can see that the pink colors of the spiral occur every other sequence, with the background colors filling in between. Along with values and hues chosen, this is what creates the illusion that the spiral is floating.*

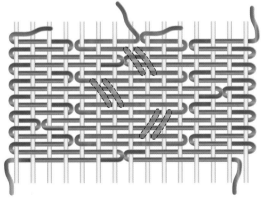

▲ *This diagram shows this jump-over regular hatching technique. The dotted lines indicate the jump-overs on the back of the tapestry.*

Regular Hatching for Transparency Practice

For practice with this technique, choose a light value for the shape and a darker value for the background. You will need two butterflies of each color: one color for the background and one color for the hatched shape. This results in four total butterflies. If you don't have two butterflies for the hatching, you'll have jump-overs on the edge of your shape, which can distort the ends of each sequence. Using two butterflies lets you keep the edges crisp by jumping over the background color somewhere in the center of the form. This has the added advantage of allowing you to splice all the ends together and makes meet and separate easier to maintain.

1. Decide what you want your shape to be. I recommend starting with a square or rectangle, but you could make it more complicated. If you need to mark the warp for this shape, do so now.

2. Start the background color with two butterflies using meet and separate and weave a little bit before starting the shape.

3. With the two background butterflies at the selvages, you're ready to introduce the hatched shape color in the center. Splice the tails together (or use the double-ended butterfly technique on page 172) and bring them out as far as you want the shape to go. Bring the side colors in to meet them.

4. Complete the sequence. You should now have the two shape butterflies meeting somewhere in the middle of the shape and the two outside butterflies at the edges.

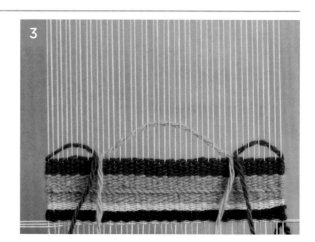

5. On the next sequence the shape butterflies will "rest." (If you're weaving from the front, tuck those butterflies between 2 warps to the back of the work before you weave anything else, as seen here.) Meet the two outside butterflies somewhere on the warp, and then relay them back to the edges. You're making one complete sequence of the background color.

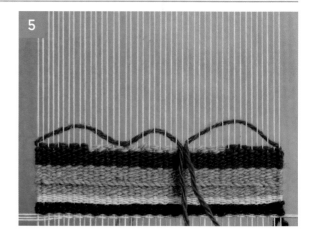

6. Take the two shape butterflies that have rested for a whole sequence and jump them over the background sequence that is woven on top of them. On the back side of the weaving, you will create two small vertical floats where this color travels over the last sequence.

7. Weave the shape butterflies away from each other to the edge of your shape. Meet the background butterflies to this point. Shift your shed. Bring the shape butterflies back to the center and the background butterflies back to the edges.

8. Continue repeating steps 3–7, adjusting where the relays of the hatched shape happen to make the form you desire. The places where the jump-overs happen should not line up. The fabric is less stable there, and you will see an area on the front that doesn't look as smooth as the rest of the surface of the tapestry. To avoid this, vary where you end the pattern butterflies, as seen in this image of the back of the weaving.

9. When you reach the top of your shape, splice the final ends together. Continue weaving the background color on top of your shape as far as you'd like.

▲ *Varying where the jump-overs occur, as seen from the back of the weaving*

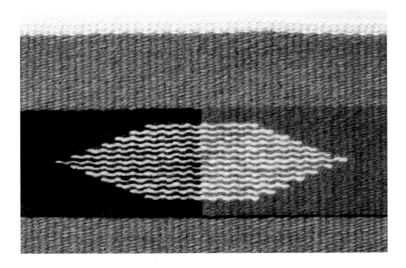

◀ *You can use this technique to make all kinds of shapes. Notice in Emergence I (see page 169) that the background colors can also change in the sequences between the regular hatching lines. For example, the diamond in the image at left has two background colors meeting in the center of a regular hatched white diamond. Experiment with making other shapes. If you change the value of the yarns you're using, can you make them float or blend into the background?*

Avoid Multiple Tails with a Double-Ended Butterfly

When you're adding butterflies in pairs such as in this regular hatching for transparency exercise, you can avoid the two tails at the beginning by making a double-ended butterfly. This is a pair of butterflies connected in the middle so that each one can be started without tails or a splice.

1. Pull off about 2 yards of yarn from your yarn ball. Start making a butterfly at the end near the ball and wind it out to the end of the yarn. Make the butterfly as described on page 115, counting the wraps around your hand as you wind it. The end of your butterfly will make the final tie.

2. Pull another 1 or 2 feet from the yarn ball, then start the second butterfly again near the ball. Wind it normally and cut the yarn after you have made the same number of wraps you used in the first butterfly.

3. Lay the free yarn in the center of these two butterflies into the shed and weave with each butterfly.

▲ In small areas where I only use a little bit of weft but still need two butterflies, I will often take a long piece of yarn and start it in the center of the design. In the next shed I then weave with both ends; at the end of the shape, the last two tails can usually be spliced together.

Floating Bars

A floating bar is a short line of another color that is inserted for design or color reasons and is woven as a complete sequence (2 picks). This technique is useful for adding little lines of color or connecting two color areas that might otherwise have a slit between them. These lines can be any width. Because the bars are created with a full sequence of yarn, you will get a solid line as you do in regular hatching. I lay in the yarn for the floating bars with a long piece inserted in the middle as shown in image 4, below. You can use double-ended butterflies as described on the opposite page or a long piece of yarn. Whichever you choose, the floating bar is made with what is the equivalent of two butterflies, so meet and separate is maintained, and there are no shedding problems. In the example shown, light yarn is used for the background color (A) and dark yarn is used for the floating bar (B).

1. Start with a background color (A) and fill in some sequences as you see at the bottom of the image to the right.

2. Decide where you want your first floating bar (B). Bring the background butterflies (A) to the selvages.

3. Cut a piece of yarn longer than twice the width of the space you want to cover and center it in the shed.

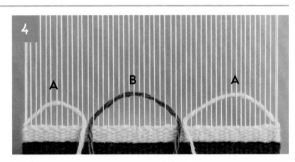

4. Bring the side butterflies in to meet the floating bar. If you are weaving from the front, put your tails to the back.

5. Change the shed and beat. Finish the sequence, splicing together the two ends of the bar.

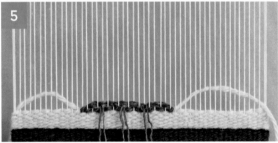

6. Weave the background colors out to the edge and continue weaving with the background colors on top of the bar you just made.

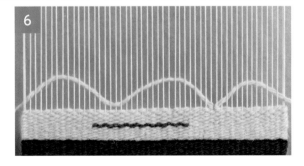

Hachures: Formalized Hatching

Hachures are a form of hatching that uses regular elongated triangular forms instead of alternating single sequences of colors. For an example of hachure, see figure A on page 162. Like irregular and regular hatching, hachures are also used to create shading, to mix adjacent colors, or to add a design element. Each hachure is formed by creating a full sequence of weft followed by successively shorter passes stepping backward several warp threads. This creates thin, elongated triangular shapes that blend the two interlocked colors.

Medieval tapestries from Europe used hachure extensively to create shading, accentuate curves in the folds of fabric, and to create pointy and interlocked shapes such as greenery. Contemporary tapestry weavers don't use a lot of hachure, since more fluid styles with more colors tend to be more popular today. But there are some contemporary tapestry artists, most often trained in France, who still use hachures expertly.

The Lady and the Unicorn: To My Only Desire, 1500.
Wool and silk, approximately 12' × 15½'.
▲ *This weaving is an example of a medieval tapestry with extensive use of hachure, especially in the clothes of the figures and in the animals.*

Elizabeth J. Buckley, *Fossil, Feather, and Light*, 2013.
Cotton, linen, silk, and wool, 25" × 18".

▲ *Elizabeth J. Buckley is a French-trained tapestry weaver in the United States. This tapestry is an example of contemporary use of hachure. This piece was woven sideways.*

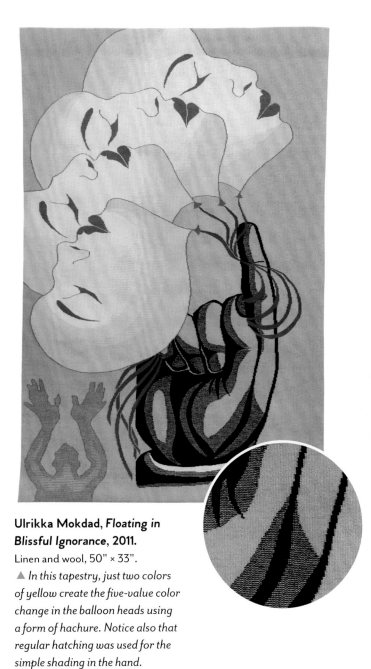

Ulrikka Mokdad, *Floating in Blissful Ignorance*, 2011.
Linen and wool, 50" × 33".

▲ *In this tapestry, just two colors of yellow create the five-value color change in the balloon heads using a form of hachure. Notice also that regular hatching was used for the simple shading in the hand.*

9 Closing Up the Holes

The kind of tapestry weaving covered in this book is often called slit tapestry because a hole or slit is formed where wefts of different colors meet. Closing up these holes is an important part of the tapestry process and is most often done using some form of join. The most common type of join is sewing the slits. Other joins include warp and weft interlocks and some hatching variations.

Up to this point in your tapestry weaving, you may have created only tiny 1-sequence holes at the relay, where two wefts meet and then separate again in the next shed. When the relays are stacked on top of each other, a vertical slit forms, as seen at right. When weaving two colors next to each other vertically for longer than about ½ inch, the integrity of the textile can become compromised. Therefore, some sort of join should be used to support the weave structure.

A sewn slit (A on page 178) is the straightest possible vertical line you can create between two color areas. Slits can be sewn as you are weaving or once the piece is off the loom. Weft interlocks (B) and warp interlocks (C) are both constructed as you weave. They are both methods of overlapping or clasping wefts to join shape areas.

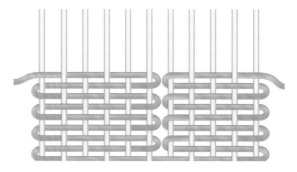

▲ *Slits form where sequences of weft stack on top of each other.*

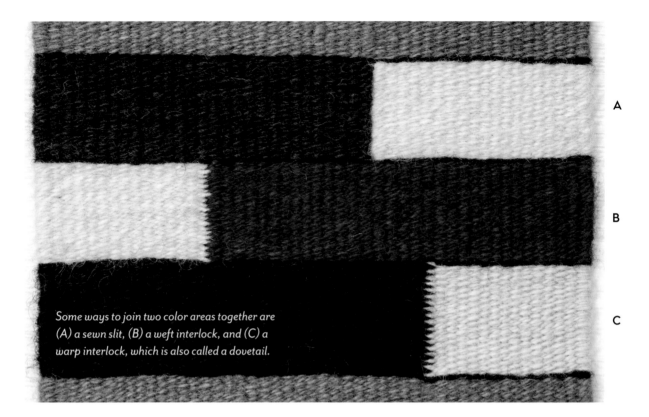

Some ways to join two color areas together are (A) a sewn slit, (B) a weft interlock, and (C) a warp interlock, which is also called a dovetail.

Both techniques B and C create a serrated appearance in the weaving, though some joins are smoother than others.

Whether you use a join and which kind of join you choose should be dictated by what you are trying to achieve in the weaving. Some joins work functionally better in a particular situation. Some require weaving from the back or that the wefts travel in the same direction in the shed. Some look very toothy, while some look quite smooth.

Sewing Slits

Sewn slits create the smoothest border between the two colors. The interlocked joins covered later in this chapter all create shape borders that have a serrated or jagged appearance where the two colors meet.

How often you sew will vary with the materials you are using and the sett of the piece. Many weavers do not sew slits until the tapestry is off the loom, but I like to sew them about every ½ inch as I weave for several reasons. Slits may start to gape open when they are longer than about ½ inch. If you use a finer weft and sett, you may need to sew them when they are even shorter.

I find that sewing slits is much easier to accomplish while the piece is on the loom than if I wait until the piece is complete and off the loom, because while I am in the middle of weaving, I can push up the most recent wefts and see where the needle needs to go to sew the slit. Sewing the slits on the loom also keeps the integrity of the fabric intact. If you have a lot of long slits that are not sewn, the textile becomes unstable, and each slit starts to act like another selvage. The edges of those unconnected areas can draw in or get wider, which not only makes sewing the slits difficult off the loom but may result in distortion of the final fabric or a rippled surface, even after the sewing is complete.

How to Sew Slits

As you weave, stop to sew the slits when they get to be ½" long, allowing the sewing thread to dangle until your next sewing session. Slits shorter than ½" don't need to be sewn unless your weaving is a very fine sett. This method of sewing slits can be done the same way regardless of whether you are weaving from the front or the back of the tapestry. This sewing technique creates a figure-8 cross between the warps, connecting the warps on each side of the slit. This seam is functionally identical front to back and invisible on both sides of the weaving, because the sewing thread passes only under the weft relays, which hide it.

I use Coats & Clark upholstery thread to sew my slits. This strong polyester thread is available in a small number of colors at fabric and craft stores. I generally use white because it is easier to see as I sew, but if you have difficulty keeping your stitches hidden, use a thread in a similar hue to your weaving. This will help make it invisible. If you do not have access to upholstery thread, any strong sewing thread will work. If you are weaving a tapestry that will be very heavy or hung sideways so there is more pull on the sewing, make sure your sewing thread is strong enough to withstand the stress and consider doubling weaker threads. I often sew 2 sequences for each stitch because it is faster and provides enough stability for the tapestries woven at 8 epi or more. For coarser setts less than 8 epi, it is important to sew every sequence as shown in the images in this how-to.

1. Cut a piece of thread long enough to sew the slit plus a good amount of extra for the tails. Thread it on a tapestry needle.

2. To start sewing the slit, make a surgeon's knot (see page 283) around the outermost warp at the base of the slit. I am right-handed, so I start my sewing on the right side of the slit; you may want to reverse this if you are left-handed. Tuck the thread tail to the back after you tie the first knot and let the final tail hang on the back. The sewing will be tightened up and the tails sewn in during the finishing process.

3. Bring the tapestry needle up through one weft relay on the side of the slit where you tied the knot. As you do this, bring the needle behind that warp and pull the needle through. The sewing thread will come out the back of that warp. You do not need to reach to the back of the tapestry to pull the needle through, just poke it out the slit and pull it toward you.

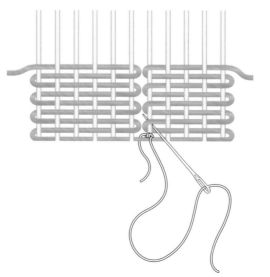

4. Using your needle, slightly separate the weft sequences on the other side of your slit. Insert the needle from front to back around only the warp. Do not pass the needle through any weft relays on the second side of the slit.

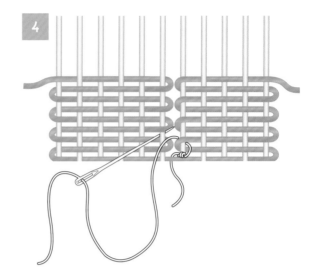

5. Repeat steps 3 and 4 (as seen in 5a) until you have sewn all the way to the fell line (5b). Remove the needle from the sewing thread and let the thread dangle. Rethread the needle when you have woven another ½" and are ready to sew the slit again.

6. Tighten up the sewing periodically by using your needle to tug the stitches, starting at the bottom and working upward.

7. At the top of a slit, do not tie a final knot. Instead, leave a 4"–5" tail until the piece comes off the loom. In the finishing process described in chapter 15, you will tighten up the slits and tie a final knot at the top of the line of stitches.

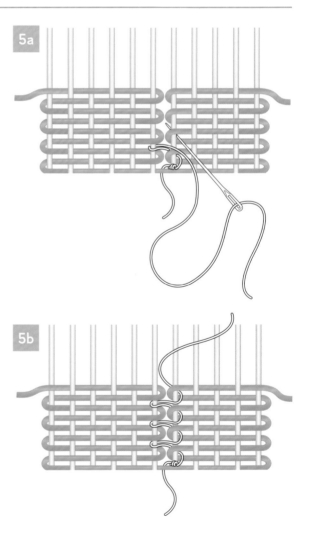

Leaving Slits Unsewn

There are many tapestry artists who use open slits as a prominent part of their work. Alex Friedman and Silvia Heyden are two excellent examples. Their use of long, unsewn slits provides interest and texture in their designs.

Silvia Heyden, *Feathered Relief*, 1992.
Linen, 71" × 47".
▲ *Silvia Heyden's weaving technique often involves wedge shapes and open slits. This tapestry was woven sideways.*

Alex Friedman, *Flow 7: Seafoam*, 2016.
Wool, wool bouclé, silk, and cotton, 46" × 34".
◄ *Alex Friedman frequently leaves long, unsewn slits in her work, providing texture, shadow, and thematic interest.*

Hanging a Tapestry Sideways

Tapestries are often displayed 90 degrees from the way they were woven. Medieval European tapestries were almost always woven sideways, and current Aubusson and Gobelin weavers in Europe continue this tradition. Today it is often done in keeping with the direction of the prominent lines in the work. A horizontal line is much easier to weave smoothly than a vertical one, so sometimes the best solution for a design is to weave it sideways.

When a tapestry is hung sideways, gravity will pull the slits open. Therefore, take extra care to sew the slits well on tapestries that will be hung from the weft instead of the warp. For more information, see How to Sew Slits on page 179.

Weft Interlocks

In this joining method, two wefts are clasped around each other between 2 warps, as seen below. Do this only to avoid slits and not as a general practice. If multiple relays do not stack on top of each other to create a slit, there is no need for an interlock. New weavers tend to want to clasp *all* their wefts as they relay, which creates a bump in the weaving and will be much more visible than just leaving small slits.

You can make weft interlocks either with the yarns moving in opposition (in meet and separate) or with the wefts moving in the same direction. The placement of the interlock with raised and lowered warps, and which of the wefts wraps over the other one, both affect the look of the final join.

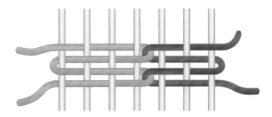

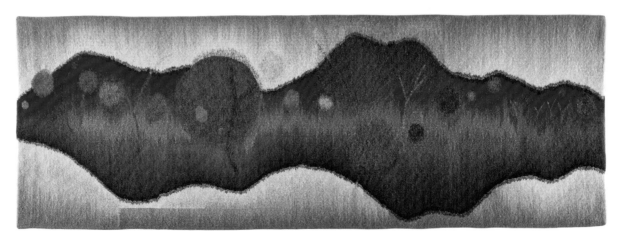

Rebecca Mezoff, *Lifelines*, 2017.
Wool and cotton, 24" × 72".
▲ *This tapestry was woven 90 degrees from the way it now hangs.*

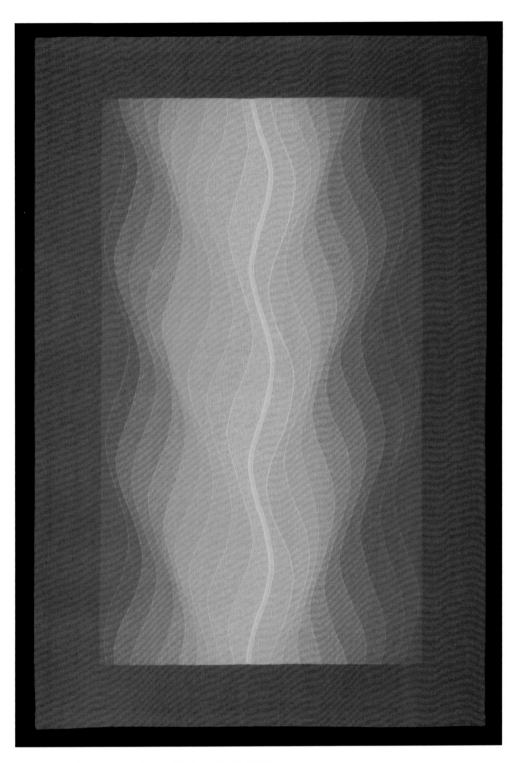

James Koehler, *Harmonic Oscillations XLIII*, 2008.
Wool, 65" × 44".

▲ *James Koehler's* Harmonic Oscillations *series includes woven frames, and the vertical lines were all formed with weft interlocks.*

Meet-and-Separate Weft Interlock

In this weft interlock, the butterflies move in meet and separate, as seen in the diagram on page 182. To make this join smooth, it is important to understand, first, the correct way for the wefts to travel over or under the warps on each side of the join, and second, which weft should wrap over the other one.

1. Working with the butterflies always moving in the same shed, bring your two butterflies together.

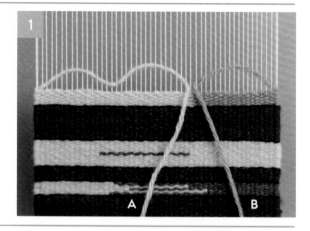

2. Shift your shed. Decide which butterfly will drop over the other one by choosing which side of the warp that just came forward you want the weft interlock to be. For example, in the image at right, butterfly B drops over butterfly A, and the wefts interlock on the right-hand side of the warp that popped up when you shifted your shed in this step. Had butterfly A crossed over first, the weft interlock would have happened on the left of that warp.

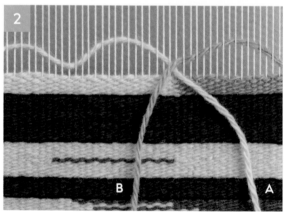

TIP

Creating Consistent Joins

Allowing the perfect amount of weft where the yarns relay around each other is the secret to making these joins look uniform. If you leave too much weft in the turns, the interlock will look messy. If you pull the interlock too tight, you will have difficulty making the join look consistent, and this may affect the weft tension.

Often weft interlocks cause the warps to spread. The warp spacing will return to normal when you reach the end of the join and begin weaving on top of it again.

3. Pick up the butterfly that was underneath and return it. Then return the first butterfly (3a). Return butterfly (B) to the selvage (3b).

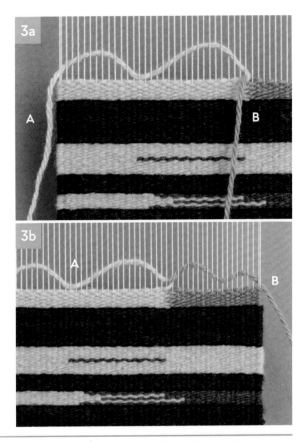

4. Before you shift your shed, pull out any extra weft to keep the interlocks crisp. Pinch one of the weft relays just inside the warp as shown at right and pull the weft tail of the other color firmly to remove any extra weft bubble.

5. Shift your shed and beat. You have completed one interlock with wefts moving in meet and separate.

6. Repeat steps 1–5, always making sure to drop the same butterfly over the other one. This gives the most visual consistency to the join.

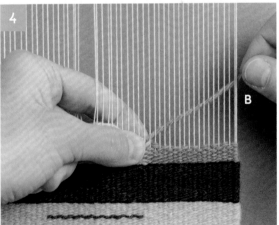

Weft Interlock with Wefts Traveling in the Same Direction

There may be times when you want to weave with your butterflies traveling in the same direction as seen in this diagram. Sometimes the design elements demand a vertical join near a selvage or in a very narrow area where having butterflies moving in the same direction is the easiest thing to do. You can use this join when working from either the front or back of the tapestry.

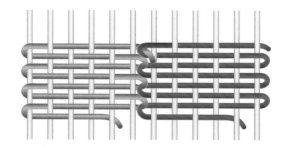

1. Set up your butterflies in the same shed and moving in the same direction.

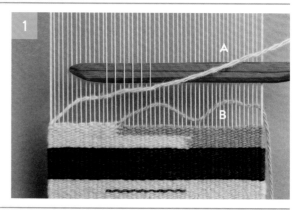

2. Change the shed and beat. Return butterfly B to the interlock point as shown here.

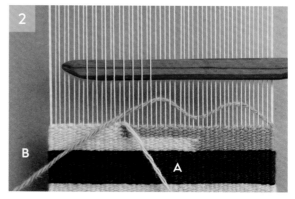

3. Drop butterfly B over butterfly A. Pick up butterfly A, wrap it around butterfly B and return it to the selvage. You have completed one interlock with wefts traveling in the same direction (3a). Image 3b shows the next pick. Notice that the interlock only happens one time in the sequence. In this example, it occurs when the wefts are moving from right to left.

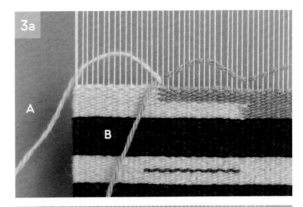

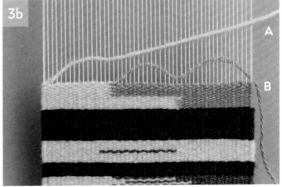

Warp Interlocks

Another way to join two color areas without creating a slit is to use a warp interlock, also called a dovetail. In this technique, both colors wrap a common warp. Warp interlocks are used in many tapestry traditions to create serrated or toothed joins (see Diverse Warp Interlock Traditions on page 189).

This technique can be done with the wefts moving in opposition or in the same direction, and it looks the same woven from the front or the back. Because most of what you are weaving is done in meet and separate, practice it that way here.

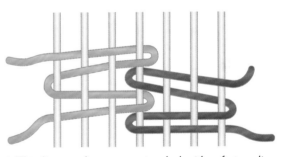

▲ *This diagram shows a warp interlock with wefts traveling in meet and separate.*

▶ *A woven warp interlock with a join occurring every sequence. Note that at the join, the weft tends to build up vertically due to the extra weft around that warp.*

Practicing Warp Interlocks

When this join is done with single alternating wraps of two colors around one warp, twice as much weft is introduced around that warp as would normally be there. As a result, this join will build up higher along that warp if done for extended distances. To keep this from happening, you can do the join every other sequence as seen at right.

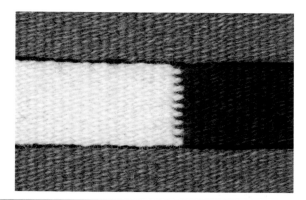

1. Choose the warp around which you want to create a warp interlock. If that warp is raised (as it is in the photo to the right), both wefts will go behind the warp, as this image shows. If the warp you want to create the interlock around is lowered, move on to step 2 now. Bring your two butterflies together on either side of that warp in meet and separate.

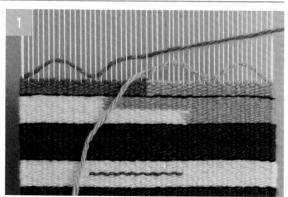

2. Shift the shed and beat. If you already put both wefts under a warp in step 1, return the butterflies to the selvages. Otherwise, the empty warp that popped up in the second shed is the one you will wrap both wefts around. Decide which weft will wrap first and make sure that you wrap it first on every sequence. If you are not consistent with this order in your interlock, the colors will not alternate evenly and you will see it in the final join.

3. Wrap the warp and return the weft on one side, and then do the second side before shifting the shed and beating.

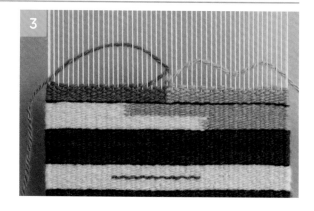

4. Repeat steps 1–3.

Diverse Warp Interlock Traditions

Rio Grande weaving is a term used to describe Hispano weaving particular to New Mexico. Weavers in this tradition use many variations of the warp interlock join, which cause tiny serrated patterns where vertical sections of color come together. The most common join they use is the simple warp interlock join described on page 187. Rio Grande weavers often call warp interlocks "dovetails."

Rio Grande weaving frequently is very patterned, with diamond shapes repeated symmetrically. Wefts all travel in the same direction, and Rio Grande weavers put two wefts in the same shed when colors move over. Depending on the thickness of the weft, you may or may not see these doubled weft areas. Warp interlocks of wefts traveling in the same direction are used to make vertical lines in this tradition.

Scandinavian weaving traditions also use the simple warp interlock join described here, as shown in the Robbie LaFleur tapestry below. This tradition frequently uses warp interlock joins that are woven in groups. Multiple weft sequences are built up around the warp before a similar set is created with the other color on top of it. The results are characteristically pointed or square.

Don Leon Sandoval, *Tribute*, 2016.
Wool, 85" × 54".
▲ *Don Leon Sandoval is a master weaver in the Rio Grande tradition. His tapestry Tribute uses dovetails in the vertical lines in the star shapes called* valeros.

Robbie LaFleur, *Great Grandmother with Chickens*, 2000.
Wool and cotton, 23" × 19½".
▲ *Robbie LaFleur studies, writes about, and weaves traditional Norwegian-style tapestry. Her tapestries follow the warp interlock techniques common in Scandinavian countries.*

Using Hatching for Joins

There are many creative ways of using hatching (see chapter 8) to join areas that would otherwise have slits. Hatching one color area into another to lightly blend the colors or to create a serrated edge on a form also effectively creates a sturdy join. The diagram at right shows a solid color to the left with hatches traveling into the lighter color to the right every so often. The photo below shows the finished result of this procedure.

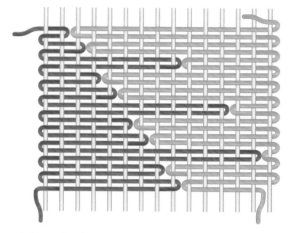

▲ *Using hatching to create a decorative join*

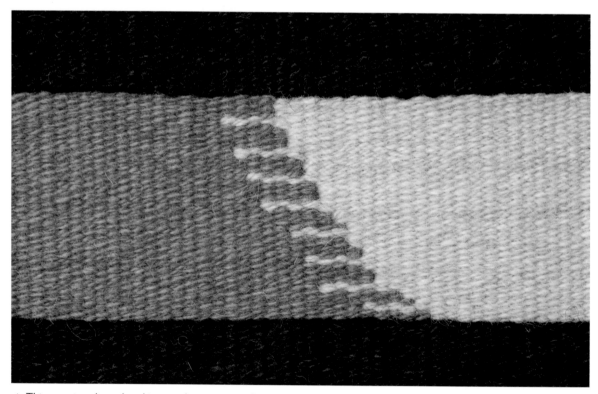

▲ *This weaving shows hatching used to join two color areas in a similar manner to the diagram above.*

Another way to use simple hatching to join color areas involves creating a serrated outline between two colors areas. The photo and diagram at right illustrate one variation of this idea, but you could vary the height of the single warp wrap or the wider sections of the weaving.

I frequently use regular hatching with jump-overs (see page 169) to join adjacent areas. The detail of my tapestry *Lifelines* (below) shows the regularly hatched dark outline between the lighter and darker blue areas. This piece was woven sideways, and the every-other-sequence bar technique (called regular hatching) results in no slits to sew and creates a mottled wide outline between color areas.

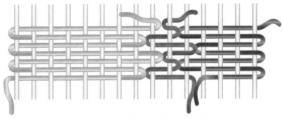

▲ *Using a narrowly hatched color area between two forms as both an outline and an easy join*

▲ *The finished result of this use of hatching*

Rebecca Mezoff, *Lifelines* (detail), 2017.
Wool and cotton, 24" × 72".
◀ *The entire piece can be seen in on page 182.*

10 Āngling

In weaving, angles are created by a repeated progression of small steps moving across your warp. Angled forms are particularly well suited to tapestry weaving because the place where the two wefts meet — the relay — moves over frequently, and the small slits at the edge of each step are unnoticeable.

Determining the Steepness

The angle you create will change depending on how many warps your sequence moves over for each relay or, for steeper angles, how many sequences are stacked up before moving the angle to the next warp. You could use a protractor to measure the angle of the line formed between the two colors in the angles illustrated below. These diagrams show various angles made by moving over different numbers of warp threads each

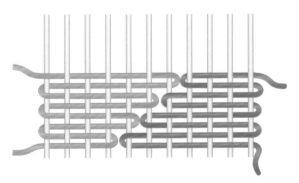

▲ *An angle made by stepping over by 1 warp every step*

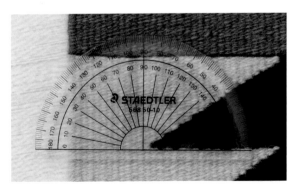

▲ *You can use a protractor to measure the size of the angle in degrees between the horizontal and diagonal lines.*

193

sequence or by stacking weft sequences on top of each other before stepping over.

To produce a shallower angle, move the weft relay over 2 warp threads for every sequence. The resulting angle is closer to horizontal than the one shown in the diagram on the previous page. You could make the angle even shallower, or closer to horizontal, by stepping over 4 or 6 warp threads for each sequence.

To make angles steeper, or more vertical, than the one on the previous page, stack two weft relays on top of each other before moving over 1 warp. You can make the angle even steeper by increasing the number of sequences stacked up before moving over.

The resulting angle of any of these combinations will be slightly different for each weaver, due to variations in how hard you pack the weft, as well as what yarn you use at what sett. If you want your diagonal line to be straight, consistency in your weaving is important. As you continue to practice these new skills, your beating will become more uniform and you will make straighter angles.

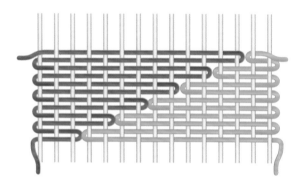

▲ This angle is made by stepping over 2 warps every sequence.

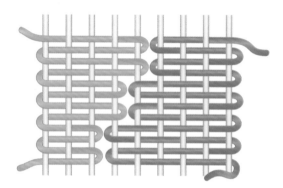

▲ A steeper angle is made by stacking 2 sequences before moving over 1 warp.

Basic Angle Practice

Start your practice with an angle where the sequences move over by 1 warp for each step. Choose two colors of weft with contrasting values so you can see what is happening.

1. Start weaving with your butterflies in meet and separate (see page 132). Decide which direction the diagonal will move and which color will advance over the other color.

2. Bring the wefts together and return to the selvages for 1 complete sequence.

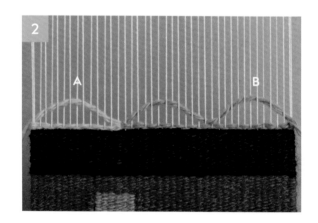

3. In the next shed, move the advancing butterfly (A) over the other butterfly (B) by 1 warp. The advancing butterfly is the one that is moving on top of the other color. (See Remembering Where to Relay on page 197 for more explanation.) Bring butterfly B to meet it. Return them both to the selvages. You have created one step, and it should look something like this.

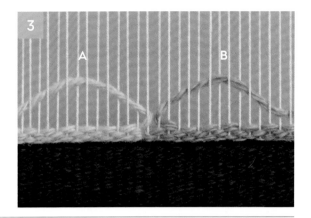

4. Repeat this stepping movement on each sequence until you have woven a couple of inches. As you weave, watch carefully to make sure you step over just 1 warp each time. Notice how the diagonal line varies if you fail to step over or step over by more than 1 warp.

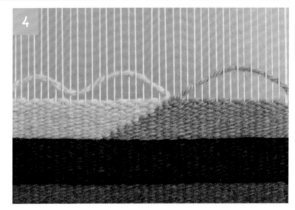

Even Steeper

Now try the same thing but with a steeper angle. Practice the same steps as you did above, but this time complete 2 sequences before advancing to the next warp, as shown in the steeper angle diagram on the previous page and in the photo at right. This will create a steeper (or larger by degree) angle than you made the first time. Weave a couple inches of this angle.

If you would like to try even steeper angles, continue to stack up sequences before moving your relays over by 1 warp. At some point, if the slits you are creating are long enough, you will need to sew them before you move over. See page 179 for how and when to sew slits.

Straight Angles, Hills, and Valleys

Because tapestry weaving is done on a grid, steps are formed as a diagonal line is built. For angles that are shallower than the ones you practiced on the previous pages, you can manipulate the character of the line by taking advantage of hill and valley threads. It is possible to weave the same angle with the same weft in a way that looks either very stepped or very smooth.

The images at right are the back and front of the same weaving; the weft is stepped over by 2 warp threads on each relay, as seen in the diagram on page 194. To understand how to make the smooth line appear on the front of your tapestry, remember the idea of hill and valley threads from chapter 6: as you weave, the weft goes over or under each warp, creating a "hill" or a "valley."

In the illustration on the right, arrow 1 is pointing to a valley weft thread, and arrow 2 is pointing to a hill weft thread. The valley thread will sink down a little farther than the hill thread as more sequences are placed on top of it. This difference in "step" height has an impact on the smoothness of the lines you create. If you were to fill in the shape on top of what is woven here, 1 would be a smoother transition than 2.

Every time a weft passes under a warp it creates a valley thread. Due to the over/under nature of tapestry weaving, this happens every other warp thread in a particular shed. You therefore can create the smoothest possible angle by moving your sequences over by an even number of warps on every step. Shallow angles are the smoothest when a valley thread occurs at the end of each sequence in the receding shape, as seen in #1 in the diagram on this page.

front

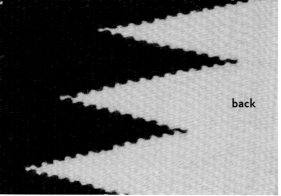

back

▲ *The images above are the back and front of the same weaving; the weft is stepped over by 2 warp threads on each relay, as seen in the diagram below.*

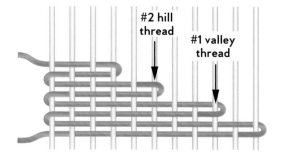

#2 hill thread

#1 valley thread

If the sequence moves over an odd number of warps each time, the diagonal line formed will have smooth areas where the valley threads were and steps where the hill threads were. If the first relay occurs on a hill, the next will occur on a valley, then a hill, then a valley, and so on. This is visible in the diagram on the previous page: 1 is at a valley thread and 2 is at a hill thread 3 warps over. When woven, the resulting line looks like the angle indicated by the red arrow in the photo at right.

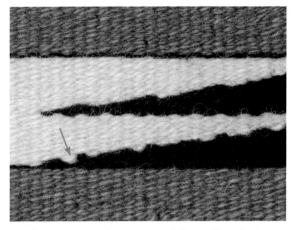

▲ *The red arrow indicates an angle formed by relaying on every 3rd warp.*

TECH TALK

Remembering Where to Relay

Some people like to memorize a rule and follow it. These two sayings can help you make sure your hills and valleys happen in the correct places to create the smoothest possible line without any other techniques:

- "Receding color wraps on a raised warp."
- "Advancing color returns on the lowered warp."

The "advancing color" is the one moving over on top of the other color. "Raised" and "lowered" warps refer here to the position the warp is in after the shed is shifted and you're ready to return your wefts.

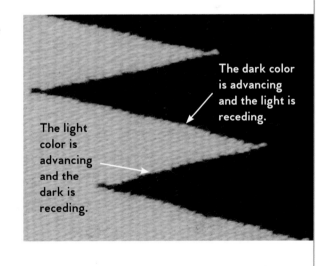

The dark color is advancing and the light is receding.

The light color is advancing and the dark is receding.

Practicing Shallower Angles

To practice making some straight lines with shallow angles, choose two colors of weft. Use contrasting values so you can see what is happening.

1. Decide which direction the diagonal will move and, weaving with your butterflies in meet and separate (see page 132), start closer to one side of the warp than the other. Make the first angle one that steps over by 2 warp threads on each sequence, as in the diagram on the left on page 194.

2. Bring the wefts together. Shift your shed.

3. The yarn that is going to be the bottom, or receding, color of the angle (A) should wrap around the warp that popped up when you shifted your shed. Return both butterflies to the selvages.

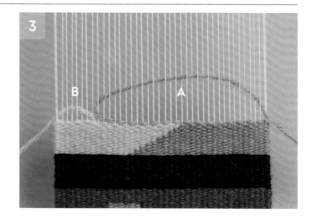

4. Shift your shed. On the next sequence, move the advancing butterfly (B) over the other one by 2 total warps.

5. Return both butterflies to the selvages. You have created one step.

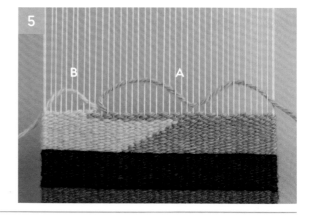

6. Repeat steps 2–5 to create a consistent stepping movement by shifting your relay over by two steps each sequence.

7. Repeat this exercise, stepping over 4 warp threads for each sequence.

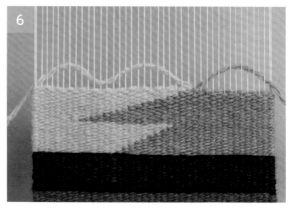

Keeping Lines Straight When Your Shape Changes Directions

When making a symmetrical shape like the angular shape in the images below, it is tempting to think that you should line up where the wefts relayed on the bottom half of the form when you weave the top half. Unfortunately, if you do this, the diagonal lines on the bottom half of the shape will be smooth and the ones on the top half will be jagged if the angles move over by 2 or more warps per step.

This is because the advancing color on the bottom half of the shape becomes the receding color on the top; the hill and valley thread combinations that make the smooth line have shifted by 1 warp. In the image below left, notice how the relay points on the top and bottom of each triangle match up but the bottom line is smooth and the top is bumpy. The bottom line had valley threads at each turn, and the top had hill threads at each turn.

To avoid the straight and jagged combination, shift where the relays happen by 1 warp thread. Do this when a shape reverses direction, as in the image below right. At the point of the triangle, change the number of warps you move over to an odd number for one step, then return to the even progression you were using. For example, if you were stepping over by 2 warps every sequence in one direction, when you turn around, for the first step you will move your sequence over either 1 or 3 warps. Then you will be back on track with the relays happening on the appropriate hill or valley thread and you can go back to moving your sequence over 2 warps every step. If you are trying to get the point in a specific place, you can also move over by an odd number for the last step on the bottom side of the triangle and resume using an even number of steps on the top side of the form.

In the image below right, you can see that I stepped over by 2 warps every time. The arrows at the bottom of the image show that I went over 2 warps to the last point. When I returned, the three arrows on top show where I went over 3 warps for the first step. (You can also count the warp ridges in the weaving.) After that, I returned to stepping the angle 2 warps at a time. The red lines indicate where the steps are for the next sequence.

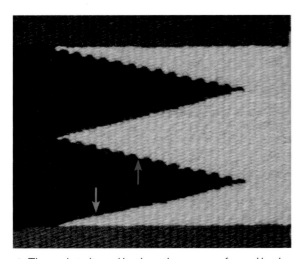

▲ *The angle indicated by the red arrow was formed by the receding color wrapping on a raised warp, which produces the smoothest possible line. The angle indicated by the blue arrow was formed by the advancing color wrapping on a raised warp, which makes the line jagged instead of straight.*

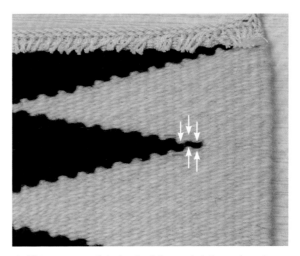

▲ *This image is of the back of the work. It is much easier to see steps in the weaving from the back, as opposed to the front, which is quite smooth, as seen in the top photograph on page 196.*

Using an Uneven Number of Sequences in Each Step

Each combination of steps and sequences produces a particular angle, which could be measured in degrees with a protractor. But what if the angle you want to make falls between successive combinations of steps and sequences? For example, if stacking up 2 sequences before moving over gives you an angle of 60 degrees, but stacking up 3 sequences gives you an angle of 70 degrees, how can you create a 65-degree angle? There are ways to create intermediate angles for both steep (larger) and shallow (smaller) angles.

To create an intermediate angle where multiple sequences are stacked up, take advantage of hill and valley threads to make a smooth angle. In this case, the rules about wrapping on raised or lowered warps don't apply, because you'll be stepping over by 1 warp every time. One warp will be raised and the next will be lowered. If you didn't watch the hill and valley threads and just wove 2 sequences on one step and one on the next (2, 1, 2, 1), the line would not look smooth if the doubled sequences fell on hill threads. This is because the hill steps are already slightly higher than the valley threads. If, however, you make the doubled sequence fall on a valley thread, as seen in the diagram at right, you can make the angle much smoother, as seen in this photograph. The lower stepped valley threads are doubled and the higher stepped hill threads are not. This gives you the intermediate angle you want, while also creating the straightest line possible.

For shallower angles that move over multiple warps with each sequence, you can alter the number of warps you move over each time. Perhaps the diagonal line you need is best created by moving over 3 warps every step. In this case, if you simply step over 3 warps evenly, and if you

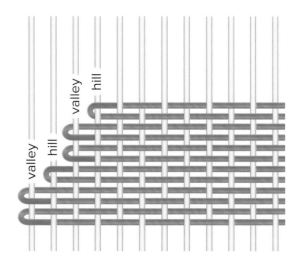

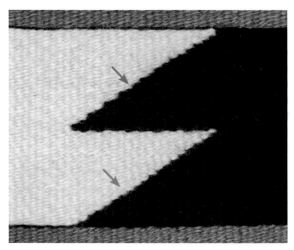

▲ *Notice the sequence and placement of hill and valley threads in this diagram to achieve the line indicated by the red arrow. The blue arrow indicates what happens when the 1-sequence steps occur on a valley thread instead of a hill thread.*

are not planning to use an eccentric outline (see page 251), your angle will have one bumpy step followed by one smooth step because of the hill and valley threads. But you can achieve the same angle by alternating advancing two and four steps on each sequence, as seen at right.

▶ *In the diagonal with the red arrow, the sequences were moved 3 warp threads each time. In the diagonal indicated by the blue arrow, the sequences were moved 2 warps, then 4 warps, then 2 warps again, and so on. The angle is the same, but when alternating even numbers of warp threads, the relays can all be made on valley threads.*

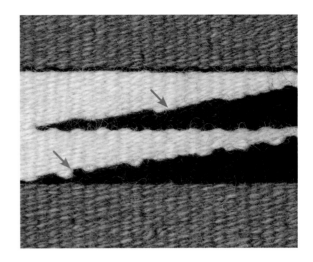

TIP

Make an Angle Sampler

Once you have experimented with various angles, I recommend weaving a full angle sampler. This will tell you which combination of steps and relays give you a particular angle when paired with your weaving style, weft, and sett. Weave each angle and label it with what warp and weft you used, what the sett was, and what the combination of steps and sequences was to get that angle. Make sure to weave each angle large enough to measure it with a protractor, as seen on page 193. Measuring the angle in degrees allows you to choose a step sequence that will match the diagonal lines in your cartoon. Knowing what those angles are before you start weaving a piece can help you avoid making corrections in your angle that will result in a jog in your otherwise straight line. This will become clearer when you learn about using cartoons in chapter 12.

Breaking Up Large Color Areas

When filling in large areas with a solid color, use more than one butterfly of the same color. This avoids draw-in and prevents you from having one butterfly travel over wide areas. So far you have done this using irregular hatching and multiple butterflies of the same color.

Using a cutback — an angle in the weaving made with the same color — is another way to break up large areas of a single color. This technique can add subtle texture by creating diagonal lines in large areas of the same color. The small slits that are created allow more give in the piece than does weaving a long distance with one butterfly. When building up shapes, cutbacks allow you to continue weaving just one section at a time as

well. See page 32 for more about weaving shape by shape.

I suspect tapestry weavers started using cutbacks when multiple technicians were weaving the same very large tapestry. When weaving just one section of a tapestry at a time, it is more efficient for the weaver to keep their body positioned in one place instead of shifting back and forth to weave a wide area. Cutbacks go through the center of a solid-colored area of the tapestry and allow adjacent areas to be filled in later, without slits.

Cutbacks can also be used by people weaving line by line (see page 32) to create subtle patterning in areas of solid color. Successive diagonal lines tend to create zigzag patterns or complete diamonds. I most often see simple one-step diagonals used, but the angle could be anything you want.

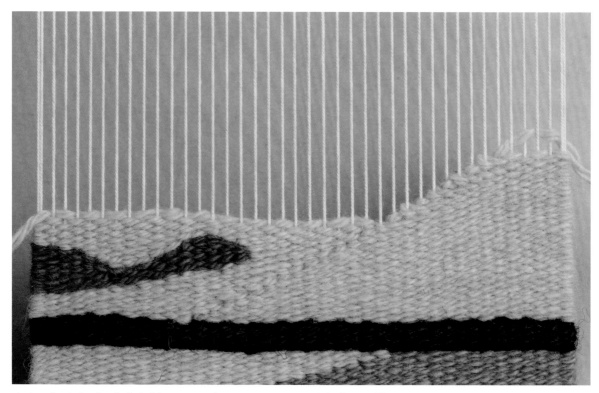

▲ A cutback divides the light blue-green color area, creating a subtle diagonal line.

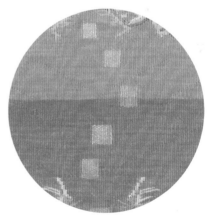

**Barbara Heller, *Tzimtzum –
Transcendence*, 2016.**
Linen, cotton, wool, and rayon, 48" × 96".
◀ *The detail above of Barbara Heller's
tapestry shows her use of cutbacks to
break up solid colored areas and add
subtle patterning.*

11 Vertical Growth

Because the images woven in tapestry are created on a grid structure, creating horizontal lines is easier than creating vertically oriented lines or curves that travel up the warp. You can make lines travel vertically up the warp using a technique known as pick and pick, as well as wrapping warps with joins. Leaving slits unsewn also has the effect of suggesting vertical lines.

Pick and Pick

This technique creates narrow vertical stripes in the direction of the warp by alternating two colors of yarn in successive picks, with each line covering 1 warp thread. Because you use different colors in each of the two sheds, the resulting vertical stripes switch colors.

If you alternate one pick of dark violet and one pick of light violet, as seen at right, the dark yarn will cover every other warp thread and the light yarn will cover the alternate set of warp threads. Pick and pick is not a technique woven in meet and separate. This causes some difficulties at the edges of forms, where the two colors have to wrap around each other. It also means that if you have

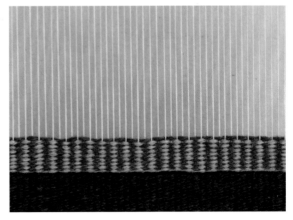

▲ *Pick and pick creates vertical stripes*

solid-colored sections of weaving on either side of the pick and pick — even if one of the colors is the same as what you're using in the pick-and-pick section — you have to use separate butterflies.

The number of warp threads in your pick-and-pick section and whether the edge warp is raised or lowered when you start the pattern will influence how you wrap the two wefts at the edges of your form (which may or may not be at the selvages of your weaving). I will teach you two different edge treatments: technique 1 is an all-purpose treatment that you can use for most occasions, while technique 2 is reserved for a more specific instance. As you practice, it will become clear when technique 1 does not cover the edge warp; in those cases you will use technique 2.

You can always use technique 1 for the edge treatment when you are weaving over an odd number of warps. This technique causes the two wefts to cross over each other at the selvage, creating a tiny striped color pattern along the edge of the pick and pick section as seen at right.

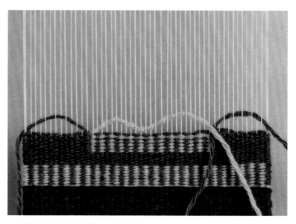

▲ The upper pick-and-pick section is surrounded by solid color, which is formed with separate butterflies of the dark violet. Notice that there are three dark violet butterflies and just one light violet butterfly in this pattern.

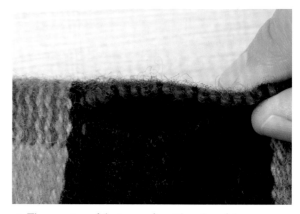

▲ The crossing of the two wefts at the edge of the pick and pick area in technique 1 creates tiny lines of alternating colors.

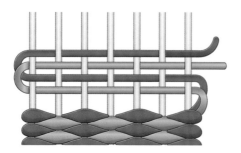

Technique 1
▲ This diagram shows pick and pick used over an odd number of warps. In this case, the vertical stripes on each side of the pick-and-pick area will be the same color.

When weaving pick and pick over an even number of warps, sometimes technique 1 will work on one side (as seen in the diagram on the previous page), but you will need technique 2 (as seen in the diagram below) for the other side. You do not need to memorize any special formula to determine when to use which edge treatment. Simply watch the weaving: if you have an uncovered warp on the edge of your pick and pick, use technique 2. For all other cases, use technique 1. Be aware that technique 2 creates a float, which you want on the back of the tapestry, as seen in the photo below right.

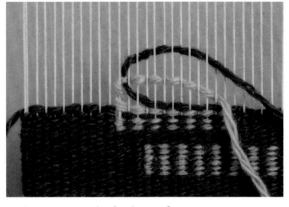

▲ *A woven example of technique 2*

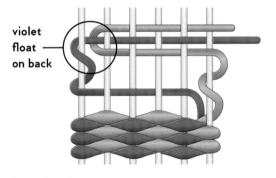

Technique 2
▲ *This diagram shows pick and pick used over an even number of warps. In this case, the vertical stripes formed on each side of the pick-and-pick area will be different colors.*

▲ *Technique 2 creates a float on the back of the weaving.*

TIP

Odd or Even?

Open one of your sheds. Look at the 2 selvage warps. If one is up and one is down, you have an even number of warps. If both are up or both are down, you have an odd number. This is faster than counting all of your warps.

Pick-and-Pick Practice

To practice pick and pick, you will weave a stripe all the way across your warp. If you prefer, you can do this exercise over just part of your warp and fill in the rest with a solid color or another pattern. In this case you will have slits at the edges of your pick-and-pick section.

Start by figuring out whether you have an even or odd number of warps (see Odd or Even? on the previous page). Choose two contrasting values of yarn so you can more easily see what is happening. (In the directions that follow, yarn A is light violet and yarn B is orange.) Then make two butterflies (see page 115), one of each color. The butterflies will follow each other in successive sheds.

1. Start one color (A) at one selvage and pass it from one side of your warp to the other. Shift the shed and beat.

2. In the next shed, enter the second butterfly (B) from the same side you started the first color. You will have two tails at one selvage. Take the second butterfly across to the other side, shift the shed, and beat. At this point you should see dots of alternating color.

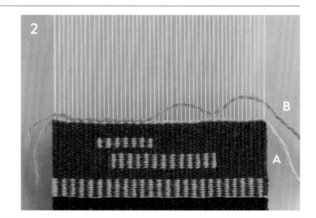

3. Refer to techniques 1 and 2 on pages 206 and 207 to create the correct edge treatment, depending on whether you have an even or odd number of warps. If you have an odd number of warps, you will use technique 1. If you have an even number of warps and you find that using technique 1 for the edge treatment leaves an uncovered warp on the edge of your pick and pick section, use technique 2.

TECH TALK

A Pick by Any Other Name

You may see pick and pick referred to as *half-pass* in other tapestry books or in workshops. As you will recall from chapter 6, the words *sequence* and *pass* mean the same thing: 2 picks are woven so that all of the warps are covered by that color. *Half-pass* literally means half-a-pass, or 1 pick. The pick-and-pick technique uses alternate picks of each color, or half-a-pass of each color, at a time.

The word *duite* is a French term for "pass" or "sequence." *Demi-duite* is the French term for half-pass. Demi-duite is often referred to as a separate technique in tapestry, but it is really just a variation of pick and pick.

TECHNIQUE 1. Image 3a shows yarn B dropping over Yarn A. Yarn A will then wrap around and behind yarn B and return in the alternate shed. This action creates a small X on the edge. If you are weaving from the front, leave a little slack in yarn A. When the next color returns, it will pull the X to the back of the weaving.

Image 3b shows yarn B returning and the place the wefts cross being pulled to the back.

TECHNIQUE 2. After bringing the 2nd pick of yarn A across as you did in step 2 on the opposite page, yarn A should be traveling behind the edge warp. Wrap yarn A around the edge warp twice, and after shifting the shed, return the yarn, creating a float as seen in the bottom photo on page 207. Shift your shed again and return yarn A to the other side. This will make a very small vertical float in yarn A where it jumps over the yarn B pick.

The top photo on page 207 shows the procedure for technique 2 expanded a bit. Remember that you're creating stripes up the warp, so the stripe that goes on the edge is the color you'll use to wrap that edge warp.

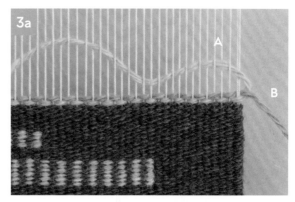

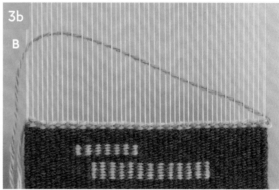

▲ *When weaving from the front, pull this butterfly a little more firmly to encourage the place the two yarns crossed to move to the back.*

4. Continue to alternate colors, one per sequence, with yarn B always following yarn A. Notice the vertical stripes starting to form.

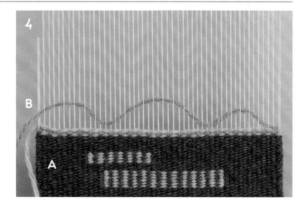

Vertical Stripe Patterns

You can shift the vertical stripes over 1 warp by weaving 2 picks of the same color in a row. By changing the frequency with which you do this, you can create all kinds of patterns.

Following the same pattern of weaving as you just practiced, try putting 2 picks in a row of one color before returning to the pick-and-pick pattern as seen at right. This will shift the vertical lines over by 1 warp. What happens if you put 3 picks in of one of the colors before resuming the pick-and-pick pattern?

Play with other patterns using the two colors you started with. See if you can create little checks or a checkerboard pattern.

▲ *Weaving 2 picks of the same color in a row will shift the vertical stripes over by 1 warp.*

TECH TALK

Double Weft Interlock

This join is woven from the back, interlocking the two wefts in both directions in the sequence. It is a good option for making very straight vertical joins. By making two double weft interlocks — one on each side of the line — it is also an effective way to make 1-warp vertical lines. I won't cover the double weft interlock technique in this book because it is woven from the back, but it is worth looking into on your own if you are interested in making thin vertical lines and have the option of weaving part or all of your piece from the back.

VARIATION

Shaped Pick and Pick

Pick and pick is most often created in non-rectangular forms. It is likely that you will want to use this technique to create effects of shading and movement in all kinds of shapes. Working shaped pick and pick creates floats, though, so it is not possible for the back to be clean.

There are no specific directions for using pick and pick in shapes, but as you experiment with doing this, remember these tips:

- It is easiest to do shaped pick and pick when weaving from the front. Watch carefully for any uncovered warps as you put in each pair of picks. Make sure one of the picks covers the warp.

- Use the technique 2 edge treatment (as seen on page 207 and described on page 209) to make sure a warp is covered.

- Make sure that each sequence in your weaving aligns with a full pass in the pick-and-pick section, one half-pass of each color. You may be tempted to weave the full pass pattern of pick and pick next to 1 pick of regular weaving because it mimics the normal meet-and-separate pattern. You should avoid this temptation, though, because then the pick-and-pick section will have twice the total number of weft rows as the rest of the weaving.

- You will have to float both the pick and pick and the background butterflies a lot to make the structure work; this is normal. Make the floats on the back.

Michael Rohde, *Golden*, 2014.
Wool, 47" × 36½"
▲ *Michael Rohde used pick and pick to create the gold simulations of text in this tapestry.*

Demi-Duites

The term *demi-duite* is a way of referring to using just 1 pick (or a half-pass) of a color. Because the yarn only travels over every other warp and does not return, this creates a dotted line, as seen at right. This technique does not create a full sequence, and like pick and pick, it requires filling in the other pick of the sequence with the background color, with another color, or by making weft floats on the back.

Demi-duites can also be used to add small bits of color to areas of the weaving, as seen in the middle photo at right. Usually this is done with floats on the back.

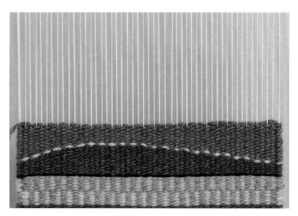

▲ *A demi-duite line woven in white*

Invisible Weft Sequence Join for Vertical Warp Wraps

You can weave very narrow shapes, including 1-warp wrapped vertical lines, using a thin support yarn to hold together the slits. It's the most elegant way to do this, as it's nearly impossible to sew a slit on either side of a warp that is wrapped, as seen in the bottom photo at right.

To accomplish this, weave in an invisible weft every 2 or 3 sequences to create a join that does not distort the warp wrap. The thread should be thin enough to disappear between the regular weft sequences. I use a regular polyester-cotton sewing thread of similar value to the weft yarns.

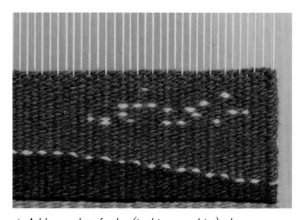

▲ *Add your dot of color (in this case white) where you want it to show and float the background color (in this case violet) around it on the back.*

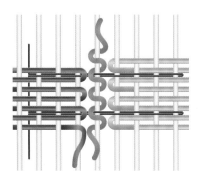

◀ *This diagram shows an invisible weft sequence join (sometimes called a bar join) using a thin thread to invisibly "stitch" a 1-warp wrap.*

▲ *A 1-warp wrap with unsewn slits on either side*

Invisible Weft Sequence Join Practice

Practice using this join to hold together the slits on either side of a 1-warp vertical line. You will weave in the thin support weft, creating the bar join, after 2 sequences of the regular weaving. The bar join is woven in a full sequence so it does not change your shedding. Set up this sample with three color areas in meet and separate: two larger solid areas and a single warp wrap line in the center.

1. Weave 2 sequences with these three colors.

2. With all the butterflies in the same shed, open the other shed and weave a piece of sewing thread or thin yarn across the two slits, as seen here. The more warps you travel over, the stronger the join will be, but make sure you go under at least 2 warps on each side of the slits.

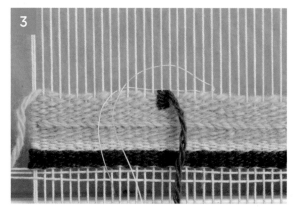

3. Shift the shed, then bring the sewing thread back to where you started the sequence. This makes a full sequence with the sewing thread. If you are weaving from the front, bring both ends of the thread to the back and leave them there.

4. Leave the thread on the back of your work until you are ready to make another join. The thread will float up the back and come back into the shed for the next join.

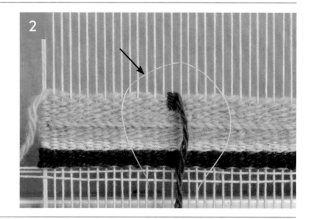

5. Shift the shed again (5a), and weave a couple more sequences before doing another join (5b).

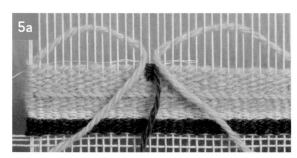

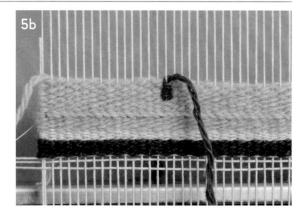

◀ On the right side of this sample, 4 sequences were stacked up before moving over 1 warp. Where the light color was a valley thread, the steps are slightly angled. Where the light color was a hill thread, the steps are more prominent. On the left side of the sample, the cutting of the corners technique (shown below) was used, and the resulting steps appear smoother.

Cutting Off the Corners

When weaving vertically oriented angles or curves, the grid structure creates many small steps, which can be quite evident depending on your materials and sett. This is simply the nature of tapestry weaving and a signature feature of the medium. In general, the more vertical a line becomes, the more stepped it will appear. It is possible, however, to make a steep angle (created with multiple sequences stacked up) appear smoother by "cutting off the corners." This process softens the corner of the step that is made when a weft steps over 1 warp, making it look less square. To make this work, you need to weave the receding side of the shape 2 sequences higher than the advancing side. You will not be able to weave completely line by line. Alternatively, you can build up one side of the shape first (see chapter 13).

The photo above shows angles where 4 sequences are stacked up before moving over 1 warp thread. On the left side, the cutting-off-the-corners technique has been used to smooth out the corners of each step. This technique was not used on the right side.

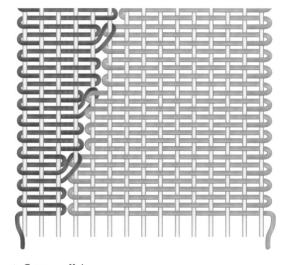

▲ Cutting off the corners

Cutting Off the Corners Practice

This technique can be used to cut the corner off steps in all sorts of steep lines and is not limited to straight diagonal lines. To practice, work an even diagonal using two contrasting colors. In the steps that follow, yarn A is red and yarn B is pale pink.

1. Weave 2 full sequences of both colors using meet and separate (see page 132).

2. Weave 2 more sequences of the color that will be receding. In this example, yarn A is receding.

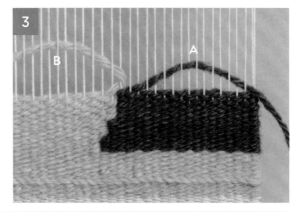

3. Pick up the advancing color's butterfly (yarn B) and weave the first pick of the next sequence. Instead of relaying back where it meets the receding color (A), bring your advancing butterfly up to the top of the step already woven, change your shed, and return that butterfly to the edge.

4. Weave 1 more sequence with the advancing butterfly (B) but stop 1 warp short of the relay you made in step 3. Make sure the total number of sequences in each color is the same.

5. Repeat steps 1–4 for each step in your diagonal line.

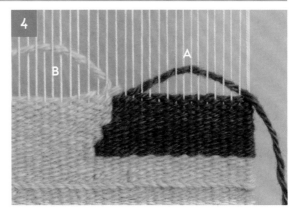

Other Ways to Make Vertical Lines

There are other ways to make vertical lines in tapestry weaving that may not be as common as pick and pick but can work well to suggest lines that travel in the same direction as the warps. Unsewn slits, short single warp wraps, and creative use of hatching are three such techniques.

Ruth Manning, *Pensar*, 2015.
Cotton and wool, 22" × 9".

Unsewn Slits

When viewing a piece of art, your brain will fill in details that are not overtly present to convince you that you are seeing something recognizable. As tapestry weavers, we can use this phenomenon to our advantage. A great way to suggest a vertical line is to use an unsewn slit in the middle of a solid-colored area. The slight disruption of color and shadow caused by the slit is often enough to convince the viewer's brain that a vertical line really exists there. This works well when the piece is hung in the direction it was woven.

Single Warp Wrap over a Short Distance

Wrapping a single warp for a short distance creates slits on either side of the wrap, and if the rest of the textile is firmly woven, the structure is not adversely affected. If your warp wraps are less than ½ inch high, this technique is fine.

Single Warp Wrap with Hatching

Another variation of the single warp wrap is to use short hatches to keep slits from forming. Note that the resulting vertical line is not as smooth as it would be if you used the invisible weft sequence join. If you use a thinner weft for the warp wrap, the hatches can connect between weft sequences of the main color. If the weft is all the same size, you might step the adjacent wefts over, as seen opposite, at far right.

Sarah Swett and Ruth Manning have used this idea to great effect in some of their work. Swett's piece *Pen and Ink* (opposite) uses the technique extensively: several unsewn slits suggest many vertical lines. Manning often uses open slits as part of her portrait tapestries. In a small piece, a vertical warp wrap might make a line that is too wide for the image. A slit can create the illusion of a thinner line where none actually exists.

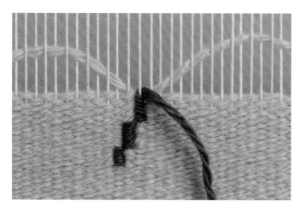

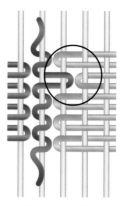

▲ It is tempting to try to sew the slits on either side of a warp wrap, but I find this is almost impossible and prefer to use the invisible weft sequence join discussed on page 212 instead.

▲ A thinner weft can connect the rest of the weaving between adjacent warp wraps.

▲ When using thicker wefts, it is important to step the adjacent color over to make the short hatch and avoid lice, which could be created with two wefts in the same shed.

Sarah C. Swett, *Pen and Ink*, 2009.
Wool, 18" × 18".

12 Designing

So far everything you've woven has had a fairly simple design, but as the techniques get more complicated, you will need a cartoon to guide your weaving. After learning some preliminary tapestry design concepts, you can turn those ideas into a cartoon from which you can weave.

Design versus Cartoon

Your design is the plan for your project — your overarching vision for the finished tapestry. Some tapestry weavers make full-color designs in paint or a digital medium, while others may only create simple sketches, leaving much of the interpretation for the weaving process.

A cartoon is a drawing of the major forms and color areas in a tapestry that is used as a reference while you weave. The cartoon is the same size as the tapestry you will weave, and it can be hung freely behind your warp, attached to the warp, or held under the warp and copied onto the warp threads with a permanent marker. The method you choose will depend on the sort of loom you use, how complicated your design is, and how much of a guide you want while you weave.

Though it can be fun to weave shapes without a guide, if you want to maintain the proportion and placement of forms in the design, using a cartoon is a good idea.

Design Concepts

Before you can make the cartoon from which you will weave, you need a design. There are entire books about designing for tapestry weaving, but the following few tips should get you started on your own tapestry designs. One of the most important aspects of design is color (see chapter 5). Here are a few more important characteristics of tapestry that have an impact on design.

What Are You Trying to Express?

This is perhaps the first thing to ask yourself as you work on a design. I think designing is easier if you can articulate the feeling you want the viewer to experience from the work. It could be as simple as joy or happiness or more nuanced like fear or depiction of the feeling from a particular memory or place.

I am a big fan of abstract ideas in tapestry. I find this medium incredibly expressive due to the depth of color and texture in yarn. There is nothing wrong with depicting realistic scenes in tapestry, but I encourage you as a beginner to look at some of the best-loved tapestries from history and today and to consider how they deal with their subjects. Most tapestries have a fairly flat picture plane, meaning there is not a lot of dimension expressed. Many are very graphic without a lot of shading or hatching between color areas. Others have a very mystical, blended quality with lots of hatching and weft bundling (see pages 161 and 49, respectively).

Students frequently show me a photograph and say, "I want to weave this." Usually they mean they want to weave the actual image in the photograph. Creating photorealism in tapestry is difficult, unless you weave at very close setts or at very large scales. I encourage my students to step away from depicting a particular scene with photographic realism, and instead to capture the feeling in the photograph by isolating colors and forms that are more readily expressed in tapestry. My argument is that we should work with the grid-based characteristics of the medium, outlined later in this chapter, when designing. Leave the realism to photographers.

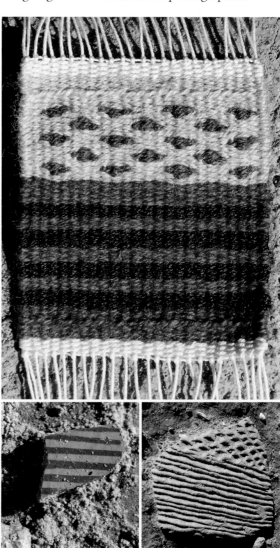

▲ *During an artist residency at Petrified Forest National Park, I wove a 2" × 2" tapestry every day based on things that I saw. This example shows how I took design elements from two potsherds and created the tapestry above.*

Margo Macdonald, *Little Deschutes*, 2013.
Wool and cotton, 36" × 34".

▲ *In this piece, Margo Macdonald wove an image of a particular place she loves and worked the latitude and longitude into the image.*

Marcia Hanson Ellis, *SuperNatural*, 2016.
Wool, cotton, and glass beads, 41" × 32" × 1".
▲ *The vertical lines seen here appear smooth because they were actually woven sideways. You'll learn more about when to turn your cartoon sideways later in this chapter.*

▲ *This detail shows how steeply vertical lines are formed by making small steps. Notice how the horizontal lines are smooth curves.*

Simplification

Students often want to put much more detail into their tapestry designs than is reasonable at setts of around 8 epi. This is especially true at the smaller dimensions that portable looms dictate.

Most weaving done on a loom starts with a square grid created by vertical warps and horizontal wefts. Because tapestry is weft-faced, you will have many more rows of weft traveling horizontally than you will have warp ends. Any forms that are moving vertically up the warp will be stepped, as seen in the detail below. Whereas a painter could make a smooth brushstroke, a tapestry artist must stack up passes and then step over to the next warp thread, creating a step, or jog, in the line being formed. There are many techniques that can help you smooth out these lines (see chapters 10, 11, and 14), but the structure of the medium dictates that they will exist. The more warp ends you have in an inch, the smaller those steps will be.

Before you are tempted to increase your epi to get more detail in each inch, consider why you weave tapestry and whether you really want to imitate other media. Some people describe tapestry as "woven painting," and I would like to push back on this idea. Tapestry is not a painting rendered in yarn. It is a completely different medium with its own structures and expressions. Painters can put paint wherever they want on a canvas, and they can also change parts of their composition as they work. Tapestry is built from the bottom to the top; if you want to change something you have already completed, the process of unweaving is difficult. Fiber is a rich and engaging medium, and if you are going to spend a long time creating a woven image, it should reflect the beauty of weaving in and of itself. Simplification of design is part of tapestry's appeal. Celebrate this fact instead of emulating other visual media. Do not get sucked into the habit of attempting to fill your weaving with detail. Simplify.

I have encouraged you to make your designs simpler, but how do you do that? Let's say you are starting with a photograph you love. Think about what it is about that image that you love so much. Why did you choose it as a subject for your weaving? Is it the color? Or maybe you love the value changes caused by a light source, a particular form, or the repetition of certain shapes. If you can pinpoint what you are drawn to, it will be easier to isolate those components in your tapestry design. Then you can start working with those elements to express your idea.

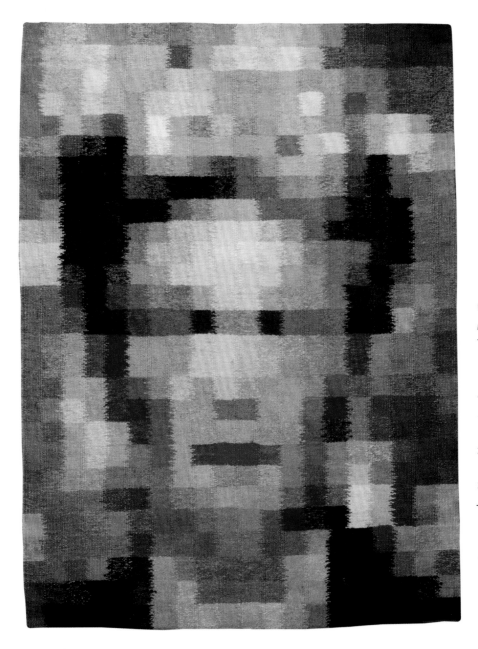

Michael Rohde, Reality, 2014.
Wool, alpaca, silk, and llama, 43½" × 32½".
◀ *In his pixelated series of tapestries, Michael Rohde has woven images taken from portrait photographs that are very roughly pixelated. When seen from across a room, these images are very recognizable as particular people. When seen close up, they appear simply as colored squares.*

The Tapestry-ness of It All

Understanding the basic characteristics of tapestry weaving is important before you launch into design. You have developed a feel for these throughout the book and as you have woven your samples, but here are a few that pertain specifically to designing tapestry.

RIBS. Tapestry weaving creates a characteristic rib that runs along the warp. All tapestry will contain these ribs to some extent; the size of the rib can be larger or smaller depending on the size warp you use and your sett (see chapter 4). The ribs provide a certain amount of texture to the image, so there will always be some suggestion of lines in the direction of the warp. In her tapestry *Cordes Sensibles* on page 59, Suzanne Paquette uses a thick warp, which creates a prominent rib structure in her weaving. In *Emergence V* on page 59, I used a much thinner warp, which makes the surface of the tapestry quite flat.

LINES AND STEPS. Horizontally oriented lines and curves can be made quite straight by paying attention to hills and valleys or by using eccentric outlines (see page 253). But vertically oriented lines will always contain steps in tapestry. You learned some ways to lessen the effect of these steps in chapter 11, but they will always be present to some extent. These steps are a defining characteristic of tapestry weaving. Knowing steps will happen is important to consider while designing in this medium.

FINE DETAIL. If you weave a tapestry at 8 epi, there are only eight possibilities in 1 inch for moving your weft horizontally. Often this means the form you want to weave, if small, can only be approximated. Some weavers solve this by putting more warps in an inch. And while this is a possibility, I believe there is value in learning to simplify designs so they can be woven at wider setts.

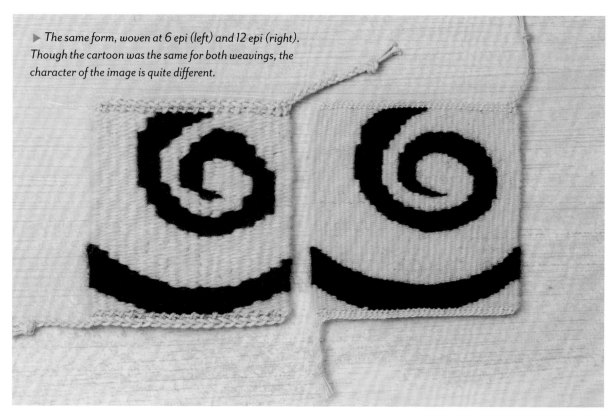

▶ *The same form, woven at 6 epi (left) and 12 epi (right). Though the cartoon was the same for both weavings, the character of the image is quite different.*

▲ Joyce Hayes, *Etude 3*, 2012.
Linen, sewing thread, and polyester; tapestry mounted on hand-painted watercolor paper, 5½" × 8½".

TAPESTRY IS A TEXTILE. Tapestry is a fabric, which means that there is flexibility and movement involved. When painting, you can apply a bit of paint to one spot of canvas and be reasonably sure it will stay there. Tapestry images are created at the same time the structure of the fabric is created. This means that the warps can shift around somewhat, moving closer together or farther apart. Very precise placement of design elements, especially small ones, is difficult (at least while you are learning). I advocate embracing flexibility as you weave your first pieces.

Scale: Size Matters

Most weavers new to tapestry will start with samples or tapestries 1 to 2 square feet. Eventually you'll want to consider how to best express your ideas in terms of size in this medium. The way a tapestry is viewed actually depends somewhat on the size of the piece. Think about how you approach a piece of art. If you walk into a gallery or a business and view a Helena Hernmarck tapestry such as the one pictured on the next page, you are most certainly going to stand quite far away from it. Her work is very large, and to see it all, you automatically stand back. Your viewing experience of Hernmarck's work is one of architectural scale and appreciation of how all the colors and forms work together in a large format.

By contrast, how might you look at a small-format tapestry, such as the one above by Joyce Hayes, who weaves at high setts with fine silk thread? When viewing her work in an installation, you cannot help but step close to look at the beautiful colors and forms that are so small.

In some respects, small-format work has a disadvantage in tapestry installations. As humans we are prone to get close to small things to study their details and delight in their tiny accomplishment.

Large pieces dominate a space and encourage us to stand back to take it all in. We are less likely to notice small irregularities of craftsmanship in a large piece compared with a small one, simply because of the tendency to study small work at close distance. Generally large works are also displayed in large spaces that allow distance for viewing.

Ways to Design for Tapestry

Some of you are reading this chapter with a sinking heart. You may be thinking, "I didn't go to art school, and I can't draw." Please believe me when I say you do not need to be able to draw to weave tapestry. If you have not spent much time looking at tapestries, do some library or Internet research. There are several excellent national and international tapestry organizations that feature artist portfolio pages online. As you browse, look at the subject matter. Notice which images attract you and see if you can figure out why. Follow your favorite tapestry artists online. Some of them talk on social media about their process and inspiration. Try some of their methods. While playing with ideas and materials, you will discover your own preferences for image and method.

Helena Hernmarck, *Folk Costume Details*, 2006.
Wool, linen, and cotton, 183" × 116".
◀ *Helena Hernmarck's work does not follow traditional Gobelin tapestry practice. Her use of multiple weft bundles of different sizes consisting of yarns in various colors and textures creates a sense of depth that can't be achieved using the techniques taught in this book. Hernmarck's skill at combining these weft bundles, along with the color choices she makes to enhance the effects of light and color, allow her to achieve striking illusion in a weave structure that up close is quite textured. (The smaller work is Hernmarck's sample for the full-size tapestry above.)*

The following is a short summary of some ways of designing. If any of these practices appeal to you, seek out further resources to advance your skills. While I believe anyone can learn to draw with practice, it isn't a requirement for tapestry design. Drawing, after all, is just making marks on paper.

COLLAGE. This method of designing for tapestry has become popular again in recent years. It does not require any drawing or computer skills. I most often see design collages using torn paper, but you could use many other materials as well. Paper collage is a quick and easy way to simplify your design ideas because the tearing of paper is imprecise and encourages you to let go of details.

ART JOURNALING. I use this term to encompass a wide variety of other collagelike activities. Art journaling could start with torn paper, photographs, pages from books, scraps of fabric or yarn, or almost anything you can glue to a page. Your assemblage can then be modified with any of a range of art materials, including acrylic paint, watercolor, marker, pencil, stamps, or ink. The idea is to free yourself up to play. Watch what colors and forms emerge that might make a beautiful tapestry design.

Molly Elkind, *Red Letter Day* (collage), 2015.
Hand-cut paper, 12" × 8".

Molly Elkind, *Red Letter Day*, (weaving) 2016.
Cotton, wool, and synthetic, 35½" × 26".

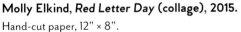

▲ *Molly Elkind used paper collage (left) to design the tapestry (right).*

TRACING PAPER. I am a big fan of this tissue-thin paper, which can be used in multiple layers to help you see various options in a design. You can put it over a photograph and trace the lines that are the most interesting to you. This is a good way to simplify potential forms from a photograph. You can also make multiples of a shape and then reorient some of them: moving the layers of tissue paper around can help you see new forms.

MASKING. Use a mask to isolate parts of a photograph or collage you're working on. You can make a mask by cutting a square out of a piece of cardboard or by cutting two L-shaped pieces of paper or cardboard and overlapping them. This allows you to change the size of your mask and play with what details you want to include or exclude.

DRAWING/PAINTING. Of course, some of you do have excellent drawing skills. Drawing is an amazing way to train your eye to see things. To practice really looking at something, spend some time sketching without placing too much emphasis on the outcome. After all, if you must draw that tree in the park, you will be forced to study it carefully, and that is the thing that leads to artistic inspiration. And if you are skilled at drawing or painting, you can draw your own cartoons. The trick is to keep them simple enough to weave.

COMPUTER DESIGN. Computer-based image-editing software or drawing applications for tablets can be excellent for tapestry design. In addition, you can use a computer to modify any design created in the ways above by adding color, erasing some lines, pixelating, adding layers, resizing, or just about any transformation you can imagine.

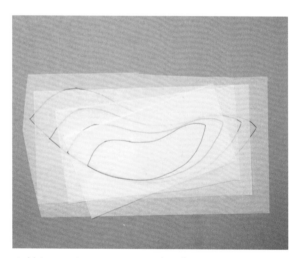

▲ *Using tracing paper to visualize design options*

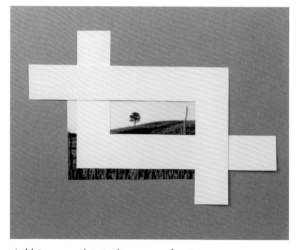

▲ *Using a mask to isolate parts of an image*

Give Yourself Time

In my own design process, when I think a design is completed, I leave it sitting out in my studio for a week or two. I look at it frequently and think about whether it still feels right. It can take time and distance away from a design to know for sure that you want to invest hours weaving it. Sometimes it takes several months for me to be satisfied with a design, and occasionally my initial idea changes drastically by the time I finish weaving the tapestry. Allow yourself this extra time before diving into weaving a new design, especially if it is a large endeavor.

Making a Cartoon

Once you have a design, you will need to create the cartoon, a full-size reference from which you will weave. The loom you are weaving on will determine to some extent how you create your cartoon and how you use it at the loom. If you use a small frame loom, it can be fairly easy to manage a cartoon by attaching it to your weaving or copying it onto the warp. Using a larger cartoon with a high- or low-warp loom with beams can require a few extra steps. You will practice using a cartoon in chapter 13 when you weave with curves.

Enlarging Your Tapestry Cartoon

Unless you are able to draw your cartoon at full size, you need to enlarge it to the size your tapestry will be. There are many ways to do this. For the methods described next it is helpful if the original drawing is a multiple of the final size. For example, if your final tapestry is 20 inches wide, the drawing could be 10 inches wide. When enlarging, you simply double the size with a 200 percent enlargement.

USE A PHOTOCOPIER. If your design is smaller than 8 × 10 inches, your home printer or copier may do the job. Otherwise, photocopy shops are your friends. Even basic printing stores in many places have large-format scanners and printers. Copy shops will usually print in black and white up to 36 inches wide for a reasonable price. For very large tapestries, when my sketch is larger than a letter-size sheet of paper, I have had my design scanned on a large-format scanner. I then use Photoshop to resize the digital version to the dimensions I need to be printed.

USE A PROJECTOR. If you have access to a digital projector, project your design onto a large piece of paper attached to a wall. Move the projector closer or farther away until your design is the size you need, then draw the projected lines onto your cartoon paper.

Material for Your Cartoon

You can make cartoons for small pieces on regular notebook paper. For larger pieces, plain bond paper that comes in large rolls works well, as does the large paper that copy shops use for enlargements. I take the paper enlargement from the copy shop and trace the design onto 0.005 mm clear-lay acetate. This film is sturdy and can be pinned to the tapestry repeatedly. Since I weave my large-format pieces from the back, I can trace the cartoon and then flip the acetate over, which ensures the final tapestry is oriented correctly.

Attaching the Cartoon

Remember that the cartoon is simply a reference for what you are producing. How exact you need the shapes to be will influence how you choose to use your cartoon. If you have many small shapes that need to be precisely realized, you want your cartoon to be as close to the woven surface as possible; you can even mark the lines directly on your warp. If you are weaving something with larger shapes and are able to rely more on your learned knowledge of making those shapes as you weave, you may only need the cartoon to hang behind the warp. You'll rely more on your eyes to create the forms and will use the cartoon largely for reference.

Regardless of whether you sew the cartoon on, hang it behind the weaving, or mark it on the warps, you should line up the bottom of the cartoon with the first part of the piece that will show. If you have completed the hemmed header, align the bottom of your cartoon with the soumak row (see page 124), since this is the first thing that will show in your tapestry.

Which Direction to Weave a Cartoon

As you learned in chapter 11, in tapestry it is much easier to weave horizontal lines and curves in a smooth manner than it is to weave smooth vertical lines and curves. This is something to consider when deciding which direction to weave your cartoon.

If the piece has a strong vertical feel and lots of long vertical lines, you might decide to rotate the design sideways, turning the verticals into horizontals. There can be some structural drawbacks to this approach, though. A tapestry is strongest when it hangs from the warp, meaning the direction it was woven. If you rotate the design 90 degrees to weave it, the finished piece will hang from the weft. For small pieces, this is inconsequential. But if you are weaving a very large piece sideways, sew slits securely so they do not fall open. In addition, take extra care making the hems for pieces that will hang sideways — especially large pieces — as the corners tend to buckle some if the hem at the edge is narrower than the rest of the weaving.

Sometimes you do not have a choice in orienting a design. If there are prominent lines in both directions, for example, determine which lines will

▲ The same design woven in two directions: the example on the left was woven sideways, and the example on the right was woven vertically, as pictured. Notice which lines are smooth and which are stepped in each example.

most effectively express the feeling or message you want to convey. Would the piece be more successful if some of the forms were smoother than others? If so, weave the tapestry so that the lines you want to be smoothest are horizontal.

Marking the Design Directly on the Warp

Whether you weave large tapestries on a beamed loom or small pieces on a frame loom, you can mark your cartoon design directly onto the warp. To do so, pin on the cartoon, transfer the lines with a permanent marker (see the tip on page 233), and remove the cartoon before weaving. I like the immediacy of the lines right on the warp, and I enjoy not having to fuss with the cartoon rattling around behind the tapestry. If your tapestry is very small, you may be able to just hold the cartoon behind your warp with one hand while you transfer the lines from the cartoon onto the warps with a marker. Most of the time, however, you will need to fasten the cartoon onto the warp before marking the cartoon lines on the warp threads.

Marie-Thumette Brichard, *Laminaires 3*, 2014.
Wool and silk, 67" × 50".
▲ *This piece was woven sideways, which means that the long verticals we see in the final tapestry were worked as horizontals, which are easier to weave.*

Use T-pins to secure the bottom of the cartoon through the already-woven portion of the tapestry, which might be just the waste yarn. Make sure the cartoon is held right against the warp either with your hand or with a longer stick (if the tapestry is larger), then mark all the places where the lines on the cartoon intersect the warps. If your tapestry is so large that the whole cartoon will not fit on the warp at one time, you will have to transfer it onto the warp in sections as the warp is advanced.

Sewing on the Cartoon

Some people stitch their cartoon directly to the weaving, adding lines of stitching as the weaving climbs upward. If you can reach a hand behind the weaving, you can do this easily using a straight sharp needle and some regular sewing thread; use a curved needle for this task if you cannot reach behind the weaving because it is too wide or if you are using a loom with a continuous warp and there is another layer of warp in the way. Either way, stitch loosely with a contrasting color of thread. You will want to repeat the stitching as you weave higher on the warp. If the piece is large, you may need to cut the lower stitching to free the cartoon. Avoid rolling the cartoon onto a beam with the tapestry, and do not allow the cartoon to get caught between the tapestry and the loom as you advance a continuous warp.

Sewing on the cartoon may distort both the cartoon and the woven forms, especially if you weave from the front and have lots of tails or bits of yarn on the back of the weaving, since the weft tails can push the cartoon away from the weaving. You may be able to accommodate for that by marking a vertical line on the cartoon and marking a corresponding warp in your weaving; keep the two aligned as you weave. Additionally, transfer horizontal marks from the cartoon to the warp with permanent marker to help you keep the cartoon and weaving aligned in the other direction. Cartoon distortion will not be an issue if you weave from the back and your tails are facing you.

Instead of sewing on the cartoon, you may also attach it with T-pins or strong magnets. Pins can easily be moved, but they tend to distort the weaving and the cartoon a little bit. Magnets are the easiest to reposition but may also be detrimental because they can be moved so easily. Although rare earth magnets are strong enough to hold a cartoon through a thick tapestry, they can be dangerous if swallowed and so are particularly hazardous if you have small children or pets.

TIPS

Transferring the Cartoon to the Warp

WARPS ARE ROUND. If you draw your cartoon directly on the warp, you will find that the dots disappear as you weave because the warps will rotate. Twisting the warp as you transfer the cartoon so that the mark goes all the way around will keep the dots from disappearing as the warps rotate.

THE MARKS CAN FADE AS YOU WEAVE. You may periodically need to darken them so you do not miss a dot.

DO NOT MAKE THE DOTS TOO LONG. Just mark the point where the warp crosses the line on the cartoon. If your dots turn into little lines, it becomes more difficult to know when to change colors as you weave.

Hanging the Cartoon behind the Warp

Many tapestry weavers using high-warp looms simply hang the cartoon behind the warp. Vertical tapestry looms often come with special cartoon bars for this purpose. If your high-warp loom does not have a cartoon bar, such a support is easy to make. It can be as simple as tying a string to each side of your loom. The cartoon can be draped over the bar or string and then secured.

TIP

The Joy and Sorrow of "Permanent" Markers

For years I have used Sharpie permanent markers to mark my warps. The standard ones I used to buy are no longer guaranteed to be water- or heat-proof. Sharpie now makes an industrial marker that is guaranteed to be waterfast and bleed-resistant up to 500°F (260°C). I recommend looking for a marker with similar guarantees.

If you weave at a fine sett with light colors, you may want to test the markers with a woven swatch or on some fabric first. Imagine weaving a large tapestry in very light colors. You put in months and months of work, and after you steam it, you notice there are black streaks in the light-colored areas. The marker you used on your warp bled when it was steamed. Though this is an unlikely occurrence for tapestries with fairly thick weft bundles (think 8 epi or wider setts), it would be unfortunate to ruin a tapestry in this way. So test marks first on a lightly colored piece of cotton fabric, let the marker dry, then wet it. Watch carefully to see if the marker bleeds.

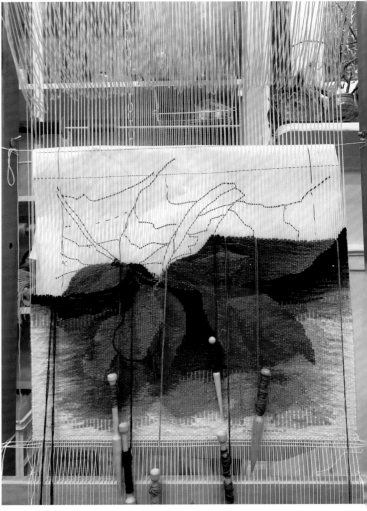

Tommye McClure Scanlin, *Fall Returns* (in progress). Cotton and hand-dyed wool, 20" × 17" (finished dimensions).
▲ *Tommye Scanlin has tied a string across the back of this Ashford tapestry loom and hung her cartoon over it for reference. Note that Scanlin does not mark the pattern on the warp but secures the cartoon by sewing it with long basting stitches to the parts of the tapestry that are woven. Some of these stitches are visible in this photo near the top of the weaving.*

13 Curve Appeal

In tapestry weaving, the warp and weft are in their most comfortable positions when they move at right angles to each other. This means that creating curves involves a little bit of illusion, because for right now, we want all the wefts to continue traveling perpendicular to the warp. Curves are just angles that change slope. In chapter 10 you learned to make the step patterns even so that the diagonal line created was straight. When making curves, you'll change the ratios of steps over and sequences stacked up to create a line that is not straight but curved.

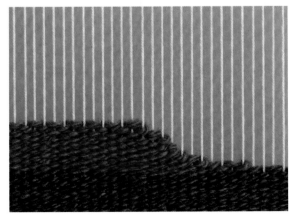

▲ *Stacking sequences to create a curve*

Weaving One Shape at a Time

Before you explore how to build curves so they look as smooth as possible, it's important to understand the difference between weaving tapestry shape by shape instead of line by line. For the most part, everything you've woven so far has been done a line at a time. You've filled in the whole warp from selvage to selvage before changing the shed and beating in your bubbles. This is an excellent way to learn meet and separate (see page 132), and in most cases, you can continue to weave this way going forward. But now that you know how to make a cartoon (see page 229) and are learning to make more shapes, you should know that you can also weave one shape at a time.

There are several reasons you may want to do this. In some cases, your chosen equipment may make weaving a shape at a time more efficient or more ergonomic. Some techniques, such as eccentric outlining (see page 253), require it. And some people find they perceive the shapes they're forming more accurately if they weave them separately. As you experiment with curves, we will compare weaving one shape at a time with weaving line by line.

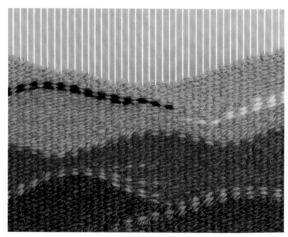

▲ *Building shapes one at a time is a common practice, especially on high-warp tapestry looms.*

Bottom to Top: Shape Order

In chapter 1 you learned that tapestry is built like a brick wall, from bottom to top. Each brick has to be supported by the bricks underneath. In tapestry, elements that come later can't be woven until the supporting fabric has been woven underneath it. This concept directly applies to weaving tapestry one shape at a time. You will never weave a shape in the middle of your warp with empty warps below it — unless you intend to leave that warp free for some reason. In that case, you will have to use some kind of knot to keep the weft from sliding down and filling the empty warps.

This means that there is an order in which shapes must be woven. All shapes or parts of shapes that are underneath other shapes have to be woven first. For example, in the diagram below, note that there is a gold shape (#4) extending over part of the pink shape (#3) underneath it. The bottom part of the pink shape has to be woven first or the gold shape will extend over open warps. However, the top part of the pink shape (#5) must be woven after the gold shape (#4) because the gold shape provides the support for the top part (#5) of the pink shape.

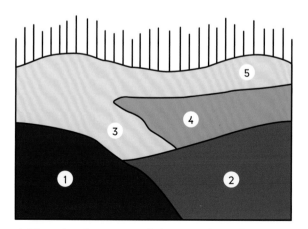

▲ *The order of weaving each shape is indicated by the numbers.*

Building Shapes versus Weaving Line by Line

There are several reasons why you might choose to build shapes one at a time versus weaving all the way across your warp in a line. Weavers have to make their own decisions about what works best for them.

Equipment. High- or low-warp beamed looms with reeds and beaters are great candidates for weaving line by line. As the reed in the beater is pulled forward, distorted warps in the reed indicate immediately that the tapestry is changing width. In addition, you can create a very uniform fabric because this sort of beater presses in the weft more evenly than a tapestry fork or bobbin. On the other hand, for people weaving on high-warp looms using bobbins, weaving a shape at a time is more efficient.

Bobbins. People who weave shape by shape very often use bobbins to organize their weft, put it through the shed, and tap it into place. When your tool does all of these things, you don't have to put it down until you change colors. This increases the efficiency of weaving one shape at a time.

Concentrating on one area at a time. Especially in larger pieces, working all the way across the weaving means you have to pay attention to many areas of a tapestry all at once. Some weavers like to make one or two forms at a time because they can focus more exclusively on them.

Ergonomics. When weaving a large tapestry, if you weave line by line you have to move your body along the loom as you put in each pick. Many weavers who work on large low-warp beamed looms solve this problem by raising the loom high enough so that they can stand at it and using locking treadles to keep the shed open. This allows them to walk along the loom as they weave. Sliding loom benches are another option. Weavers using high-warp beamed looms, however, must sit in front of the loom. For them, it would be difficult to weave all the way across a tapestry that's more than a couple feet wide without moving their body. In these cases, building shapes on the warp right in front of them makes sense.

Making and Using a Cartoon to Weave Curves

It is possible to weave vertical lines, square forms, and angles without a cartoon. But curves introduce the need for some guidance. Here you'll practice making a cartoon to guide you in weaving curves. I suggest you weave this cartoon twice. The first time, weave it line by line as you have been doing throughout the book so far. The second time, build up the shape underneath the curve first and then fill in the area above it. The two weavings should look the same if you followed the dots carefully and used the same cartoon. Either way of weaving curves is appropriate if the shapes are not going to be outlined, which you'll learn about in chapter 14.

After weaving the cartoon two times, with both approaches explained below, note how the experience differed each time. Was one way easier to make the shape than the other? Do the two weavings look the same or are they slightly different?

Setup

Enlarge the cartoon at right or draw a similar one on a piece of paper. It does not have to be exactly like my example. Make sure the drawing is approximately the same width as your warp.

Review the options for attaching the cartoon to your weaving as discussed on page 229. I suggest you align the cartoon behind your warp and attach it with one of the methods described. For this first example, I also recommend transferring the curve right onto your warp with a permanent marker. Make a dot on the warp every time the design line crosses it. Remember that warps can turn, so you may want to rotate the warp and mark all the way around it.

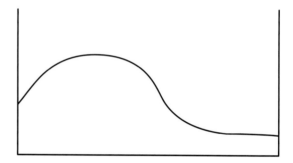

Weaving Line by Line

1. Choose two colors and wind two butterflies of each. If your warp is quite narrow, you can do this exercise with one butterfly of each color, but make sure they are moving in meet and separate (see page 132).

2. If you haven't yet marked the cartoon on your warp as indicated in the setup instructions, do so now.

3. Set your butterflies in as shown at the bottom of this diagram. There is a band of color (A) that goes along the entire bottom of the cartoon, so start two butterflies of yarn A in meet and separate and weave until you get to the cartoon line, where you'll start the second color (B).

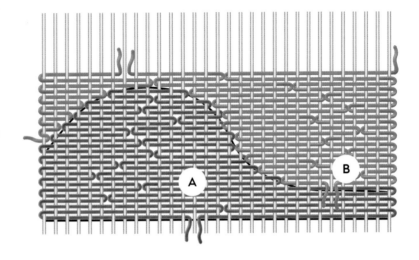

4. Enter the two butterflies of color B as indicated. At this point, the innermost butterfly of color A will weave just to the cartoon line, where the innermost butterfly from color B will meet it.

5. Continue having the innermost butterflies of each color meet along the cartoon line. The point where these relays meet is going to create the curve between the two colors.

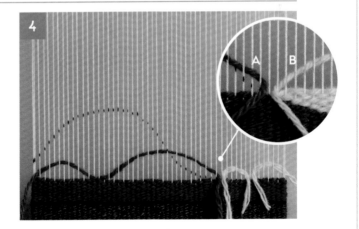

6. Add another butterfly of color B when you reach the point on the left side of the cartoon where color A starts to curve in. Make sure you're entering the new butterfly so it is working in meet and separate.

7. Splice together the two butterflies of color A when you get to the top of the color A hill shape, or if you don't have room, tuck the butterflies to the back of the weaving.

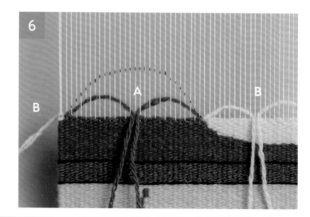

8. Continue weaving with the remaining three butterflies of color B in meet and separate above the hill shape to finish the cartoon. Splice two of the ends together and leave the last one as a tail.

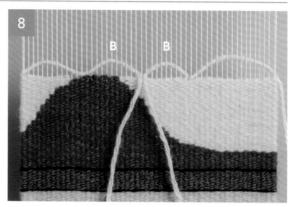

Weaving a Shape at a Time

Now you'll weave the same thing by building the hill shape first and filling in the rest of the area after the hill is woven.

1. Draw the same cartoon onto your warp again.

2. Make two butterflies of your hill color (A) and start them as shown at the bottom of the diagram on the right.

3. Weave back and forth in meet and separate, matching the edges of your woven shape to the cartoon line. Make sure the two butterflies forming the shape meet in random places so you don't create a slit. If you use two butterflies to weave this shape, you can splice them together when you get to the top.

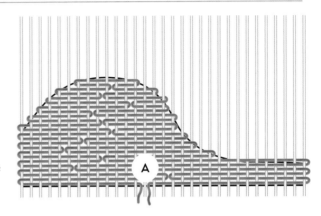

4. Fill in the spaces around your hill by starting two color B butterflies in the low spot on the right side of the cartoon. Weave in meet and separate, trying to match the number of sequences in each step. This is easiest to see by looking at the places where the weft returned at the edges of the shape. You can gently push the weft up to count the sequences (as shown in the inset), as this makes them easier to see. When you reach the top of the hill, let the two butterflies of color B rest.

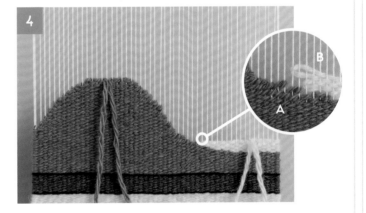

5. Enter one color B butterfly from the selvage at the low point on the left side of the cartoon. Make sure this butterfly is set up to weave in meet and separate with the butterfly next to it from the already-finished hill. To make sure you're doing this correctly, see Shapes in the Wrong Shed? on the next page. Continue filling in that area until you're back at the top of the hill.

6. Weave with the three remaining color B butterflies in meet and separate until you have completed your cartoon.

Shapes in the Wrong Shed?

When new tapestry weavers first attempt to weave one shape at a time, the thing that tends to confuse them the most is how to keep meet and separate working.

You *must* make sure that you are weaving adjacent color areas in meet and separate even if you are weaving them sequentially instead of at the same time, as you do when you weave line by line. If you don't weave shapes that are next to each other in meet and separate, you will not be able to move your butterflies over without putting two wefts in the same shed. As you build up shapes, you'll know something is in the wrong shed when there are two wefts going under the same warp as your fill-in weft moves over a step. The images below show how the weaving will look if the new butterfly is in the wrong shed and how it should look if it is correct.

Once you can recognize that you are placing two wefts in the same shed (sometimes you'll hear weavers say, "It doesn't weave"), fixing it is as simple as following the steps outlined on page 136. If you're just starting a new butterfly to make a new shape, reversing where the tail of the butterfly starts will fix the problem.

Tail Tip for Looms without Shedding Mechanisms

One way to quickly know which way to enter a new butterfly when building up shapes is to notice where the tails are in a particular shed. On a pipe loom, for example, you may notice that the tail from the shape next to the one you are about to start is on the right side of the shape. If you also know you started the shape in the shed held open by the shed rod or top of the loom, the weaving is telling you that in that open shed, the tail of the new shape has to start on the left or opposite side of the new shape. This will create meet and separate between adjacent shapes.

If you're using a loom with a shedding device like a Mirrix or a loom with treadles, the problem with this method is that both sheds look the same and you probably can't reliably remember in which shed the last shape started. In that case, using the other tips presented and learning to read your weaving will unravel the problem.

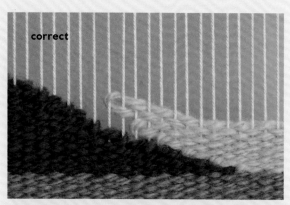

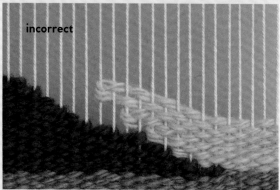

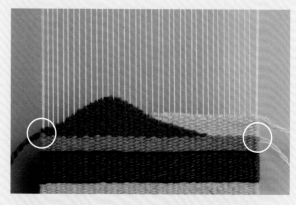

▲ *After weaving the darker teal hill shape with the tail started on the left selvage, start the lighter color on the right selvage to ensure meet and separate.*

Smoothing Out the Steps

There are several techniques you can use to make the illusion of a curve stronger to the viewer's eye. For example, you can outline shallow angles and curves (see page 254). In chapter 11 you learned about cutting off the corners of steps (see page 214), and you will use this method again later in this chapter to smooth out steeper steps. You also were introduced in chapter 10 to how helpful hill and valley threads are to smoothing out angles (see page 196), and you'll explore that more now.

Hill and Valley Threads with Shallow Curves

The hill and valley thread concepts that you learned about in relation to angles apply in the same way to curves. Remember that a hill thread creates a slightly higher step than a valley thread. If you can arrange your relays with the receding color on valley threads on the front of the weaving, you will maximize the smoothness of the line you are weaving.

This can result in making some judgment calls as you weave. Working all the relays of the receding butterfly on valley threads on the front means that you lose half of the choices of warps when creating your shapes. This is not always practical, and there will be plenty of times when you need to make the edge of a step occur on a hill thread. You will often have to decide between creating a more jagged line and making the shape look right. However, if you're weaving a shallow curve, paying attention to the hill and valley threads is the first technique to use to make curves appear smooth.

Weaving a Shallow Curve with Hill and Valley Threads

When you weave a shallow curve, you can either weave the curve line by line or build the cradle, or bottom part, of the curve first and then fill it in with the second color. The instructions below are for weaving line by line. If you want to weave one shape at a time, first weave the background color (A) up to the top of the curve and then fill in the central color (B) with two butterflies, matching the weft relays on each side of the curve. You'll fill in the remaining part of the background color (A) after weaving all of shape color (B). There are more specifics about how to weave a curved shape this way in the circles portion of this chapter (see page 248).

1. Draw a cartoon for a curve similar to the one on the right and mark it on your warp.

2. Start weaving with two butterflies of your color A in meet and separate (see page 132).

3. When you get to the shallow curve marked on your warp, bring your color A butterflies to the selvages.

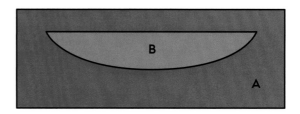

4. In the next shed, insert two butterflies of color B starting in the center. Bring them outward to the cartoon line on each side of the shape. Bring the color A butterflies to meet them. Shift the shed.

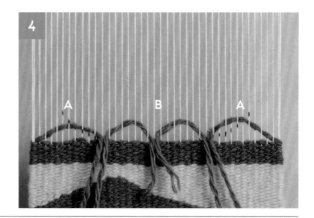

5. Look at the hill and valley threads. In this design, color A is the receding shape on each side of the curve. The relays in color A need to be made on valley warps, which means they will wrap the empty warp that came forward when you shifted the shed. Wrap that warp, then return the color A wefts to the selvages. You may not be exactly matching the cartoon to do this. Return the curve butterflies (color B) to meet somewhere inside the shape.

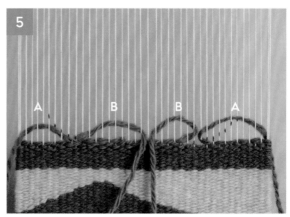

6. Continue to weave, approximating the cartoon as carefully as you can, while also making sure the background color always wraps a raised warp before returning to the selvage. This creates a valley thread in the receding color. Take care not to create a straight angle. It is tempting to simply back each background butterfly off by 2 warp threads to allow the turns on valley threads, but if you make the steps all the same, your form will have diagonal lines and not curves on the sides.

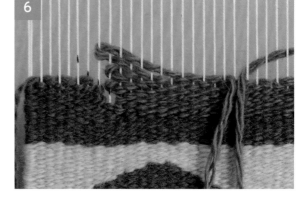

In this exercise you may have experienced the frustration of trying to make relays happen on valley threads and not being able to create your form the way you want. In a shape where the curve starts out quite flat and then gets steeper as it does on the left side of this example, it will at some point become impossible to use all valley threads to turn on. If you did that, you'd never get a steeper angle. You can see in the image above how I wove the left edge of the curve. The curve initially started out with smooth steps due to the background being on valley thread, but when the angle got steeper, I had to change the step pattern to every warp thread and then quickly to stacking up sequences on one warp.

Cutting Off the Corners

If you've forgotten how this technique works, refer to page 214. As any curve or angle gets steeper, this technique can help take a little visual bite out of the corner of the stairsteps created by vertically oriented lines. You'll practice using this technique in Weaving a Vertical Curve on the next page. But first I will explain a few visual tricks that you can use to make a curved vertically oriented line look smoother.

Making Curved Vertical Shapes

Curving vertical shapes are some of the most difficult forms to render accurately in tapestry weaving because there are only as many choices to place the weft as there are warps in an inch. If you are weaving at 8 epi, for example, there are only eight points in every inch where your weft can relay to make your image. You could simply follow the lines on your cartoon to create the curve, hoping that the design line and the warp intersections line up enough to give you a reasonably curvy line. But all too often the line on the cartoon can lead you astray.

When weaving a vertically oriented curve, it is important to realize that there is a long edge that is completely flat, as seen in line A below. It is tempting to make the line go over 1 more warp for a short distance, but this results in a small square jog that appears out of place in the smooth flow of the line.

In the diagram below, each of the columns on the graph paper represents 1 warp. You can vary the height of the steps, however, by stacking up different numbers of sequences along each warp.

Area A indicates the portion of the curve that needs to be straight. The desire to make that line look more curvy leads some weavers to try to add more steps to that portion of the design, but the curve will look smoother if it is just woven straight, stacking up sequences. Area B indicates a shallower portion of the curve. At the top of this curve you can see you are moving over by more than 1 warp on each step. If you can plan those moves so that the receding color is on a valley warp, the top portion of the curve will be smoother. Area C contains some steps that have more weft sequences stacked up. You could use the cutting-off-the-corners technique to make a couple of those steps smoother.

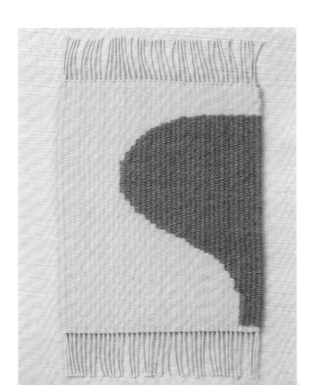

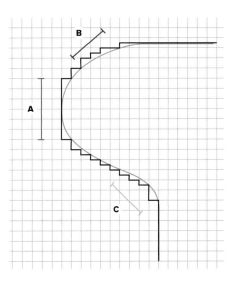

Weaving a Vertical Curve

To practice some vertical curves, start by drawing a cartoon with a curving vertical line; use the example below if you'd like. The directions that follow explain how to weave this curve in shapes rather than line by line.

Earlier in this chapter you learned that when weaving shape by shape, you must weave underlying shapes first. In this diagram, the first shape you must weave is #1. You can weave that shape all the way up to the red line before starting #2. When both colors have reached the red line in the cartoon, the color you wove in area #2 becomes the receding color (#3), and you must weave that before area #4, which you'll weave last.

1. Transfer your cartoon to your warp.

2. Weave area 1 of the diagram. Notice that the steepest part of that curve (C in the diagram on the previous page) contains several fairly steep steps. You'll stack multiple sequences up to reach the cartoon line before moving your wefts over.

3. Fill in area 2 with your second color. On the steps that are at least 2 weft sequences, you can use the cutting-off-the-corners technique (see page 214) to smooth out the steps slightly; however, if you get to a point where you only have 1 weft sequence in each step, you can no longer use this technique.

4. Finish the exercise by weaving area 3, then area 4.

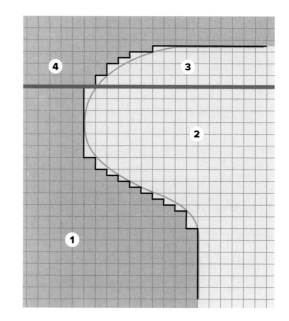

Make It Curve

Your curve may differ significantly from mine. As you're weaving it, keep in mind the following tips:

Make the vertical areas of curves absolutely straight for longer than you think you need to.

Use the cutting-off-the-corners technique when you fill in with the second color for steep steps with multiple weft relays stacked up.

Set up your weaving so that the receding color creates a valley thread at the weft relays to make a smoother line on the front for shallow angles.

Circles

In tapestry weaving it is very difficult to render circles in a way that makes them look perfect to the viewer. I often use circular-like forms in my work, but I usually do not attempt to make them look perfectly round. To make perfect-looking circles, you would need to make both smooth shallow angles at the bottom and the top and very even vertical curves at the sides. The transition from the low-angled curve to the vertical curve is very quick. Despite my entreaties to give up perfect circles, many of my students really want to try them. If that is true for you, here are some tips.

DIVIDE THE CIRCLE INTO QUADRANTS. Realize that a full third of the diameter of the circle's top, bottom, and sides should be straight, as seen in the diagram at right. This is the single most important tip for making round-looking circles.

MATCH SIDE TO SIDE AND TOP TO BOTTOM. All four quadrants should have the same step patterns. This means you'll be most successful if you count sequences and mirror them when you weave the other quadrants.

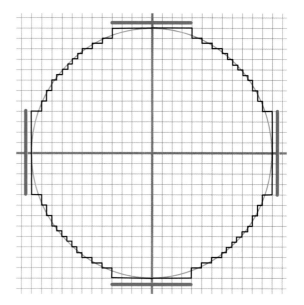

TIP

Resist Making Extra Tabs!

When you are weaving vertical images, if you do not actually make the parts of the curve that should be the straightest fully straight, little square bits protrude from the curve. This makes the weaving look like it has tabs. The furthest extent of your curve should be the longest straight portion of your weaving. This little heart would look better without the tabs on each side.

Weaving a Circle

One way to weave a circle is to form the cradle for the bottom of it first, fill in the cradle, weave the top half of the circle, then fill in the background color last.

1. Choose two colors for your circle. Make two butterflies of the background color (A) and one or two butterflies for the circle color (B). Make a cartoon for your circle by tracing a round object or using a drawing compass.

2. With color A, weave a base for your circle in meet and separate (see page 132).

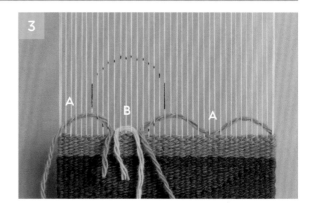

3. When the base is woven, attach your cartoon with the bottom of the circle resting on the line of weaving. Mark the circle onto your warp with a permanent marker. Color B is shown in the photo to remind you to set up the A butterflies in meet and separate.

4. Following the dots on the cartoon as a preliminary guide but matching the steps on each side of the circle, weave the two outside parts of the circle's cradle at the same time. Weave until you reach the point where the circle starts to curve back in again. You will find that your two cradle butterflies are weaving in the same direction in the same shed. The circle butterfly that goes between them will be moving in the opposite direction, completing your meet and separate correctly.

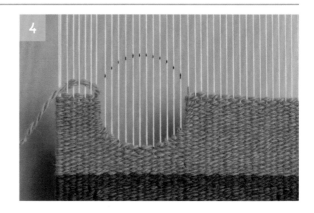

5. Fill in the cradle with the circle color (B) by starting it as indicated in image 3. The three butterflies should be in meet and separate even though they are not all in a line at this point. You can prove this to yourself by opening the shed all the way across with your shedding mechanism or a shed stick, then verifying that when the three butterflies are loose in the shed, they are moving in opposition to each other.

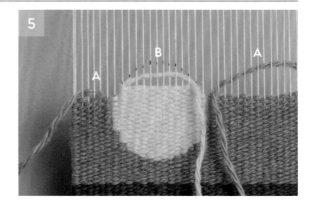

6. Finish weaving the rest of the circle.

7. Fill in the background color around the circle, matching the number of sequences in each step as you go. Your two A butterflies will not be in meet and separate when the circle butterfly drops out. You can either drop one of the A butterflies and continue weaving with just one butterfly above the circle or fix your shedding problem with one of the techniques on page 136.

14 Outlining

Tapestry is most often woven so that the weft travels perpendicular to the warp. However, there are times when you may want to include an outline in your weaving either to smooth out the edge of a shape or to serve as a border between two forms. You can do this by weaving around the edges of forms. When the weft does not travel perpendicular to the warp in this manner, it is called eccentric weaving. The split weft technique is another way to create a crisp line between two shapes.

Weaving Eccentrically

Many weavers find weaving eccentrically attractive because it frees them from the grid: they want to be able to make weft yarns go in any direction and make curves that aren't stepped. The drawback of weaving eccentrically is that as soon as the weft leaves its perpendicularity to the warp, it starts to behave badly. Any amount of eccentric weaving will pull the warp out of alignment. If the eccentric bit is limited to a few sequences, you'll never notice this. But if you weave eccentrically for long distances, the warps will shift to try to regain their perpendicular alignment to the weft.

There are many tapestry artists who use the eccentric distortion of the fabric intentionally, as Silvia Heyden does in her tapestry *Preludium*, shown on the next page. Weavers who employ wedge weave (see next page) in their work manage eccentric weaving in a special way while maintaining a mostly flat fabric. If you want the surface of your tapestry to remain flat, it is best to limit the use of eccentric weaving to outlines of just a sequence or two.

Silvia Heyden, *Preludium*, 2005.
Linen, 39" × 45".
◀ *Tapestry woven with eccentric wefts causes the buckles in the fabric, which are intentional in this case.*

Wedge Weave

Woven completely eccentrically, wedge weave is balanced so it forms characteristic scallops at the selvages. The scallops are formed because the weft is weaving in a non-perpendicular way to the warp, which pulls the warp out of alignment. But because this weave pattern is symmetrical, the warp is then pulled the other direction when the pattern shifts, and the fabric remains flat.

Connie Lippert, *Acer rubrum*, 2006.
Linen and wool, 25" × 24".
▶ *Connie Lippert is a master of wedge weaving. This piece demonstrates the symmetrical diagonal lines and the scalloped edges characteristic of this style. It was woven sideways, so the scallops characteristic of wedge weave appear on the top and bottom of the piece.*

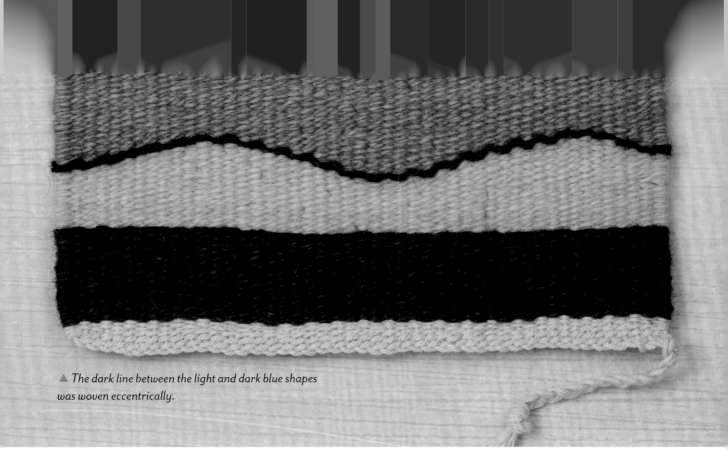

▲ *The dark line between the light and dark blue shapes was woven eccentrically.*

Eccentric Outlines

In chapter 13 you learned about building up shapes and which shape has to be woven before another to make a structurally sound fabric. To do an eccentric outline of a shape, you have to weave the shape you will outline before you can outline it. That seems kind of obvious, but it means that the contour of the outline is determined by the underlying shape.

The first thing to consider is that the outlined shapes have to be fairly horizontal in nature. When you try to outline shapes that have steeper slopes, the weft of the outline has to float from one warp to the next, as seen at right. The steeper the angle is, the longer those floats are, and pretty soon the "outline" looks as if you have a bunch of floats on the surface of your fabric. The angle that can be outlined without looking like floats depends somewhat on your weft size and warp spacing, but generally, angles of 30 degrees or less can be effectively and smoothly outlined.

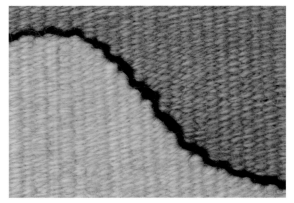

▲ *Notice the outline of a steep-angled curve looks like floats or errors on the surface of the weaving.*

When weaving eccentrically, the weft also has to travel a lot farther than it would if you were weaving perpendicular to the warp. This means you'll have to put more weft into the outline picks than you put into your regular weaving, which can make bubbling tricky.

Outlining a Shallow Curve

As you practice creating a solid outline in a contrasting color over a shallow curve, remember that it takes 2 picks of weaving to create a solid line. If you weave only 1 pick, your outline will be dotted. Make sure you weave the underlying shape first before applying the outline.

1. Weave a low-angled hill for your first shape. Make the slope of the angle step by 2 warps or more for each sequence.

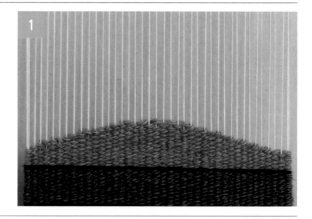

2. For your outline color, cut a piece of yarn that's long enough to weave 2 picks along the edge of your shape plus some extra for tails and bubbling.

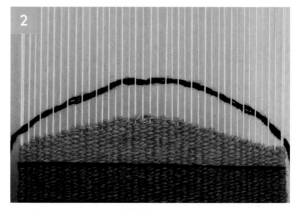

3. Lay your outline color over the curve, with the center of the piece of yarn in the middle of the curve. Getting enough weft into an eccentric outline without creating puffs of weft yarn on the surface is tricky, so don't be surprised if it takes a few tries to get this right. One trick is to leave the shed open as you lay the yarn in, gently pulling more weft into the space as you beat a little at a time. You can also do this with your fingers pinching the weft and index finger stuck through the warp, pushing it down into place.

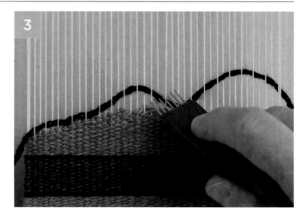

4. Shift the shed and tap the weft into place. Bring the two tails of the outline yarn back together and, if you have a fairly flat top to your curve, splice the ends together. Otherwise tuck the tails to the back.

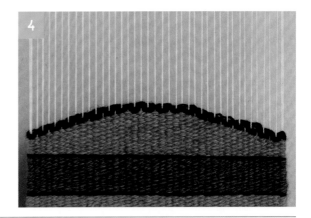

5. Fill in the color on top of the curve as discussed in Weaving a Shape at a Time on page 241.

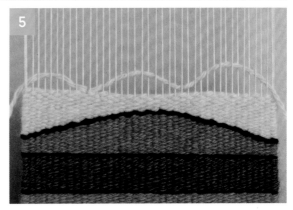

Fixing Shedding Problems

The meet-and-separate system of wefts moving in opposing directions in the same shed allows you to move colors around wherever you want in tapestry weaving, but this gets thrown off quite easily when you begin weaving shapes. As you add shapes or they move over one another or are completed and butterflies drop out, you can find yourself constantly struggling to keep your wefts in the correct shed. This is a normal part of tapestry weaving! You learned some ways to fix the shed in chapter 6. Using an eccentric outline is another way to fix shedding problems for low angles or curves while also smoothing out the steps in the

form. This accomplishes the same thing as using a half-pass to shift the shed, but it is done at an angle, and often you can continue weaving with the same butterfly.

In the diagram on the next page, the blue shape was woven before the red shape. For an elegant way to both smooth out the steps of the blue line and shift the shed so that the red shape can weave next to it, start the tail of the red butterfly at the top of the blue shape, then weave down the side and across the bottom of the red shape in the same shed. When the shed is shifted and the red butterfly reverses direction, the edge of the interface with the blue shape will be in the correct shed.

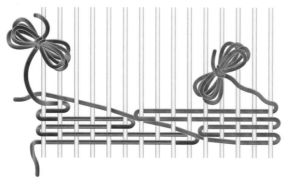

▲ *This diagram shows the use of an eccentric outline over the edge of the blue shape to shift the shed so that the red shape can be woven next to it.*

Another shedding problem that is common and can be fixed with an eccentric outline happens when building hill-shaped forms. In Outlining a Shallow Curve on page 254, you wove a shallow curve with two butterflies. Your outline should have been easy to weave exactly in the way I described without shedding problems. However, if you weave that curve with one butterfly, you'll find that half of the hill is in one shed and half is in the other. If you just lay an outline weft over the curve in this situation, half of the curve will weave normally, but the other half will have two wefts in each shed, resulting in lice along that half of the shape. To fully outline this shape, shift the shed on half of the hill by starting the weaving where the shedding problem occurs, weaving to the bottom of the hill, shifting the shed and weaving all the way across the top, then shifting again and ending the outline sequence in the center where you started the first butterfly.

Shifting the Shed with an Eccentric Weft

Here you'll practice with an eccentric outline of a different color, but remember that the eccentric weft can be hidden by making it the same color as one of the forms you're weaving. Of course, eccentric outlines are not practical if your curves are too steep, so keep the design to a low-profile hill or curve. This procedure also works when filling in a cradle, as you did in the circles section of chapter 13.

1. Weave a simple hill shape with shallow curves using one butterfly.

2. Open your shed across the top of the shape and look to see whether the two sides of your hill are in the same shed or two different sheds. Notice that the warps on the right side of the shed stick are ready to weave, but the warps on the left side are in the wrong shed.

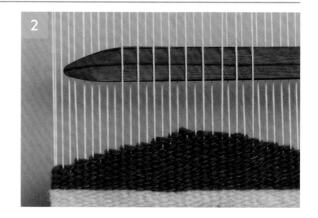

3. Choose an outline color that contrasts with your hill form. With your shed still open, identify which side of the hill is ready to be woven. Start the tail of the butterfly at the top of the shape and weave down that side.

4. Shift the shed, then return the butterfly up and over the entire shape to the other side.

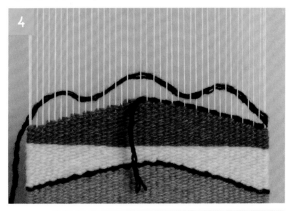

5. Shift the shed again and return the outline butterfly to the top of the shape where you started. End the butterfly here.

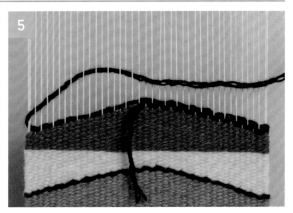

Split Weft

Now that you have some experience outlining shapes, I'm going to show you a little bit of magic. The woven structure of tapestry creates a wavy line in the direction that the weft is traveling. This is because the weft creates hills and valleys as it travels over and under each warp. Where the weft goes *under* a warp to create a valley thread on one pick, it will go *over* that warp and create a hill thread on the next pick. The hill sinks into the previous valley a little bit, creating the characteristic wavy line shown in the top diagram below.

The split weft technique lets you straighten out that line and make the border between two colors very crisp and straight. If you divide in half the rice-shaped bits of weft across one pick of weaving, as seen in the bottom diagram below, you can make the color change happen in the middle of the pick, straightening out the line where the colors change. To do this you'll have to be able to divide your weft in half. If you're using a single strand of a 1-ply yarn at a time, this technique is not possible. However, if your weft is made of 2 or more plies and you can divide them, or if you are using multiple strands of weft bundled together, you can do the split weft technique.

The secret to this technique is that two colors are woven in the same pick. Half the weft in that pick will be the color you've been weaving, and half will be the new color. The weaving below demonstrates the difference between a horizontal line using the split weft technique and one without. This technique can be applied to straight horizontal lines or to any shallow curve or angle you could outline eccentrically.

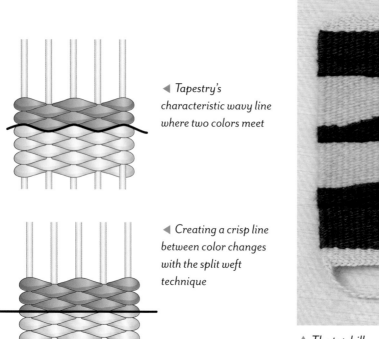

◄ *Tapestry's characteristic wavy line where two colors meet*

◄ *Creating a crisp line between color changes with the split weft technique*

▲ *The top hill was woven without the split weft technique. The bottom hill was woven in the same way, but with a split-weft outline added.*

Making an Outline Using Split Weft

The split weft technique can be used in any instance you'd be able to use an eccentric outline, including over any shallow angle or curve.

1. Weave a solid area of one color.

2. Split your weft in half or use a portion of your weft bundle that is approximately half the size of your regular bundle; it doesn't have to be exact. For example if you are using three yarns together, use one strand of one color and two of the other. If you're using a strong 2-ply yarn, such as Harrisville Highland, you can use a fishing swivel to unply the yarn (see the next page).

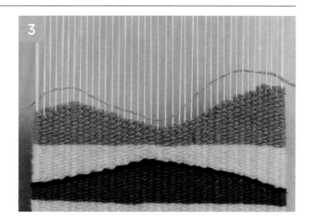

3. Lay the half-size piece of the color you were weaving with into the next shed. Bubble as you usually would and tap this into place. Do not shift the shed.

4. *In the same shed*, lay the half-size piece of the second color on top, bubble normally, and tap it into place. Shift your shed. Note that in the image, the gold yarn is not yet beat in for demonstration purposes.

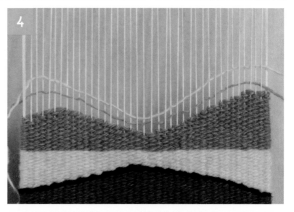

5. Continue weaving with the new color. Putting in only 1 pick of additional weaving to accomplish the split weft technique will change your shedding. If you are using it all the way across your weaving as shown here, this doesn't matter. However, in most cases it means that the shapes surrounding the one you just outlined will now be in the wrong shed. To fix this you'll need to add an extra piece of the second color in the next shed to bring everything back to the way it was before you put in the one pick of split weft outline.

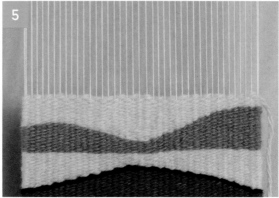

NOTE: It is important that the two half-size lengths of weft are placed in the same shed. If you shift the shed between the two colors, even though the weft is about half the normal size, you will not see the straight-line effect. As a result, this technique creates lots of tails. Those can be worked in later with a needle.

Swivel Technique to Unply Yarn

Some worsted weight 2-ply yarns, such as Harrisville Highland, have strong enough individual plies that you can take the plies apart and recombine them to create a yarn with 2 different-colored plies. This is a great way to take apart the plies when you're doing the split weft technique explained on page 258. It also allows you to recombine two different colors of weft for a kind of weft bundling (see page 49). I use welded-ring ball bearing fishing swivels in size 5 or 6 for this. The swivel allows the twist to travel out of the yarn as you pull the plies apart. It is easiest to start this procedure with 2-yard or shorter lengths of yarn. You cannot ply yarn together with a swivel.

1. Use warp to attach the swivel to something sturdy like a doorknob or tie it to a heavy piece of furniture.

2. Cut a piece of yarn 1–2 yards long. If you're going to combine two colors, cut two pieces the same length, one of each color.

3. Use a slip knot (see page 282) to tie one end of one piece of yarn to the free end of the swivel.

4. Walk to the end of your yarn and separate the 2 plies.

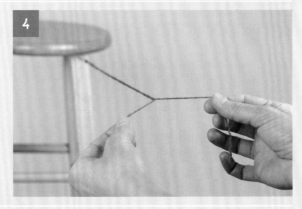

5. Using gentle pressure on the yarn, pull the two pieces apart to encourage the swivel to turn. As the plies untwist, pinch sequential pieces of the yarn between your index finger and thumb. You'll be gathering little loops of yarn in the palms of both hands.

6. When you have unplied the whole piece of yarn, pull the end of the slip knot to release the yarn from the swivel. Lay the two bundles of unplied yarn down far enough away from each other that they won't become tangled. If you're unplying another color, do that now. After unplying, you'll have four bundles of yarn, 2 plies of each color.

▲ *If you're going to put two different-colored plies back together, you must do this within about 10 minutes of unplying them. The yarn has memory and, if done soon enough, will retwist with a ply of the same kind of yarn. But if the unplied yarn sits around too long, the memory is lost.*

7. To re-ply the yarn with two different colors, match the ends of the 2 plies and pinch them in your left hand. Hold the two bundles of yarn loosely in your right hand. While pinching the two yarns together with your right hand, drop the end you're currently holding in your left hand and allow twist to reenter the yarn.

8. Run your left hand down the 2 plies that are dangling to encourage them to twist back together.

9. Pull out another length of the 2 plies, allow the yarn to dangle and twist together. Continue this procedure until the 2 plies have retwisted and you have a piece of yarn with 2 different-colored plies.

15 Finishing Up

After you finish the body of your tapestry and have added the header at the top and some waste yarn, you can take the tapestry off the loom. At this point, however, you're not quite finished; there is still work to be done. You must clean the wool fuzz from the tapestry, then finish the tails and slits. The tapestry also needs to be steamed and prepared for installation.

Final Cleanup

Before cutting the warps to release your tapestry from the loom, remember that you planned some extra warp for whatever finishing technique you are going to use (see chapter 6). First loosen the tension on your loom; this keeps the warp from springing back violently and will ensure your tapestry remains square. Making sure that you leave enough extra warp for your planned finishing technique, cut the warps and release the tapestry from the loom. Then set it aside and let it rest for a day or two. This allows all the fibers to relax after being under high tension for so long.

When you are ready to prepare the tapestry for display, follow these steps:

1. **VACUUM.** You may find that your tapestry has wool particles or other debris clinging to it. I find that wool dust is most evident on and around my large floor looms, but even a tapestry on a small loom can collect particles. I use a regular household vacuum with a clean, nonbrush attachment on the end of a wand. *Do not run a floor vacuum over your tapestry*; the beater brushes meant to pull dirt out of rugs will

▲ *Use a dedicated attachment to vacuum your tapestries.*

▲ *To hide weft ends on the back of the tapestry, unply the yarn (A), then put each ply on a needle and sew it up or down the adjacent warps (B).*

destroy your weaving. Purchase or clean a dedicated vacuum attachment for tapestry weaving or get a small handheld vacuum that you use only for your tapestries. Mark it as your tapestry vacuum attachment and keep it somewhere it will not be used for household dirt. With the tapestry flat on a table, run the vacuum attachment over it on both sides to remove any accumulated debris. You may need to vacuum it again prior to steaming.

2. **MANAGE THE WEFT TAILS.** I like my tapestries to have clean backs. After vacuuming, I spend some time stitching in all the tails. I divide the weft bundle or 2-ply yarn and stitch part of it up the warp channel and the other part down the same channel or an adjacent one. How you do this depends on what kind of yarn you use. If you use very fat singles yarn that cannot be divided, leave your tails hanging. Stitching them in will create distortion on the surface of your weaving. If you use a plied yarn, unply it (A) and stitch the plies in separately (B). If you use a weft bundle with multiple singles, you may be able to stitch several singles in together depending on how thin they are.

3. **SEW SLITS AND FIX IRREGULARITIES.** If you did not sew your slits while the piece was on the loom, do so now. If you adjusted the warp tension at any point by pulling out a loop of warp and pinning it to the tapestry (see Fixing Uneven Warp Tension on page 159), work that loop of warp out to the nearest selvage now as shown on the next page. Also, if there are slight irregularities in the corners of the work — perhaps one corner sank at the beginning or end — you can gently adjust the wefts on the warp at this point if you used twining instead of knots at the beginning and end. Do not try to drastically adjust the shape of the tapestry off the loom, as this can pull it permanently out of shape; only minor shape adjustments can be made.

▲ *A loop of warp in the center of the tapestry is being worked to the edge. The loop was created to fix uneven warp tension while weaving.*

4. HEM. Use whatever method you want to finish your hems now. I cover various ways to do this starting on the next page.

5. STEAM. The tapestry is steamed before the final knots are tied because this allows the warp and weft to shrink freely without being distorted by the finishing. Lay the tapestry flat on a table. Before you begin steaming your piece, make sure the surface under your tapestry is heat and water resistant. Apply steam liberally to the entire piece; you will be able to see the slight bubbles that happen in the weaving flatten out with the steam. If necessary, you can steam some areas more heavily than others. For example, if part of the tapestry is wider than other parts, you can steam the wider parts more heavily to

try to get those fibers to shrink more than the rest of the piece. Because the tapestry needs to be lying flat, clothes steamers that must remain upright while steaming will not work. I use a clothes steamer with a wand attachment.

Allow the tapestry to dry overnight on the table. In the morning, look at it from the side at eye level. If there are remaining buckles in the fabric, steam those areas again to see if you can flatten them out. Allow the tapestry to dry again before moving it.

TEMPERATURE CAUTION: Keep track of what kinds of fibers you used in a piece. You cannot decrease the temperature of a steamer, so if you used fibers that cannot withstand high temperatures like cotton and wool can, you should use an iron with a lower temperature setting.

IRON ALTERNATIVE. Many people do not have a clothes steamer and don't want to purchase one. A clothes iron with a steam feature will do the job almost as well, especially for smaller tapestries. The main advantage of a steamer over an iron is that the steamer does not have to touch the tapestry. It is tempting to put the iron on the surface of the tapestry, but pressing the iron into the tapestry will flatten the ribs and change the character of the work. You should hover the iron above the work, and if you want to steam the fibers more, use a damp pressing cloth.

Blocking

I hear people use the word *blocking* a lot in relation to tapestry weaving. Blocking is done in knitting projects and refers to washing the object, arranging it in the desired shape and dimensions, and letting it dry. That is basically what we do when steaming a tapestry, so in that sense, I do block my work. But if "blocking" to you means soaking the piece, nailing the edges of the tapestry to boards, then letting it dry, I do not do that to my tapestries. I prefer to control issues with selvages and weft tension in the weaving so that the finished work is nearly square. Remember that if you aggressively block a tapestry with nails, it will eventually resume its original shape, especially if it gets wet or is hung in a humid environment.

Shrinkage Considerations

Tapestries benefit from a good steaming to flatten out inconsistencies in the weaving and to allow the fibers to bloom a little bit. Of course, the high heat and moisture of steaming also causes wool and cotton fibers to shrink a bit. This has the advantage of making the tapestry much flatter. However, if you planned a form to be a certain number of inches high, especially in the warp direction, that form will get shorter during steaming. Cotton warp will shrink more than wool weft. The percentage of shrinkage is greater in the direction the warp runs than the weft direction.

The extent of the fabric shrinkage depends on many factors. Establish a baseline for yourself by carefully measuring the length and width of your first tapestry samples before and after steaming. In future projects with those materials, you can correct for the shrinkage by weaving your forms a little higher.

If you use materials other than cotton and wool for warp and weft, I recommend testing them in a sample weaving before exposing a completed tapestry to high heat and moisture with steaming.

Finishing Tapestries with Hemmed Headers

If you use the hemmed header with the soumak line fold (see page 122), follow these steps to complete the finishing. To hang a tapestry with hemmed header, see page 275.

Secure the Warp Ends

After the steamed tapestry has dried, tie the knots in the warp to secure the ends. I use a half Damascus knot (see page 281) to secure the warp ends. The benefit of this knot is that it turns the warp ends toward the back of the tapestry.

1. Place the tapestry facedown on a table. It helps to place a weight on top of the piece to keep it from moving.

2. Carefully unravel some of the waste yarn holding the tapestry together at both the top and the bottom of the piece. To do this, I carefully cut it every 3"–4" between the warps and pull it out in pieces. Do not cut a warp! If the piece is very wide, it can be helpful to leave the last few sequences of waste until you are ready to tie the half Damascus knots to make sure the twining and header do not slide down your warp.

3. Tie half Damascus knots from one warp edge to the other. After the knots are tied all the way across, work the last 3 warps up into the hem with a needle to secure the line of knots, as shown at right. At this point, the warps will be folded back over the tapestry.

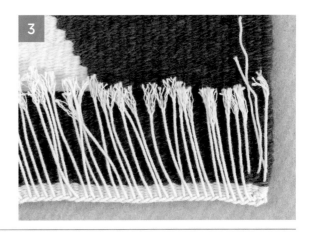

4. Secure the warps to the hem using one of the following methods: With either a sewing machine or by hand, go across the warps twice using a straight stitch, making sure they are all held down, as shown at right. Alternatively, tie another row of half Damascus knots.

5. Trim off the warp ends, leaving only ⅛"–¼" beyond the stitches. The warp ends should easily fold into the narrow hem this header creates.

Attach the Velcro and Twill Tapes

After securing the warps, you are ready to prepare the top of the tapestry for hanging with Velcro and the bottom with a hem. For the top, I stitch Velcro to heavy cotton twill tape. I like having the twill tape behind the Velcro to keep the plastic parts of the Velcro from touching the tapestry. Twill tape is also easier to hand-sew than Velcro is, and the last bit of stitching must be done by hand, regardless of whether you use a sewing machine for the rest.

For the Top

1. Cut a piece of twill tape about 1" longer than the width of the tapestry so you can fold the ends under. I often use pinking shears to cut the twill tape so it does not unravel.

2. Cut a piece of the fuzzy side of the Velcro about ¼" shorter than the width of your tapestry. Stitch the Velcro to the center of the twill tape. *Take care not to stitch the rough hook side of the Velcro to your tapestry.* Instead, the rough side of the Velcro will go on your hanging bar. This will prevent it from catching and damaging the tapestry when you roll it for storage.

3. Stitch the Velcro/twill-tape band to the warp-as-weft portion of the tapestry, turning under the ends of the twill tape as you stitch. Using my sewing machine, I stitch across once with a straight stitch then use a zigzag stitch to nicely tack down the top of the twill tape. This second line of stitching is aesthetic and is not necessary if you do not have a sewing machine.

4. Using your steaming method again, make a crisp, firm fold in the hem along the soumak line before stitching down the end of the twill tape. If you are using an iron, it's okay to gently press the tip of the iron to the edge of the hem, or you can hover close to the hem with the steaming iron and then press the edge flat with a towel (don't burn your fingers!). Allow the folds to dry completely.

   NOTE: It helps to use a metal ruler (or something else heat resistant) in the fold to keep the corners from pulling in, especially if the tapestry is small. On large tapestries, I lightly pin the fold down and only steam the very edge of the fold. Keep the steam away from the pins; otherwise, this steams the distortion from the pins into the tapestry.

5. After the hem is dry, hand-stitch the twill tape to the back of the tapestry. Take care that the needle does not go to the front of the work; you do not want the stitches to show on the front of the tapestry. At the top of the tapestry, catch a warp thread every couple stitches. The weight of the tapestry will rest on this hem, and you don't want the stitching to come undone.

For the Bottom

Follow steps 1–4 without adding the Velcro (skip step 2). You may want to steam the hems from the front of the tapestry one last time after all the stitching is done.

▲ *The stitching in this photo is done with white thread for demonstration purposes. I would normally stitch on black twill tape with black thread.*

VARIATION

Hanging a Tapestry Sideways

If you wove your tapestry with the design turned sideways, follow the instructions above to make your hems without adding any Velcro. Instead, you will add the Velcro hanger to the side that will be the top of the tapestry, along the selvage. Prepare a third piece of twill tape 1" longer than the top selvage of the tapestry. Machine-stitch the Velcro to the center of the third piece of twill tape. Attach this twill tape/Velcro strip to the top of the tapestry by hand-stitching all four sides.

Finishing Non-Hemmed Tapestries

If you've planned a header that does not have a hem, follow the same steps to clean up the work but instead of making a hem, finish with fringe, knots, braids, or other finishing or hanging methods.

Fringe and Knotted Edges: Warp That Shows

If your tapestry began with double half-hitch knots that are holding firmly, you can finish your tapestry by simply cutting your fringe straight and letting it hang. You can do the same thing at the top of the piece, allowing the fringe to fold over the front or back of the tapestry.

If you did not use double half hitches at the beginning and end of your piece, you can use overhand knots (see page 282) as a finishing technique. To do so, tie at least 2 warps together. These knots are difficult to tie if your warps are shorter than a couple inches; use a needle inserted in the overhand knot to place the knot close to the beginning of the weaving.

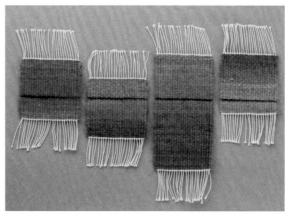

▲ *Four tiny tapestries with double half-hitch headers. I cut the fringe straight using a metal ruler and rotary cutter.*

Braided Edge

This edge treatment is popular with small-format works. It is tidy and does not require a hem. The more warps you involve in each step of the braid, the wider the braided edge will be. In the directions below you will make a braid with 5 warps, which allows you to go over the 1st warp, under the 2nd, over the 3rd, and under the 4th and last. You can use different configurations if you'd like, but the tail you're currently braiding has to go under the last thread in the group.

To practice, start the braid on the left side of the tapestry. Because you do the braid from the back, the tail of the braid will be on the left side of the finished tapestry. If you want the braid tail on the other side, start from the right side. The warp that is currently weaving will always end by going under the last warp in the group.

1. Put the tapestry facedown on a table and place a weight on it so that it does not move. Separate the 5 edge warps on the left side of your tapestry. Weave the leftmost warp over and under to the edge of the set.

2. Pick up the next warp to the right so you are again holding 5 warp threads.

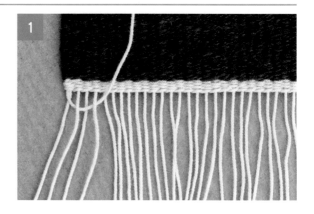

3. Weave the leftmost warp over and under the 4 warps.

4. Repeat steps 2 and 3 until your braid extends across the warp.

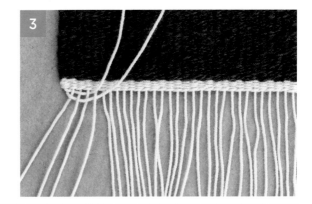

5. Finish by braiding the remaining warps in a three-strand braid and tie an overhand knot (see page 282) at the end.

6. Stitch across the warps to secure, then trim the ends.

▶ *This process results in the warp ends turning toward the back of the tapestry. You can secure them with some hand stitching, or you can stitch them down with a sewing machine along the edge between the braid and the tapestry weft. It is best to trim the warp ends within ¼"–½" of machine stitching or 1" from hand-stitching to keep them from flopping over and showing when the tapestry is displayed.*

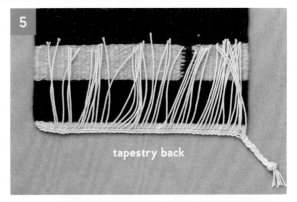

tapestry back

tapestry front

▲ *When I got to the end, I incorporated 1 more warp thread into the braid so that each of the three groups of the braid contained two strands.*

Preparing a Tapestry for Display

Tapestries can be displayed many ways. Small-format works benefit from being mounted on a larger surface and then framed. This gives them a greater presence than they might have if they were attached to the wall in their small form. You have several options for hanging larger tapestries. On page 275 I explain how I hang my larger works from invisible wooden bars with Velcro. Regardless of which method you choose, turn to page 276 for a list of necessary supplies.

Mounting Smaller Works

Small pieces can get lost when hung on a wall by themselves. Attaching them to a larger surface enhances their presence in a room. This is called mounting, and it is sometimes done with much larger pieces as well. The mounted tapestry can then be conventionally framed. I do not like to see tapestries behind glass. It not only makes them difficult to see, but if moisture is present, this may also cause the fibers to degrade. A tapestry mount could be the same size as the tapestry itself, but most often the stretcher bars I refer to in the instructions below are a couple inches to a foot larger than the dimensions of the weaving. The added surface around the tapestry helps frame the work and sets it apart from the wall on which it is displayed.

There are as many ways to mount tapestries as there are tapestry artists, but a popular method is to use the bars on which painters stretch their canvases. A neutral fabric is stretched over the frames, and the tapestry is stitched to it. The disadvantage of using stretcher bars is that if the tapestry is not well cared for at shows or in storage, anything leaning against the unsupported fabric and tapestry can cause the backing to stretch. Of course, the staples holding the fabric to the stretcher bars can be removed and the fabric re-stretched. But if the possibility of stretch in the backing concerns you, wrap the fabric around a solid acid-free foam core or archival board instead. Once you have completed your chosen mounting method, it can be framed in any way you prefer, or it may be hung on the wall just like this.

1. Assemble four stretcher bars. Use a carpenter's square, a quilt ruler, or the edge of a book to make sure that the frame is square. Once it is square, staple the corners so it cannot wiggle out of square while you work with it.

2. Cut a piece of flannel or cotton quilt batting larger than your frame. All four edges need to be able to wrap around the frame and be stapled securely to the back.

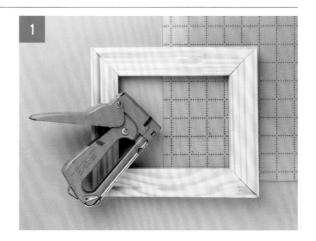

3. Fold one side over the frame and staple evenly along that edge. Move to the opposite edge and, while stretching the batting very lightly so it is not loose, staple that side down. Repeat on the other two sides.

4. Trim off the corners of the batting without folding. If needed, staple the edges again to secure the cut edges.

5. Cut a piece of the fabric on which you will display the tapestry. Make sure it is sufficiently large to wrap around the frame and cover the batting.

6. Staple on the fabric as you did the batting. Make sure that the fabric is stretched somewhat tightly. If the grain of the fabric is obvious, make sure it is lined up with the edges of the frame.

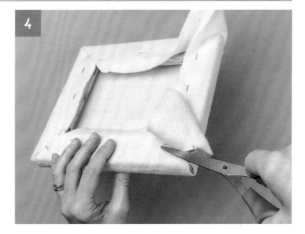

7. The corners of the fabric will need special treatment. Fold the side of the fabric so it lies against the top and staple it down. Fold the top flap over and staple it down on top of the first fold.

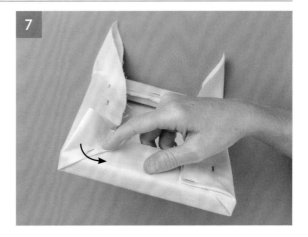

8. Loosely stitch the tapestry to the front of the mount. This is called basting and consists of long stitches that will be removed later. Sew the basting stitches straight through the tapestry and the fabric of the mount, but be careful to not pierce a warp while you do this. In the photograph for step 9, the long, loose basting stitches are white.

9. Stitch the tapestry more securely to the mount. Do this very carefully around the edges of the tapestry, or bring the needle right up through the center of the piece around a warp and down again, ensuring that you do not pierce a warp and that the sewing thread is hidden by the wefts. If the piece is small, stitching around the edges is enough. If the piece is larger, you may want to make some center stitches to support the piece. Take care not to pull stitches too tightly, which may make a visible dimple in the tapestry.

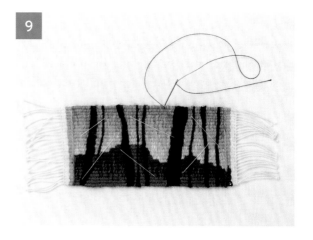

9

Optional Backing and Hanging

You can cover the back of the mount with another piece of fabric by either stapling it on or stitching it around the edges.

You can nail a toothed picture hanger to the back of the top bar of the frame or attach screw eyes on each side and a picture wire.

Tommye McClure Scanlin, *Hickory*, 2015.
Wool and linen, 29" × 19" (as woven); 42" × 24½" × 2¼" (when framed)

▶ *Tommye Scanlin mounts many of her larger tapestries in a similar way to what I've described in the preceding pages. For large pieces, Scanlin wraps the mounting fabric around archival board or foam core and includes invisible support stitches through the center of the tapestry. She then places the mounting inside a frame, as seen here.*

Hanging Larger Works

Larger tapestries are often hung from the top by some sort of mechanism attached to the wall. The method I detail here involves using Velcro to attach a hanging bar to a hem in the piece.

The hemmed header preparation described on page 268 details how to attach the fuzzy "loop" side of a piece of Velcro to the top of the tapestry. To hang a piece prepared this way, you need to attach a bar to it using the rough, or hook, side of the Velcro. I use a 1" × 2" wooden hanging bar with holes drilled in it so it can be attached to the wall with nails or screws.

1. Cut your wooden bar ½"–1" shorter than the width of your tapestry. I use a miter box to get the cuts as square and flat as possible. (Note that the edges are not mitered or cut on a diagonal.)

2. Sand the bar to avoid splinters. Smooth out the saw marks at the end of the bar. When hanging, this is the only part anyone will be able to see.

3. Using a large drill bit, drill two holes in the bar, each one the same distance from an end. For example, on my 45"-wide tapestries, I make the holes 6" from each end. These are the holes by which the hanging bar will be attached to the wall.

4. Paint the bar with any kind of paint, following manufacturers instructions. I usually use black paint so that it fades into the shadows behind the weaving.

5. Cut a piece of the rough side of the Velcro the length of the bar. Mark where the holes in the bar are and punch holes in the Velcro to match the holes in the bar. I use a hole punch for this, but you could use scissors.

6. Staple the back of the rough side of the Velcro to the bar with your light-duty stapler every 1½".

Necessary Supplies

For Mounting

STRETCHER BARS FOR PAINTING CANVASES.
They come in different lengths, and you can mix and match to make rectangular or square-shaped frames. Purchase two identical lengths for the sides and two for the top and bottom.

LIGHT-DUTY STAPLE GUN AND EXTRA STAPLES.
This is the kind of stapler that is used for wood (as seen on page 272), not the kind you have on your desk for paper.

FLANNEL OR COTTON QUILT BATTING, enough to cover the front of your frame and wrap around all four sides. I do not use polyester batting for tapestries because I don't like this synthetic oil-based material next to my work.

COTTON OR LINEN FABRIC TO GO ON THE OUTSIDE. You will need enough fabric to cover the front and to wrap around all four sides of your frame. Your tapestry will be shown against this fabric, so make sure it works well with your piece. I like to use a neutral-colored fabric and often choose linen because it has a slight sheen to it, looks natural, and sets off most tapestries. I like a smooth, solid-colored fabric without a lot of texture. Other people like to use boldly colored fabrics or pair the fabric design with the pattern of the tapestry.

IRON, SCISSORS, AND RULER OR MEASURING TAPE

SHARP NEEDLE AND THREAD. You will need two colors of thread: one that matches the tapestry and one contrasting color, for basting.

For Hanging

TWILL TAPE, ½"–2" wide depending on the size of the tapestry. I use black, but since it will not be seen on the front, the color probably does not matter. I use heavy cotton twill tape, which you can order online or request from your local fabric store. On small tapestries, I have also used grosgrain ribbon. I advise against polyester twill tape because it is thin and flimsy and melts with heat.

VELCRO, sew-on, in a similar width to the twill tape

WOODEN BAR, 1" × 2". This bar should be about ½"–1" shorter than your tapestry's width.

SAW to cut the hanging bar (or have it cut at a hardware store). You can also use a miter box, a simple plastic box that sits on the edge of a table and has slots in it. Pegs hold the wood in place so you can make a 90-degree cut with the saw that comes with the box. Available at hardware stores, a simple miter box is inexpensive and will ensure straight cuts. (I also use the miter box to cut cardboard tubes for storing larger tapestries.)

DRILL for holes in the stretcher bars

PAINT AND PAINTBRUSH

SANDPAPER (60–80 grit)

LIGHT-DUTY STAPLER, as mentioned for mounting, with silver or black staples

Labeling Your Tapestry

Tapestries are artworks that tend to remain in the possession of collectors for generations. It is important that you place documentation on the back of the work. Make a tag that includes your name, the title of the piece, the dimensions of the tapestry, materials used, and a copyright statement. In the United States, writing ©[date] and signing your name is enough to establish copyright for your work. I use either handwritten tags made of cotton fabric stiffened with iron-on interfacing or printable fabric and an ink jet printer. Letter-size sheets of printer-ready fabrics are available in many fabric stores. If the work is a gift or came from a particular event or story, consider including a paragraph about it on the label.

TIP

Photographing Your Work

If you are going to enter your work in any shows or competitions, you need good photographs. Images submitted for consideration in juried shows need to be perfectly in focus, square, well-lit, and free from extraneous elements. Unless you have some skill with photography and good camera equipment and lights, using a professional photographer to shoot your work is an excellent idea. There are photographers who specialize in shooting fiber art.

Take some time to carefully document your weaving right from the beginning. If nothing else, it gives you a reference for future projects even if you can't find the actual piece.

- The image should contain only the tapestry on a plain white or light-colored background.
- Use daylight bulbs in at least two light sources. Diffusing the light is helpful, and you can make effective light boxes for small works.

- If you don't have a way to light the piece effectively, consider shooting photos outside in the shade. Create a plain background for the piece, and make sure it is hanging straight or, if you're shooting it on a flat surface, that you can position the camera directly over the center of the piece.
- As you take photos, line up the edges of the tapestry with the viewfinder. You want to position the camera so it faces the center of the piece. Play with the camera position and angle until the tapestry appears square in the viewfinder.
- If you have some knowledge of photography, bracket the photo exposures so you can choose the best ones in the computer. Knowledge of Photoshop will also help you produce a good image. Make sure to compare the color of the photograph to the actual tapestry. Some cameras have a difficult time rendering some colors, like blue, realistically.

Conservation Considerations

You've spent so much time creating your tapestry, now you want to make sure it lasts. Keep in mind the following considerations to preserve your tapestry.

MOTHS. There are a few critters, including clothing moths, that will chew on your tapestries or yarns. The best thing you can do to defend against these invaders is to remain vigilant. Do not bring clothing, yarn, or textiles made of protein fibers into your home from an unknown source. That wonderful thrift-store rug could be infested with larvae that could damage your entire yarn stash and tapestry collection. Use moth traps near your wool items. Moth traps will not fix the problem, but they will alert you that you have a problem. Expose your yarn and stored wool items to light and air periodically and check for any infestations.

LIGHTFASTNESS. Most yarns sold for tapestry have been dyed with commercial dyes, which are fairly lightfast. Some natural dyes can fade quickly when exposed to constant light. If you are dyeing the yarn yourself or purchasing naturally dyed yarns, consider doing a lightfastness test prior to using them for a big tapestry (see page 47 to learn how). Because all dyes will fade eventually, tapestries should never be displayed in direct sunlight.

STORAGE. Tapestries are best stored rolled on sturdy tubes. Cardboard tubes with at least a 2-inch diameter work well, but the cardboard should first be covered with acid-free paper or fabric. (Historic tapestries should be rolled on acid-free tubes. If you have a historic tapestry, consult a conservator about all of the issues in this section.)

Sew a muslin cover for your tapestry. My covers are flat pieces of fabric hemmed on all four sides. They are the size of the tapestry, plus 6 inches on each side and a few extra feet on the ends. The tapestry should be rolled around the tube, in the direction of the warp if possible. This puts the least amount of tension on the weft. However, if you have sewn Velcro to a tapestry that was woven sideways, the twill tape will not cooperate with rolling, and you may have to roll the tapestry in the weft direction.

Place the cover on a table and place the tapestry facedown on top of it, centered on the fabric. Fold the edge of the muslin cover over the Velcro end of the tapestry and put the tube over the Velcro. Roll the tapestry and cover together around the tube, making sure the muslin covers the tube before the tapestry touches the cardboard.

Place the hanging bar inside the tube and put the whole bundle into a plastic sleeve or wrap it in a sheet of plastic. This is especially important for shipping to ensure against liquid and dust exposure. If you live in a moist climate, make sure you don't trap moisture in the tapestry by using plastic; in this case, consult a local conservator. Museums store tapestries wrapped on tubes and then hung on rods running through the tubes. This keeps any part of the tapestry from resting on a surface. The museum storage method is not a practical way of storing your work; but if you own a historic or valuable tapestry, it is a good idea.

Tapestries that have been mounted can be wrapped in muslin covers or acid-free paper and stored in acid-free boxes.

CLEANING. As tapestries hang, they will collect dust. This is easily vacuumed off using the same clean tapestry-dedicated vacuum attachment you used to vacuum your tapestry when it first came off the loom (see page 263). Tapestries should need no other cleaning unless they are displayed on a floor or become stained. In those cases, consult a professional conservator or rug cleaner.

Knots

Some people understand making knots intuitively, but I've found many weavers struggle with making them. In the following pages you'll learn the few knots you may need to know when weaving tapestry.

Double Half-Hitch Knot

DOUBLE HALF HITCH USED TO SECURE WARP TO WARPING BAR. This knot is useful for securing the end of your warp thread while putting on a continuous warp with a warping bar. This knot slides, so it allows you to tighten that last warp after the knot is tied. Think of the last warp thread as it approaches the warping bar as a solid material that can't bend. The knot will be made around this last warp and can then slide on that warp. If you allow that last warp thread to bend when you make the knot, the knot won't slide. When tightening the knot, grasp the very last part of that straight string near the bar. Slide the knot along this taut string away from the bar to tighten the warp.

DOUBLE HALF HITCH USED TO START A HEADER. The double half hitch is also frequently used in headers. It holds firmly and, when the tapestry comes off the loom, the header and weaving won't unravel if secured with this knot. It can be quite decorative, and I often use it with fringe in small pieces. When used for a header, this knot looks different on the front and the back. You can tie it so that you see a tiny diagonal line in each knot as in image A on page 127 or two horizontal lines as in image B on page 127. These two images are the front and back of the same piece. The knots can be tied to make either example show up on the front of your finished tapestry.

Diagonal Line Version

To make the double half-hitch knot so that a tiny diagonal line is visible on the front, follow these steps.

1. Bring the thread around the 1st warp and underneath the beginning thread, as shown in step 2 on page 128.

2. Wrap it around the same warp again, making the loop go to the left like a lowercase *d* as shown in step 3 on that same page.

3. Tighten and continue across the warp.

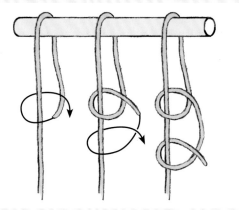

Horizontal Bars Version

To make the double half-hitch knot so that the two horizontal bars show up on the front, follow these similar steps.

1. Bring the warp under the first warp.

2. Loop around the warp, forming a shape similar to a capital *D*.

3. Repeat the same loop around that warp.

4. Tighten the knot.

5. Repeat steps 1–4 all the way across the warp. After finishing each knot, make sure to start the next one by putting your working thread under the next adjacent warp.

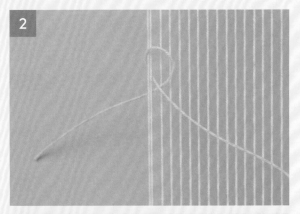

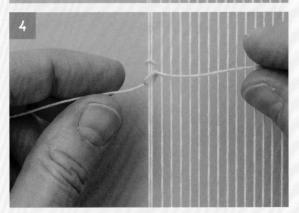

Half Damascus Knot

This little edging technique is mentioned in Peter Collingwood's *The Techniques of Rug Weaving*. He says it is so named because he first saw it on a rug made by a Damascus rug weaver. This knot is used in the finishing process to make the warp ends turn neatly toward the back of the tapestry so they can be hidden inside the hem. It is tied with the tapestry lying facedown and the warp ends pointing toward you. The images show making the knots from left to right, but you can easily reverse the directions and make the knots from right to left.

1. Starting at one end of the tapestry, hold 2 warp ends firmly.

2. Pick up the leftmost warp and wrap it over and around the 2nd warp end. Pull the knot strongly upward; the 1st warp end will now be lying along the back of the tapestry, away from you.

3. Pick up the 3rd warp end and do the same maneuver with the 2nd warp end wrapping around it.

4. Continue with each end all the way across the warp.

5. When you reach the other side, put the last warp end on a tapestry needle and run it back into the weaving under the weft along a warp rib. Repeat this with the 2nd and 3rd warp ends from the edge. This secures the ends of the row of knots.

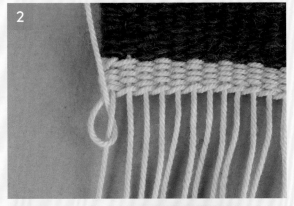

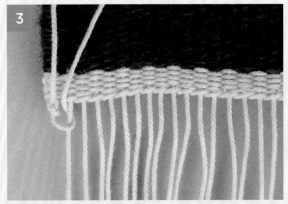

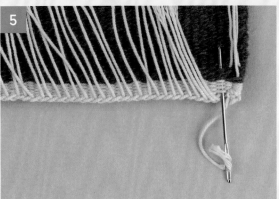

Lark's Head Knot

This knot can be used to start your twining thread. It is useful any time you need to connect a loop to a fixed point.

Fold your thread in half. Wrap the loop over and around the edge warp and bring the two tails through the loop. Pull tight.

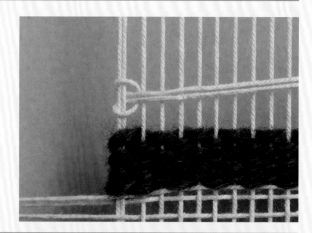

Overhand Knot

A simple overhand knot is useful when tying fringe. It is the same as the first half of a square knot but is usually made with more than one piece of thread. When used to make a decorative fringe, it can be helpful to use a needle to pull the knot up against the header of the weaving firmly.

Make a loop with your yarn and pass the working end of the yarn through the loop. Pull tight.

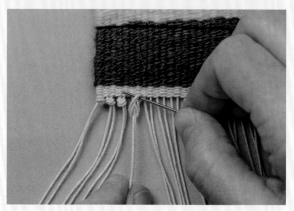

▲ Using a needle to make sure the overhand knot ends up tight against the header when making fringe

Slip Knot

A slip knot is an overhand knot but the tail is not pulled all the way through the knot. This knot is one I use sometimes when weaving on a pegged loom to secure the beginning of the warp to one of the pegs. I also use a slip knot to secure yarn to the fishing swivel, as described in the unplying technique on page 260).

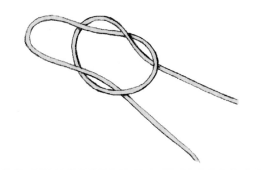

Square Knot

If you only know how to tie one knot reliably, make it the square knot. This was the first knot my dad taught me to tie, and when I do it I still think of the saying he taught me: "Right over left, left over right." The square knot is used in weaving to tie two pieces of yarn or warp together. It is strong in the direction of pull, so it can be used to join a new warp to a broken one to patch it, or for many other basic applications where the stress on the knot isn't all that great.

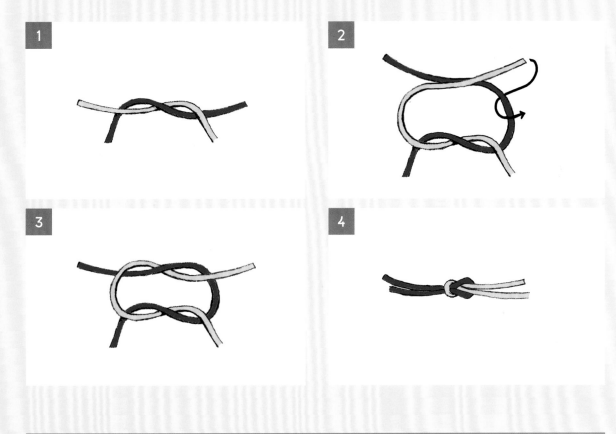

Surgeon's Knot

I use the surgeon's knot when tying the warp to the front beam of a floor loom and when starting a thread to sew slits. This knot is also sometimes referred to as a surgeon's throw.

To make this knot, do the first wrap you use when you tie your shoes — but go around twice. The double wrap grabs and holds tight when the single one won't.

Leashes

Leashes are long heddles that are used on some high-warp tapestry looms to open one of the two sheds. They are attached to a leash bar. When using leashes, one of the two sheds is held slightly open at all times by an open shed rod (A). The second shed will be pulled forward by the leashes as in (B). I use 12/6 cotton seine twine for my leashes because it is tough and holds the knots well. Most likely whatever warp you're using for your tapestry will work, but you don't want the leashes to get too thick, as that makes them harder to grasp accurately and quickly.

There are two ways to make leashes. The first method involves tying each leash individually around a bar. The second involves a string that runs along the edge of the bar around which you will secure knots. For both of these methods, you'll need a loom that has a leash bar. If you have a loom that allows you to secure the string along the edge of the bar as seen in image 3 on page 286, choose the second method. This works best if the bar is wood or has a peg coming out of the end. If you're using a homemade pipe loom with a metal bar, you may opt for the first method.

In both methods you want the length of the leashes to be the same. Whichever method you use, take a moment to set up a secondary bar that will help you keep each leash the same length as you tie them on.

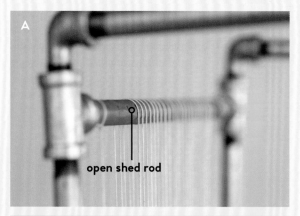

A

open shed rod

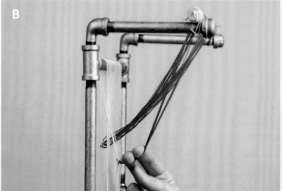

B

Setting Up the Measuring Bar

1. Insert a dowel ¼"–½" in diameter into the open shed. Tie the ends of this dowel to the sides of your loom. (If you have a large high-warp loom, you can secure this bar with strings to the top and bottom of the loom to hold it in place.)

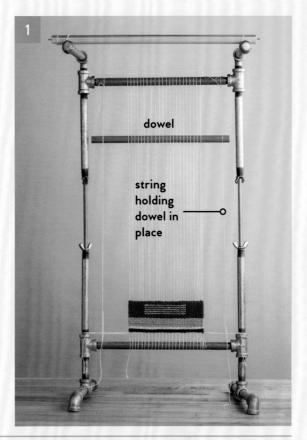

dowel

string holding dowel in place

2. The second layer of warp is behind this bar. You will only be picking up the warps for the leashes from *behind* this bar. Each leash will go between the warps on the front layer, one in each space.

Method 1

In this method you'll tie individual leashes to your loom using a square knot. The path of the leash goes around the top of the leash bar, down around the measuring bar and around one of the warps behind the bar, then back over the top of the leash bar, which is part of your loom.

1. Make one leash as indicated below and tie a square knot (see page 283) very loosely around the bar. Clip the thread, then untie the knot. Use this length of thread to measure the leashes for the rest of your warp. You will need one piece for every other warp, or half the number of warps in your piece.

2. Wrap the first leash string around the first warp that is *behind* the measuring bar, then bring both ends of that string around the front of and over the top of the leash bar.

3. Wrap both ends of the leash thread around the back of the leash bar, around the sides of the leash, and tie a square knot on the front of the leash as in the step 1 photo above.

4. Repeat steps 2 and 3 for every other warp all the way across. You are picking up the warps that are behind the measuring bar.

5. After tying all the leashes, remove the measuring bar.

Method 2

In this method you'll use one long piece of thread to tie all the leashes. Wind your leash fiber onto a large bobbin. If you run out while tying the leashes, simply tie it off to the leash bar and start a new piece.

1. Attach a piece of warp running along the length of your leash bar, if you don't already have one. This cord is often called the heddle rod cord. Large tapestry looms may come with leash bars that have pegs at the end to tie the heddle rod cord to. If you are making a leash bar for a small loom, cut a dowel wide enough to tie securely to the supports (as seen in step 1 on the previous page), then nail two small tacks or nails into the ends of the dowel and use them to attach a heddle rod cord. Tie the cord made of strong, thin warp to the nail at one end of the leash bar. Bring it across and wrap it around the nail on the other side, then bring it back and tie it off to the first nail using a double half-hitch knot. Wrap the dowel near the ends tightly with cord to stabilize it.

2. Tie the end of the leash cord on your bobbin around the leash bar with a square knot. The heddle rod cord will be trapped under this tie.

3. Wrap the cord around the bar a few times to secure it, and tie a double half hitch around the heddle rod cord.

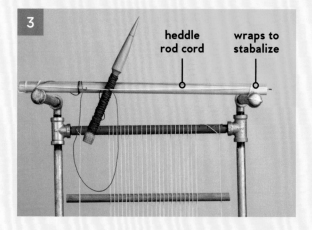

heddle rod cord | wraps to stabalize

4. Bring your bobbin of warp over the top, down and under the measuring bar, through the 2 front warps, around the back warp, and back up to the leash bar (4a). Wrap firmly all the way around this bar, then secure that heddle with a double half hitch around the heddle rod cord. You've completed one leash (4b).

5. Repeat step 4 to continue tying the leashes. Keep the spacing between each leash on the leash bar wide enough that the leash is coming away from the warp in a perpendicular aspect.

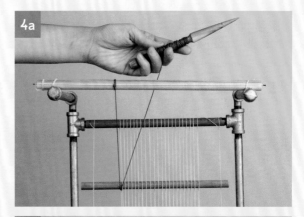

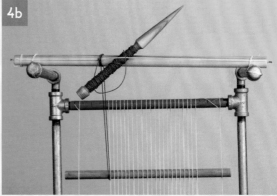

6. When you get to the end of the warp, tie the final end around the leash bar securely. Remove the dowel that served as your measuring bar.

How to Weave Using Leashes

Leashes are used to open a small section of the weaving at once. They are a good shedding mechanism for people who use tapestry bobbins because the bobbin never leaves the weaver's hand. The weaver pulls down and slightly forward on a group of leashes about 1" wide (A) and then slips the bobbin into the opened shed with their dominant hand (B). The bobbin is then used to beat in the weft (C), and the process is repeated (D).

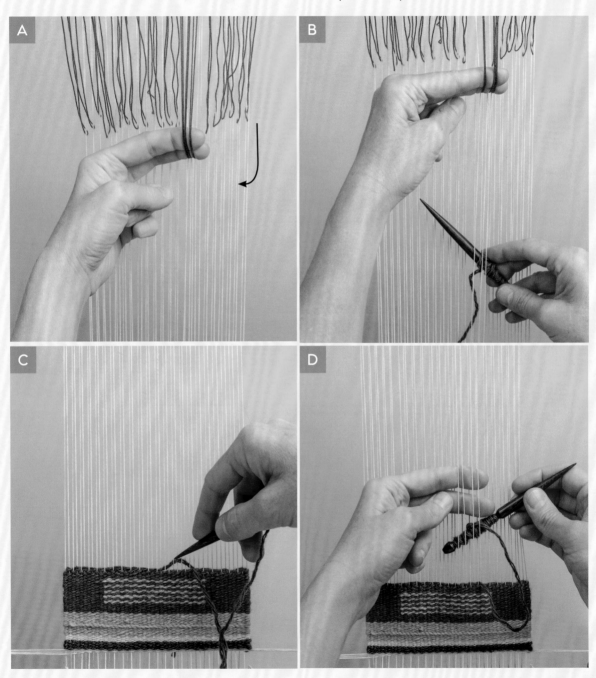

Making a Pipe Loom

You can make your own tensioned frame loom using copper pipe, galvanized threaded pipe, or black threaded pipe. You can even make a very large loom out of black pipe or scaffold pieces. In this section I'll give you plans for making two looms: a simple copper pipe loom and a galvanized pipe loom. Black pipe looms are made exactly the same as galvanized pipe looms. Note: The threaded rod that is inserted into the sides of these kinds of looms lets you make the loom longer or shorter to provide tension on the warp. The loom will also not stay together until it is warped.

Copper Pipe Loom

Materials

- ½" copper pipe, long enough for the loom plans

- 4 elbows that match the size copper you are using

- 4 wing nuts or 4 hex nuts that fit the threaded rod (These nuts need to be larger than the diameter of the pipe so they don't disappear inside.)

- 2 pieces of threaded rod that fit inside the copper pipe, 6" or 12" long (½" rod usually works for ½" pipe, but test it before buying)

For Assembly

- Tool to cut copper pipe, such as a simple rotary cutter for copper pipe (sold in the plumbing section of the hardware store and pictured below)

- Strong adhesive such as superglue, epoxy, or soldering kit

Construction

Draw the loom shape you want before visiting the hardware store to make sure you buy enough pipe. You might just go ahead and buy parts to make two of them. They're rather addicting.

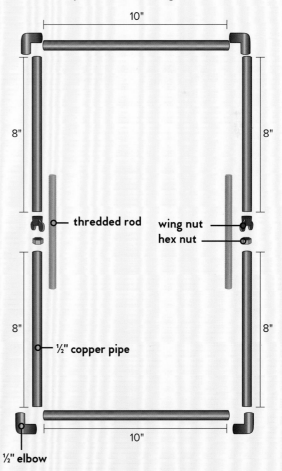

1. Cut four pieces of pipe: one each for the top and bottom, and two for the full length of the sides. Following the manufacturer's instructions, glue or solder the four pieces of pipe into a rectangle using the four elbows.

2. After the glue is dry or the solder cools, cut the center of each side so you have two U-shaped pieces of copper.

3. Screw two nuts onto each piece of threaded rod. Place the nuts in the center of the rod.

4. Insert each of the U-shaped pieces of copper onto the threaded rods as shown on the next page.

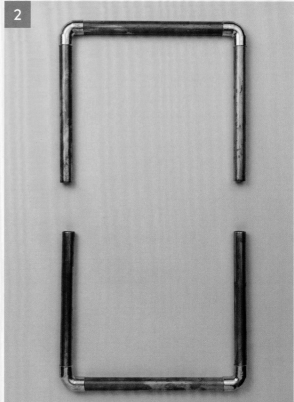

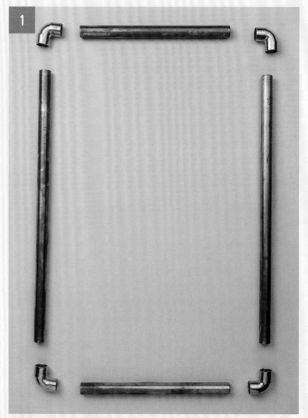

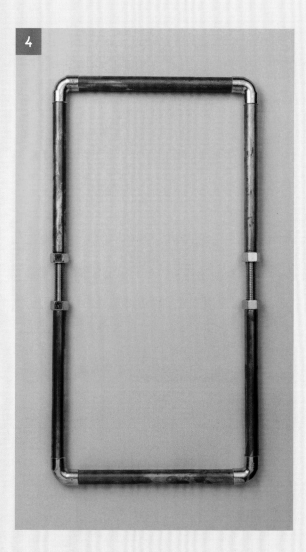

4

Consider This

Copper is soft. You can't make a large loom with ½" pipe. Keep the horizontal pieces to 12" or less and the total upright size of the loom to 28" or less. You can make a larger loom with ¾" pipe.

Glued joints can fail, especially if subjected to temperature extremes. Keep a bit of superglue or epoxy in your weaving kit for a quick fix, and if it fails while you're weaving, the worst that will happen is the loom will twist a bit. When you finish the tapestry, take the loom apart, clean off the old adhesive, and apply more.

Use nylon threaded rod instead of copper pipe if you don't like how heavy this loom is. If you know you aren't going to extend the loom a lot, use 6" lengths of threaded rod to decrease the weight.

The loom is held together by the warp. Basically you are constructing two U-shaped pieces of copper with threaded rods between them. When warped, the threaded rod allows the loom to get longer or shorter, providing tension on the warp. The loom will not stay together until a warp is applied.

Galvanized Pipe Loom

This is the easiest loom you'll ever make. Once you have all the parts, you can put it together in less than 10 minutes without any tools. Galvanized or black pipe (also called nipple) is threaded, so it simply screws together. The concept for tensioning is the same as with the copper pipe loom, but the construction is even easier. It is also simple to make this loom with little "feet" that allow the loom to stand on a table.

Materials

¼" galvanized or black pipe in these lengths (or the lengths you want for your loom):

- Six 8" pieces
- Two 6" pieces
- Two 3" pieces
- Four 90-degree elbows
- 4 tee fittings
- Two 2" pieces
- 2 end caps
- 4 wing nuts to fit the threaded rod that fits inside the pipe
- Two 12" pieces of threaded rod
- Small pipe wrench (optional)

Construction

All you have to do is screw the pieces together in the configuration shown at right and you're done. The elbows on the front of the legs tilt the loom back slightly, and the end caps on the back of the legs protect your table.

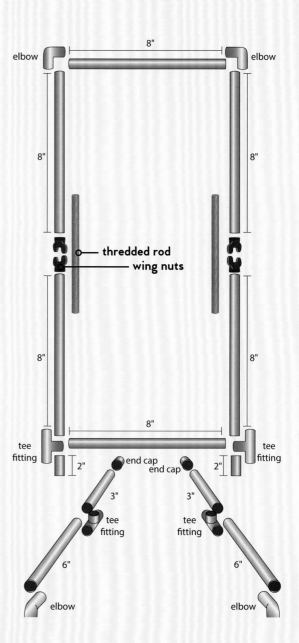

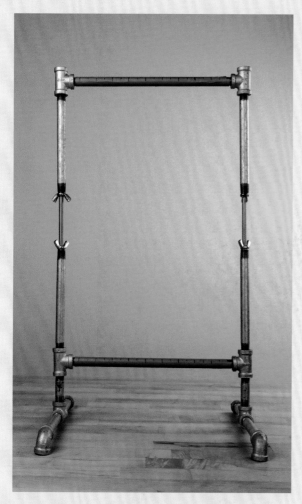

▲ *The tee fittings that I used at the top of this loom serve the same purpose as the 90-degree elbows in the diagram.*

Consider This

- Even though these pipes seem very strong, they can bend if they get too long. If you're using ¼" galvanized pipe, keep the width of your bottom and top bar to 12" or less. If you use larger diameter pipe, you can make the loom wider.

- Various combinations of screw-together parts allow you to add a leash bar (as seen on page 285) or legs and stand the loom on a table or the floor.

- This loom is also held together by the warp. The two halves will come apart until a warp is applied.

- I have found it difficult to find threaded rod that fits nicely inside ¼" galvanized pipe. The threaded rod is quite a bit smaller and rattles around inside the pipe. It becomes stable once warped, but some people don't like this feature. Make sure when purchasing threaded rod that you test its fit inside the pipe.

- It can be difficult to find ¼" galvanized pipe in lengths longer than 6" in conventional hardware stores. If you ask, they'll probably order it for you.

- It is very easy to change the length of the pipes to make different-size tapestries.

- Galvanized and black pipe nipple are interchangeable. Black pipe is usually cheaper.

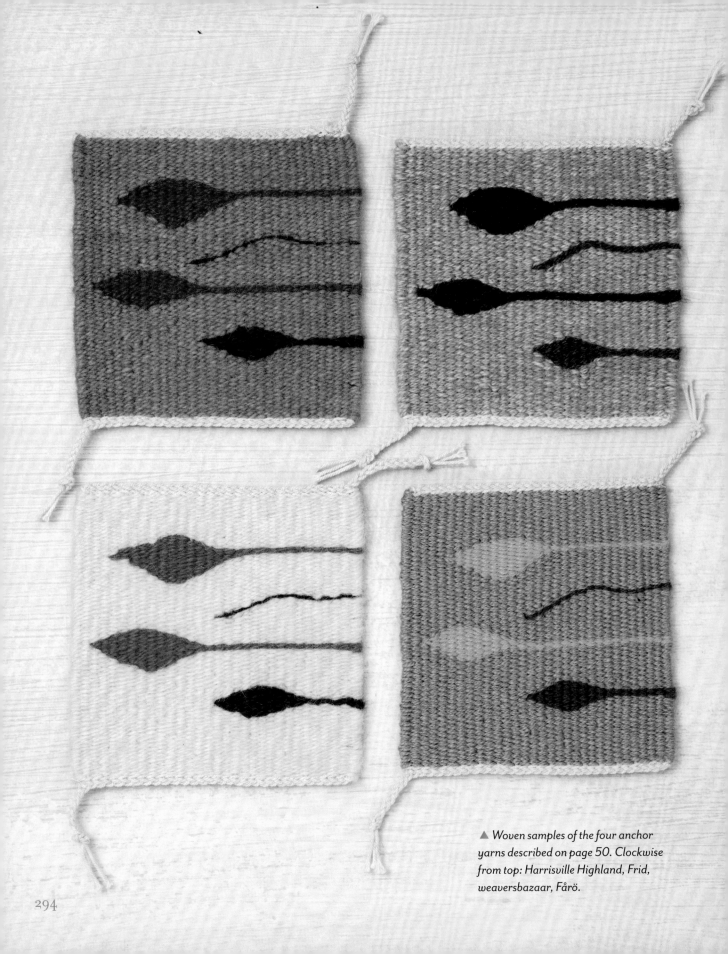

▲ *Woven samples of the four anchor yarns described on page 50. Clockwise from top: Harrisville Highland, Frid, weaversbazaar, Fårö.*

Acknowledgments

I am grateful for all the people who helped me bring this book from dream to completion. My primary inspiration for writing it was my students. Their willingness to ask questions, experiment with the answers, and then push themselves to discover the next step on their own helped me craft the way the material is taught in this book. It is my greatest wish that they take these foundational techniques and carry them forward into their own work in fiber art.

Jillian Moreno gave me the idea for this book, the confidence to start writing it, and the moral support to see the project through. She and Jane Patrick introduced me to Gwen Steege, my first editor. Gwen helped steady my first shaky footsteps. She read the first drafts of the book and offered her invaluable editorial advice. Thank you to all three of these exceptional women for starting me on this path.

For guidance on subject matter, I want to thank Elizabeth Buckley, Susan Martin Maffei, and Chrissie Freeth for advice on hachures; Donald Sandoval and Lisa Trujillo for advice on Rio Grande tapestry traditions; D.Y. Begay for her deep knowledge and kind willingness to share her knowledge of Diné weaving and culture; Robbie LaFleur for advice on Norwegian tapestry; and Michael Rohde, Sarah Swett, and Tommye Scanlin for assistance with technical details.

A huge amount of credit goes to the creative team at Storey Publishing. Michal Lumsden was the best editor I could have wished for. Her grace in steering my writing, her suggestions about clarity and content, and her good humor about the entire project were indispensable. Mars Vilaubi is responsible for the fantastic photographs in the book. Not only is he a skilled photographer, but his unflappable nature allowed what could have been a very stressful photoshoot to be fun. And Michaela Jebb made this book the gorgeous visual treat that it is. I will always be grateful for her skill with graphic design, color, and layout.

In addition to the technical assistance Sarah Swett lent on this project, a special word of thanks goes to her as my friend and colleague. Her inspiration as an artist and her support as a friend always remind me about the magic that comes from making things.

And lastly I am grateful to my family. My eternal gratitude goes to my parents, who helped me learn to think and instilled me with enough confidence to leave a career in health care and start my own business teaching tapestry weaving. Thanks to my sister for her boundless well of creativity, which has always inspired me to try new things. And always and forever to my wife, Emily, whose job it was to keep me from steering my ship straight into panic when deadlines were looming. She read drafts of the manuscript, made me endless cups of tea, and never once believed that I couldn't do it.

METRIC CONVERSIONS

WEIGHT

TO CONVERT	TO	MULTIPLY
ounces	grams	ounces by 28.35
pounds	grams	pounds by 453.5
pounds	kilograms	pounds by 0.45

LENGTH

TO CONVERT	TO	MULTIPLY
inches	millimeters	inches by 25.4
inches	centimeters	inches by 2.54
inches	meters	inches by 0.0254
feet	meters	feet by 0.3048
yards	centimeters	yards by 91.44
yards	meters	yards by 0.9144

Index

Page numbers in **bold** indicate charts; page numbers in *italic* indicate illustrations.

C

Y

Z

Fill Your Fiber Arts Library
with More Books from Storey

BY DEBORAH ROBSON & CAROL EKARIUS

This one-of-a-kind photographic encyclopedia features more than 200 animals and the fibers they produce. Find everything you need to know about each fiber's color, density, strength, and features when spun, knit, and woven.

BY GAIL CALLAHAN

Satisfy all of your color cravings, right in your own kitchen! Set yourself on the right color path with detailed advice on color theory and types of dyes, and learn how to dye your yarn using standard kitchen equipment.

BY SYNE MITCHELL

This best-selling guide covers everything you need to know to master the craft of rigid-heddle weaving. Choose a loom, set it up, and get started with a variety of fun techniques to produce beautiful and colorful results.

BY DEBORAH JARCHOW & GWEN W. STEEGE

Make stunning woven items using a variety of materials and a simple loom — or no loom at all! With innovative projects and step-by-step photos, you'll find inspiring new ways to approach the ancient art of over/under.